ITS STRUCTURE AND CONTROL

Clifford D. Shearing

Butterworths
Toronto

Organizational Police Deviance: Its Structure and Control

Printed and bound in Canada
5 4 3 2 1   1 2 3 4 5 6 7 8 9/8

Canadian Cataloguing in Publication Data

Main entry under title:
Organizational police deviance

ISBN 0-409-84880-8

1. Police corruption. 2. Police corruption - Canada. 3. Police administration. 4. Police administration - Canada. 5. Organizational behavior. I. Shearing, Clifford D., 1942-

HV7936.C85075   363.2'2   C81-095003-0

The Butterworth Group of Companies

Canada:
Butterworth & Co. (Canada) Ltd., Toronto and Vancouver

United Kingdom:
Butterworth & Co. (Publishers) Ltd., London

Australia:
Butterworths Pty. Ltd., Sydney

New Zealand:
Butterworths of New Zealand Ltd., Wellington

South Africa:
Butterworth & Co. (South Africa) Ltd., Durban

United States:
Butterworth (Publishers) Inc., Boston
Butterworth (Legal Publishers) Inc., Seattle
Mason Publishing Company, St. Paul

Contributors

Jean-Paul Brodeur
Associate Professor, Ecole de Criminologie, Université de Montréal.

Richard V. Ericson
Associate Professor of Sociology and Criminology, University of Toronto.

John Hagan
Professor, Department of Sociology, University of Wisconsin–Madison and Department of Sociology, University of Toronto.

John Alan Lee
Associate Professor of Sociology, Scarborough College, University of Toronto.

C. Peter Morden
Consultant, A.R.A. Consultants, Toronto.

Clifford D. Shearing
Associate Professor of Sociology and Criminology, University of Toronto.

Philip C. Stenning
Consultant and Special Lecturer, Centre of Criminology, University of Toronto.

Austin T. Turk
Professor of Sociology and Criminology, University of Toronto.

Contents

Foreword

The study of deviant behaviour has progressed steadily in the past several decades both in depth and range of analysis, theoretical formulations, and focus of attention. Whereas interest was once largely concentrated on the so-called "dangerous classes" and marginals like bohemians, misfits, and the mentally disturbed—denizens of the sociological zoo—we now have investigation of "respectables" up to and including corporate, political, and bureaucratic officials of national prominence (John M. Johnson and Jack D. Douglas (eds.) *Crime at the Top* [Philadelphia: Lippincott, 1978]). Sophisticated analysis of levels of deviance, its various social functions, and its embodiment in sturdy social structures and institutions are now being advanced. With all this has recently emerged an interest in the deviance of law enforcement officials up to and including secret service police operations like the RCMP Security Service and the CIA.

In Canada, media discussion of deviance within the once hallowed ranks of the Royal Canadian Mounted Police and the publicity attendant upon the investigations of the McDonald Royal Commission have sparked some sociological analysis of police deviance and its sociological and policy implications. Whereas the study of police deviance was until recently largely confined to corruption and bribery, increased insight into patterned deviance in regular police forces in both the U.S.A. and Canada has led to the introduction of the concept of organizational deviance. To a large extent the essays in this volume will contribute to sociological understanding of such organizational misconduct and its relation to the older concept of structured deviance.

One study of police occupational deviance carried out in the U.S.A. in the mid-1970s considered perjury, brutality (excessive violence), sexual deviance on the job, sleeping on the job, and drinking on duty. It concentrated on peer support or condemnation of these five kinds of deviance, but looked only briefly at the rather obvious frustrations that often lie behind perjury, or at the temptations that help explain sexual deviance on the job. Conducted by an ex-police officer now criminologist, the research instrument consisted of a questionnaire that asked each officer in a small city force to say how many men on the force he perceived to have committed each deviant act and how often such acts would be reported by fellow policemen. The result of the questionnaire—legitimated by the local police officials—indicated that 39.1 per cent of the force were perceived to have used excessive violence, 39.5 per cent to have slept on the job, 31 per cent to have indulged in sex while on duty, 22.9 per cent to have committed perjury and 8 per cent to have drunk on duty. It was also discovered that "the perceived extent of each pattern of police deviance did vary inversely with the group support as measured through the perceived 'wrongness' and risk which existed in the police organization. The extent of each deviant pattern was almost a direct function of how 'wrong' the police peer group perceived the act and the perception of how often the men thought it would be reported" (Thomas Barker, "An Empirical Study of Police Deviance Other Than Corruption," *Journal of Political Science and Administration* 6, no. 3: 264-72).

In Canada few if any such legitimated deviance studies of the police have yet been made. The reasons are not hard to fathom: No profession likes to see the extent of its occupational deviance exposed to public view, even if impersonally and reported only in a professional journal. The general norm is to dismiss such behaviour as uncommon, just a few "bad apples," and to close ranks if any outsider comes in looking for hard data. Moreover, among the police it seems that next to murder and incest, one of their most central codes is "never squeal on a fellow officer." As a result, revelations from within of dirty work in the CIA or misconduct in the RCMP, or in municipal forces, rarely occur, and when they do, subject their authors to serious sanctions from within, and general disbelief from the public. At the same time, it must be noted that when faced with hard evidence that a fellow officer is breaking the law and should be reported, many police officers experience a profound role conflict. In turn, this strain may encourage excessive drinking or even lead to suicide.

The scholars who have written the essays in this collection have had, in most cases, unusual access to the day-to-day functioning of various police forces in Canada. The writers brought together here anchor their empirical insights in a penetrating appreciation of the realities of police work and a sophisticated understanding of sociological theory. Their aim is objective, academic understanding and effective social analysis, not sensational exposure. Recommendations when provided grow out of scholarly concern and eschew easy, superficial, or premature decisions.

A central aim of this volume is to illuminate the role of the police in the reproduction of order in modern society. As Durkheim clarified decades ago, the modern industrial world is held together by an organic interdependence of its many parts, which implies, among other things, increasing specialization of function, increasing differentiation, role segmentalization, and functional interdependence. Specialization and differentiation of function have willy-nilly accelerated within police forces and will continue. Bureaucratization and role conflict are ever more visible. The ever-growing rate at which legislatures make laws and add to the burden of law enforcers, to say nothing of the passage of some laws that lack widespread popular support, add to the already heavy burden on law enforcers. The result is that our police function within an increasingly complex and burdensome lawmaking and law enforcement system. Conflicts between norms of authority, discretionary powers, and democratic principles, as well as rules demanding secrecy and protection of the police as an institution and of one's job within that structure, force the average policeman daily to walk a tightrope. Contemporary developments of unionization and "professionalization" combine to make this task no less easy. Under such conditions we can expect that the extent and range of deviance in police behaviour will grow. The increase in the number of minority groups in given jurisdictions will inevitably muddy the waters.

In short, it would seem that the publication of this book is timely. It will throw light on some key issues, encourage a deeper probing of matters of central concern, and stimulate scholars and researchers to move more thoroughly and boldly into an area of human conduct of growing significance as our world comes to see policing as an institution of strategic import. It is hoped that it will be read by relevant administrators and policy makers as well as social scientists and others directly concerned with its findings and theories. The editor is to be congratulated on bringing together such a varied and high-level collection of articles, each of which, carefully researched and tightly argued, makes a distinctive contribution to its own area.

W. EDWARD MANN
Department of Sociology
Atkinson College
York University
Toronto

Introduction*

As with so much of the sociological literature on the public police, the bulk of the research on police deviance has been undertaken in the United States of America. American scholars have focused their attention almost exlusively on police corruption,[1] so that although there is a considerable literature on this one aspect of police deviance, there is practically no general literature on the subject. This book begins to redress this imbalance by focusing attention on another aspect of police deviance, namely, organizational deviance.[2]

The American emphasis on police corruption echoes the long-standing public concern in the United States with this topic, a concern that has found its expression in a series of public inquiries and commissions that go back many decades. These inquiries, and the public and political pressures that prompted them, have fuelled several reform movements to professionalize the police service in the United States (Walker, 1977; Fogelson, 1977). Whatever else these reform movements have accomplished, it is clear from the existing literature that while they may have reduced the extent of police corruption in the United States they have certainly not eliminated it. As a result, corruption continues to be viewed as one of the distinguishing features of American public policing and an important area of scholarly attention within the United States.

In indicating how this collection of essays contributes to the development of a more general account of police deviance, it is useful to begin by considering the primary focus of the existing literature as well as those aspects of police deviance that this focus excludes.

Definitions of "police corruption" tend, by and large, to converge around the concept of "illegitimate exchange"; that is, police corruption is identified as police behaviour that results in private gains at public expense.[3] For example, Goldstein (1975: 3) in defining "police corruption" identified it as those "acts involving the misuse of authority[4] by a police officer in a manner designed to produce personal gain for himself or others." Goldstein goes on to note that this definition excludes specifically other forms of police deviance "where authority may have been abused but where there is no indication that the abuse was motivated by a desire for personal gain." In making a similar distinction, Sherman (1974: 5) writes that abuses such as "wiretapping, fabricating evidence, and even brutality are usually used to 'fight crime' and not to fatten policemen's wallets."

---

*I would like to thank Helen Boritch for her assistance in the preparation of this essay.

Despite this traditional focus, some American authors have recently begun to pay some attention to abuses of authority which are motivated to further the organizational objectives of law enforcement. This redirection of concern has been prompted by events of the last few decades, such as Watergate, which have served to publicly disclose widespread and questionable law enforcement practices on the part of the police. For example, in a recent analysis of the police, Lundman (1980: 180) moves beyond the traditional focus on police corruption by including both the "abuse of arrest discretion" and "unnecessary police force" together with "police corruption" under the general heading of "police misconduct." In this volume, we seek to elaborate upon this trend by examining the deviant activities carried out by police officers to "fight crime."

In directing attention to these police behaviours, the contributors to this book utilize the concept of organizational deviance, a concept which is well established in the organizational literature. Bensman and Gerver (1963), for example, drew attention to this phenomenon nearly two decades ago in a discussion of rule breaking for legitimate organizational purposes within an aircraft factory. Since then, the notion that deviance can and does take place to achieve legitimate organizational goals has been well documented. Recently, for example, Schrager and Short (1978: 411) defined "organizational crime" as "illegal acts of omission or commission of an individual or a group of individuals in a legitimate formal organization in accord with the operative goals of the organization. . . ." In contrasting this form of deviance with corruption, Shover (1978: 39) uses the term "organizational crime" to refer to "criminal acts . . . [intended] to contribute to the achievement of goals and other objectives thought to be important for the organization as a whole, some sub-units within the organization, or their own particular job duties." In this book the term "organizational police deviance" is used to refer to various deviant acts designed to further organizational objectives rather than promote personal gains.[5]

Although the issue of organizational police deviance has increasingly become the subject of considerable public and political concern in the United States, it is a subject which has been at the very centre of public and political debate in Canada for much of the past decade. This interest, and the commissions and inquiries which it has generated, have brought to light much empirical evidence about the existence of, and nature of, organizational deviance within Canadian police departments, and this in turn has encouraged scholarly interest in this issue. In view of this history, it is appropriate that this text should be based on the research of scholars working in Canada.

The linkage we have just noted between public debate and scholarly interest is reflected in this book in the fact that three of the contributors have been involved as researchers in three recent inquiries into the Royal

Canadian Mounted Police. Two of them, Jean-Paul Brodeur[6] and Philip Stenning,[7] have based their articles directly on research done for these commissions, while Clifford Shearing[8] has used his experience with the RCMP to assess the generality of an analysis based on data collected from a municipal police force. Similarly, one of the other contributors, John Lee, has used data disclosed during public hearings into the RCMP to inform his analysis of police-minority relations.

One of the strengths of the literature on police corruption is that scholars considering this pervasive phenomenon have consistently rejected the "bad apple" theory, so popular with senior police administrators, in favour of a structural account which emphasizes social determinants of corruption. This structural approach has been advocated by Barker and Roebuck (1973: 10), who maintained that:

> Police corruption is best understood, not as the exclusive deviant behavior of individual officers, but as a group behavior guided by contradictory sets of norms linked to the organization in which the erring individuals belong. . . .

In developing a general concept of structured deviance, Ermann and Lundman (1978) have provided a definition which focuses on the organization itself, specifying the conditions that must be present if deviance is to be considered organizational rather than individual in character. The features they include are that (1) "the action must be contrary to norms maintained by others outside the organization" (ibid.: 7); (2) "the action must be supported by the internal operating norms of the organization" (ibid.); (3) new members must be socialized to accept these norms; (4) the action must have peer support; and finally (5) the deviance must be "supported by the dominant coalition of the organization" (ibid.: 8). This definition is far narrower than that offered by Barker and Roebuck and, as Sherman (1974) has pointed out, is more a theory of the nature of the organizational factors that structure deviance than a definition of such deviance. In providing his definition of "organizational police corruption," Sherman seeks to overcome this limitation by focusing on Ermann and Lundman's fifth criterion. He writes that:

> Organizational corruption in agencies of social control may be defined as the illegal misuse of public authority in accordance with operative organizational goals for the private gain of social control agents or others participating in the agency's dominant administrative coalition. [Sherman, 1974: 482]

Unfortunately, however, in focusing on one particular organizational determinant of police corruption, Sherman also falls foul of the problem of confusing the identification of a phenomenon with its explanation. As a result, like Ermann and Lundman, Sherman limits his definition of "structured deviance" solely to deviance that has its origin in the social factors operating within the police organization. This limitation is inconsistent with

Schrager and Short's insistence, noted earlier, that in explaining organizational deviance it is imperative that factors external to, as well as internal to, the organization be taken into account.

This broader view of structured deviance as an approach to the explanation of police deviance is one shared by all the contributors to this book. This more general approach, which allows for a wide range of social and legal factors in the explanation of police deviance, is nicely summarized by Mann and Lee (1979: 19) in their discussion of the concept "structured deviance":

> When sociologists find that a set of social conditions are so arranged that the people involved are virtually pushed into frequent deviant behaviour, they speak of "structured deviance." Such deviant acts are apparently less the product of conscious choice by the people involved, than of the structure of their work and social lives. A parallel may be found in the example of a street corner that is the scene of repeated auto accidents. Eventually someone realizes that the problem is not just a series of careless drivers but a badly designed intersection.

In criticizing the narrow focus on police corruption that tends at present to dominate the literature on police deviance it is important to note that much of the literature on police discretion—in particular, research on the influence of extra-legal factors on police decision-making—can in fact be viewed as an analysis of structured organizational deviance. However, since this research has not been conceptually located within this context, its implications for the study of police deviance have not been readily recognized (Hagan et al., 1979; Meyers, 1980). This problem is one that John Hagan and Peter Morden address and seek to remedy in their essay on the influence of extra-legal and quasi-legal factors on police decision-making. In doing so, they go a long way toward illustrating the contribution that can be made to our understanding of police deviance as structured organizational deviance by explicitly considering police decision-making in this light.

In the course of their discussion of the way in which the law, and in particular the Canadian Bail Reform Act, distinguishes between legal and extra-legal factors, Hagan and Morden raise questions about the discrepancies between democratic ideals and legal prescriptions which are considered by other contributors. In addition, and most importantly, these authors consider the extent to which factors which can be considered legitimate at one stage of the process have consequences which may be illegitimate at another. This possibility, despite its importance to both the literature on police discretion and police deviance, is one which has hitherto received scant attention in the literature.

Hagan and Morden's consideration of the continuity between the established research literature on police discretion and the phenomenon of police deviance is elaborated upon by Clifford Shearing, who argues that not only is the police subculture an important determinant of organizational police deviance, but it serves to link police activity to structures of dominance within the larger society. In developing this argument, Shearing constructs a typology of responses that police officers choose between in coming to terms with the contradictions between the norms of the police subculture and the formal rules of the police organization.

John Lee in his article focuses attention on the manner in which police officers "target" certain groups of people as problem populations deserving police attention. In doing so he too relates the issue of police deviance to the general literature on police discretion by utilizing the concept of the police subculture to develop his analysis of the structure of police-minority relations. Lee draws on contemporary media accounts of police-minority interactions to provide a very rich empirical context to his analysis.

Both Lee and Shearing raise the notion that the public and senior police administrators often tacitly support organizational deviance by rank-and-file police officers. This is an issue which Richard Ericson develops in his analysis of the relationship between formal normative structures and police deviance. Taking the work of the legal scholar Doreen McBarnet (1976; 1979) as his point of departure, he argues that it is not only the informal guidelines of the police subculture which facilitate police deviance but legal rules themselves. Ericson's analysis thus serves to demonstrate that very often what police officers are deviating from is not the strict rule of law but rather the ideals of legality that the law supposedly expresses. Consequently, police deviance need not always involve an informal subversion of due process but may very well constitute activity which is consistent with both common and statutory law. In developing this theme Ericson elaborates and extends Hagan and Morden's suggestion that police deviance must be understood in terms of "the legal and institutional structures in which they work; . . . structures that encourage and even legitimate the violation of democratic norms."

Austin Turk in his essay examines a form of policing that is particularly susceptible to organizational deviance, namely, "political policing." In the course of his analysis, Turk identifies and describes the elaborate institutional and legal mechanisms used to redefine and deny the existence of police deviance. In considering the conditions under which police deviance can be successfully denied or obscured, Turk also delineates the relationship between political institutions and police organizations.

Jean-Paul Brodeur, like Turk, examines the difficulties involved in controlling organizational deviance. In considering these issues, he directs his attention to evidence that was brought before the Keable Commission (Quebec, 1981) with respect to the activities of the RCMP's Security Service (the section of the RCMP which does "political policing") and uses this to expand upon a number of the issues raised by Ericson. In particular, he examines the difficulties involved in determining whether or not activities which upon superficial examination clearly imply police wrongdoing can in fact be considered illegal. In the process, he considers the problems that arise in attempting to use the criminal justice process as a means of controlling organizational police deviance.

This issue of controlling police deviance is also examined by Philip Stenning in the final essay in the volume. Using a historical approach, Stenning outlines the political-legal framework that has evolved in Canada for the governance of the police. His discussion focuses on two principle themes, namely, "the shift from judicial to non-judicial control of the police" and the struggle between central and local levels of government for control of the police. In discussing these issues, Stenning leads the reader directly to the issue of police independence from political control—a topic that is at the very centre of contemporary debate about the control of organizational police deviance.

As will be readily apparent from this introductory discussion, the contributors to this book share common concerns and have operated within remarkably consistent conceptual frameworks, despite the fact that they prepared their essays quite independently of one another. As a consequence they have together gone a long way toward developing a general theory of structured organizational police deviance.

NOTES

1. The one exception to this is the research that has been done on police brutality as an instance of police deviance (see, for example, Lundman, 1980).
2. It should be noted at the outset that in using the term "police deviance" in this book we will be focusing exclusively on *public* police deviance. As private police now rival the public police in size (Shearing and Stenning, 1981), this means that we are excluding a vast area of police deviance from consideration. Our justification for doing so is quite simply that the area of police deviance we will be considering is so little understood that the phenomenon we do have to deal with is quite extensive enough to warrant our exclusive attention.
3. For examples of such activities, see Barker and Roebuck (1973) and Stoddard (1980).
4. This emphasis on misuse of authority distinguishes police deviance from other forms of deviance which police officers may engage in as citizens but which have nothing to do with their status as police officers (see Brodeur, below, for a further discussion of this distinction).
5. This usage of the term "organizational deviance," while consistent with the usage within the general organizational literature, differs from the way in which it has been used by some authors writing on police deviance. Lundman (1980: 184), for instance, uses the term to refer to "patterned police misconduct." Similarly, Sherman (1974) uses the term to refer to deviance supported by the dominant coalition within the police organization. In short, these authors use the term to refer to deviance with organizational causes. As we will indicate shortly, we prefer to use the term "structured deviance" to refer to deviance that is organizationally determined.

6. Jean-Paul Brodeur was a consultant with the Commission d'Enquête Sur des Opérations Policières en Territoire Québécois.
7. Philip Stenning was a consultant with the Commission of Inquiry Concerning Certain Activities of the Royal Canadian Mounted Police.
8. Clifford Shearing was Director of Research for the Commission of Inquiry Relating to Public Complaints, Internal Discipline and Grievance Procedure within the Royal Canadian Mounted Police.

REFERENCES

Barker, Thomas, and J. Roebuck
1973. *An Empirical Typology of Police Corruption: A Study in Organizational Detail*. Springfield, Illinois: Charles C. Thomas.

Bensman, J., and I. Gerver
1963. "Crime and Punishment in the Factory: The Function of Deviancy in Maintaining the Social System." *American Sociological Review* 28: 588–98.

Ermann, M. David, and Richard Lundman (eds.)
1978. *Corporate and Governmental Deviance: Problems of Organizational Behaviour in Contemporary Society*. New York: Oxford University Press.

Fogelson, Robert M.
1977. *Big-City Police*. Cambridge, Mass.: Harvard University Press.

Goldstein, Herman
1975. *Police Corruption: A Perspective on Its Nature and Control*. Washington, D.C.: Police Foundation.

Hagan, John, John D. Hewitt, and Duane F. Alwin
1979. "Ceremonial Justice: Crime and Punishment in a Loosely Coupled System. *Social Forces* 58: 506.

Lundman, R. J. (ed.)
1980. *Police Behavior*. New York: Oxford University Press.

Mann, Edward, and John Alan Lee
1979. *RCMP vs The People: Inside Canada's Security Service*. Don Mills, Ontario: General Publishing.

McBarnet, Doreen
1976. "Pre-Trial Procedures and Construction of Conviction" in P. Carlen (ed.) *The Sociology of Law*, Sociological Review Monograph, 23: 172–79. Hanley: Wood Mitchell and Co. Ltd.

McBarnet, Doreen J.
1979. "Arrest: The Legal Context of Policing" in Simon Holdaway (ed.) *The British Police*: 24–40. London: Edward Arnold.

Myers, Martha A.
1980. "Predicting the Behavior of Law: A Test of Two Models." *Law and Society Review* 14, no. 4 (Summer): 835–57.

Quebec
1981. *Rapport de la Commission d'Enquête Sur des Opérations Policières en Territoire Québécois*. Quebec: Ministère des Communications.

Schrager, Laura Shill, and James F. Short
1978. "Toward a Sociology of Organizational Crime." *Social Problems* 25, no. 4: 407–19.

Shearing, Clifford D., and Philip C. Stenning
1981. "Private Security" in Michael Tonry and Norval Morris (eds.) *Crime and Justice—An Annual Review of Research*. Vol. 3. Chicago: University of Chicago Press.
Sherman, Lawrence W. (ed.)
1974. *Police Corruption: A Sociological Perspective*. Doubleday: New York.
Shover, Neal
1978. "Defining Organizational Crime" in M. David Ermann and Richard J. Lundman (eds.) *Corporate and Governmental Deviance: Problems of Organizational Behaviour in Contemporary Society:* 37-40. New York: Oxford University Press.
Stoddard, Ellwyn R.
1980. "Blue-Coat Crime" in Richard J. Lundman (ed.) *Police Behavior*. New York: Oxford University Press. Reprinted from "The Informal 'Code' of Police Deviancy: A Group Approach to Blue-Coat Crime." *Journal of Criminal Law, Criminology and Police Science* 59 (1968): 201–13.
Walker, Samuel
1977. *History of Police Reform: The Emergence of Professionalism*. Lexington, Mass.: D. C. Heath and Co.

Chapter 1

The Police Decision to Detain: A Study of Legal Labelling and Police Deviance

*John Hagan and C. Peter Morden**

One of the most disturbing features of contemporary criminal justice is the consistent finding that many more people are detained prior to trial than are jailed after sentence. One of the first researchers to observe the consistency of this pattern, Daniel Freed (1973), has gone so far as to suggest a statistic, the "imbalance ratio," to estimate how pervasive this pattern is in any particular jurisdiction. This ratio is based on a comparison of the size of the pre-trial population of a prison system and its sentenced population. Freed's research, and the research of others (e.g., see Feeley, 1979: 236), regularly reveals just how imbalanced this ratio is.

In this essay we will be concerned with the role police play in creating this imbalance by detaining suspects for bail hearings. The potential dimensions of this problem in Canada are suggested in a finding by MacKaay (1976: 8) that 53 per cent of all accused at a Montreal "Municipal Court" were still in custody at the time of their initial appearance. We will suggest in this paper that the decision to detain a suspect for a bail hearing constitutes a form of legal labelling; we will be concerned with the causes and consequences of this type of labelling.

A police decision to detain a suspect for a bail hearing can be regarded as extra-legal, in cause and consequence, if it is based on criteria that are not authorized by law. Such decisions constitute a form of police misconduct or deviance. Thus Lundman (1980: 5) notes that "misconduct by police patrol officers includes abuse of discretion, [and] . . . . Abuse of discretion exists when police patrol officers base their decision on factors . . . such as the behavior or demeanor of the citizen, that are not part of the criminal law." In so far as the behaviour or demeanour of suspects is the basis of police

---

*Authorship is alphabetized.

decisions to detain, independent of other legally recognized criteria for decisions to detain, these decisions can be characterized as extra-legal, and as a manifestation of police deviance.

However, the criminal law is not always as definitive a guide to the legitimate uses of police discretion as might initially seem the case. Indeed, the law seems intentionally vague and ambiguous on many issues that confront legal actors, particularly the police. H. L. Hart (1961: chap. 7) refers to this characteristic of legal language as constituting the "open texture of the law." Beyond this, Bernstein et al. (1977: 367) note several additional problems that complicate the drawing of any simple division between legal and extra-legal bases of case decisions.

> First, there is considerable variation from one jurisdiction to another in the procedural law that stipulates what factors are legal versus those that are extra-legal in criminal justice decisions. Second, what is specified in a statute as legal for one stage of criminal justice processing may not be legal for another stage, e.g., community ties (flight risk) is generally a legal consideration for pre-trial release status decisions, but not for plea bargaining or sentencing decisions. Third, some variables ordinarily placed in the "legal" category (e.g., prior record of convictions) may themselves have resulted from some combination of consideration of legal and extra-legal variables in some prior processing.

The above three factors and the problems noted by Hart all complicate the study of pre-trial detention decisions. To begin with, we will see that Canadian bail reform legislation has left the criteria to be applied in these decisions vague. In turn, this has led to variation between jurisdictions in Canada in the factors that are given quasi-legal recognition in the administration of this law. Beyond this, some factors (e.g., measures of community ties) that have achieved a level of quasi-legal recognition as influences in pre-trial detention decisions are nonetheless contrary to legal expectation in the influence they directly or indirectly exercise at later stages (i.e., conviction and sentencing). Finally, it is possible, even likely, that aspects of suspects' prior legal records used in making pre-trial detention decisions are the combined products of legal and extra-legal variables that have operated at earlier points in the suspects' previous contacts with the law.

The implication of the preceding discussion is that no hard and fast distinctions can be drawn between legal and extra-legal factors in police decisions to detain. Instead we will speak of three overlapping categories of influence that we will characterize as legal, quasi-legal and extra-legal. A central point we wish to make in this analysis is that the study of police deviance will be made too narrow by any perspective that considers problematic only those influences that are explicitly extra-legal, or accepts as *non*-problematic those influences that in *appearance* are legal, or ignores the range of influences that have some legal legitimacy but can be characterized more accurately as quasi-legal in character. The problem is that the borders of police deviance are as uncertain as the laws that define them. The analysis that follows is intended to illustrate this point.

Pre-trial Detention as a Legal Label

The legal parameters of pre-trial detention are outlined in the Bail Reform Act of Canada. This Act was formulated following recommendations of the Ouimet Commission (1969), which in turn was informed by Friedland's (1965) major study of bail. Prior to the Bail Reform Act (referred to hereafter as the B.R.A.), the majority of offenders were processed by way of police arrest, with following decisions regarding bail usually made by magistrates. Thus Friedland found that approximately 90 per cent of all charges followed from police arrests, with 40 per cent of those arrested being detained prior to trial. Most significantly, Friedland found that being detained had an adverse effect on the accused's likelihood of conviction and severity of sentence. The implication is that being a "pre-trial detainee" can have disadvantaging consequences at crucial, later stages. This means that factors leading to pre-trial detainment are important not only in determining this decision, but in determining those that follow as well.

The B.R.A. was intended to address those problems by avoiding all unnecessary arrests and periods of incarceration prior to trial. Prior to the Act, the accused was bound to request his own release and then justify why he should not be held in custody. However, the Ouimet Commission reasoned that since people unconvicted of a crime are presumed to be innocent, the onus for justifying the detention of an accused prior to trial should be on the state. Thus section 450(2) of the Act states that the accused has a right *not* to be arrested (without warrant) for the majority of offences (i.e., summary conviction offences and dual-indictable/summary-offences), unless the arresting officer has reasonable and probable grounds to believe either that the accused will fail to attend trial (i.e., the flight risk posed by the accused is large) or that the immediate release of the accused poses a threat to the "public interest." In the absence of an arrest, the officer is empowered to issue an appearance notice to the accused (which is subject to confirmation by a justice of the peace).

At this point it should be noted that the B.R.A. does not indicate on exactly what "reasonable and probable grounds" an officer might infer that an accused will fail to attend trial, nor the circumstances under which the immediate release of the accused might pose a threat to the "public interest." It is this "open texture" of the Canadian Bail Reform Act that makes it impossible to draw a fine line between legal and extra-legal influences on pre-trial detention decisions. As we will note later, quasi-legal criteria have emerged to give this law operational meaning.

Meanwhile, if an arrest is made, the accused must be released without unreasonable delay, unless the arresting officer is not convinced that release is justified (s. 452). In such cases the onus to release the accused shifts to the officer in charge of the station. Section 453 allows the officer in charge an extended range of release options for all offences carrying a maximum sentence of five years or less. These include release by way of summons;

promise to appear; and recognizance without surety not exceeding $500. If the officer in charge decides to continue custody, the accused must be brought before a justice of the peace within 24 hours (s. 454). Appearance before a justice may take place at a police station, in a detention facility, or in Provincial Court. The justice is bound in turn to release the accused on an undertaking, without conditions, unless the prosecutor "shows cause" why a more onerous form of release or continued detention is justified. However, the prosecutor is entitled "reasonable opportunity" (with up to three days permitted for remand purposes) to prepare his case.

It should be clear from this discussion that the B.R.A. has structured police discretion with the intention of forcing police officers in most cases to invoke powers of arrest and detention as a last resort. At the same time, the B.R.A. has increased police responsibilities and powers by enlarging the scope of release alternatives at the disposal of police. These additional resources encourage a "quasi-judicial" function by police in their determination of which release option, if any, to exercise (see Kelly, 1976: 152). Thus, in an effort to confine the majority of bail decisions to the primary stage of criminal processing, the B.R.A. simultaneously curtails police powers of arrest and detention while augmenting police powers of release.

For the accused who is denied release prior to trial, the net result is an accumulation of socio-legal facts which insinuate that, despite all benefits of the doubt granted to the accused by the B.R.A., he is too untrustworthy, dangerous, desperate or morally corrupt to be released. Stated more succinctly, the B.R.A. "makes pre-trial detention a salient piece of negative information about an accused" (Koza, 1974: 48). It is in this sense that the B.R.A. may in effect act as a legal vehicle whereby the implicit label "pre-trial detainee" is disadvantageously applied by police to accused persons.

New Criteria and Prior Research

We have noted that the B.R.A. does not specify the criteria by which police are to make pre-trial detention decisions, other than to indicate that these decisions are to be made in light of the "reasonable and probable" grounds of flight risk and in terms of the "public interest." It is perhaps for this reason that there exists an Ontario Crown Attorney Association (OCAA) manual regarding bail decisions which lends quasi-legal authority to a more specific set of criteria to be applied in these decisions by prosecutors, and by implication, by police. These criteria include the accused's presumed strengths, weaknesses, attitudes, associations, home life, employment status, residence, medical and psychiatric history and prior criminal record (OCAA, 1976: 27–29). Much of the justification for utilizing such criteria originated from the Vera Institute's Manhattan Bail Project (Ares et al., 1963). In this project, the researchers developed a scale for identifying low-risk bail candidates (on the basis of many of the above considerations) and apparently applied this scale successfully in the reduction of failure-to-appear rates. It has since become a touchstone for both bail reform legislation and localized pre-trial diversion programs (Mahaffy, 1979; Wice, 1974).

However, recent research questions the premise that variables like those identified above accurately forecast whether the accused will fail to attend court or be rearrested. Gottfredson (1971) conducted research to determine the reliability of the Vera Institute Scale, and found that it failed to predict 43 per cent of one sample as being "successes" and 26 per cent of another sample as "failures." He concluded that the scale had little power to predict non-appearance. Feeley and McNaughton (1974) found that among released defendants, neither seriousness of offence, personal background characteristics, nor community ties were related to eventual non-appearance.

Clarke et al. (1976) conducted a major study which analysed variables related to non-appearance and rearrest of accused prior to trial. *Not* related to either event were sex, race, income, employment status and seriousness of offence. Factors which were related to non-appearance or rearrest (i.e., "erroneous release") included the time between release and final court disposition (the longer the interval, the higher the probability of flight or rearrest), criminal record of the accused, and form of bail used (the least effective being the threat of financial loss). Landes (1974) found that severity of offence and prior record were significant predictors of rearrest but did not have any power in forecasting non-appearance. On the basis of these findings, Landes concluded that the major criterion for deciding pre-trial status and bail amounts is actually the judge's anticipation of further crimes. Thus, judges, and the bail systems they work with, may actually be more concerned with the prediction of dangerousness than with ensuring trial attendance.

Finally, we look at a study which analysed the criteria associated with accused who were refused bail on the assumption that they would commit serious crimes if released. Christenson (1971) looked at an extensive list of variables upon which the decision to detain was based. Many of these criteria are the same as those used in the Manhattan Bail Project, such as family ties, prior record, seriousness of offence, employment, community relations and residence. *None* of these factors predicts the criminal activity of accused following release. Christenson observed that "at no time do the criteria individually or collectively provide a means of isolating even a small group of defendants, more of whom are recidivists than are not" (1971: 369).

We can tentatively conclude from the above studies that of the wide range of considerations commonly employed to predict post-release behaviour of accused, none is consistently demonstrated to predict accurately rearrest or failures to appear. Nonetheless, these variables are, with the encouragement of quasi-legal authority, a central part of much pre-trial decision-making. One possible consequence of this situation is suggested by Paul Wice:

> Despite the good intentions of bail reform projects, they continue to utilize release criteria that can be met only by middle-class defendants. By stressing a stable, economic family and residential lifestyle, as well as penalizing defendants for past violations of the law, these projects are unable to help the indigent, the transient and youth who fill the nation's pre-trial detention facilities. [1974: 212]

The above situation becomes a serious matter of concern when it is noted that pre-trial detention decisions can influence conviction and sentencing decisions as well. There is increasing evidence that the chances of being convicted and receiving a harsh sentence are increased if the defendant has been in custody pending trial (see Friedland, 1965; Koza and Doob, 1975; Baab and Ferguson, 1967; Rankin, 1964). As well, the converse situation has also been reported: "Pre-trial *release* directly results in greater leniency" (Farrell and Swigert, 1978; emphasis added; see also Ares et al., 1963). The effects of pre-trial detention may manifest themselves in a number of ways. For example, incarceration may hinder the ability of the accused to engage counsel and limit other activities necessary for a sound defence (such as tracking down witnesses, earning money to pay for a lawyer) (see Stanley, 1977). Similarly, an "atmosphere of guilt" may surround the defendant who appears in custody for trial because he is presumably a poor flight risk and/or a danger to society (Friedland, 1965; Skolnick, 1967; Koza and Doob, 1975).

Police decisions to detain can, therefore, be important factors at later adjudication and disposition stages. The dubiousness of this situation is that many of the quasi-legal factors (e.g., employment status) considered by police in the decision to detain can become extra-legal influences in later stages of the decision-making process. This possibility is a primary concern of the research we describe next.

The Current Research

The present research undertakes to further explore, in an empirical context, the variables that are associated with police refusal to grant bail to an accused (i.e., to hold for a bail or show-cause hearing), and the direct and indirect effects that this decision may have on conviction and sentencing. This approach differs from previous research on bail selection, as our concern is with police rather than judicial decisions to detain. One of the problems associated with the latter approach is that *final* decisions regarding bail may be made at virtually any point prior to completion of trial (see Hann, 1973; OCAA, 1976). An added reason to focus on police as opposed to court determinations of pre-trial detainment involves the greater responsibility that police have in Canada in overseeing bail determination in the majority of criminal cases. Finally, the subterranean motives police may have regarding pre-trial status (i.e., to gather information or extract statements) and the weight of influence that police recommendations have upon judicial bail decisions, also encourage an exploration of the bail question at the police level (Lafave, 1965). Underscoring our concern here is the advice of Justice Douglas of the U.S. Supreme Court that "what takes place in the secret confines of the police station may be more critical than what takes place at the trial" (dissenting opinion in *Crooker v. California* (1957), 357 U.S. 433 at 444–45).

Sample, Variables and Methods

Data for this study were derived from official records for a research project on criminal victimization. The data were gathered from September 1976 to January 1977 in the region of Peel, Ontario. The offence- and accused-related variables we will consider were abstracted from police "occurrence sheets." These sheets are typically one-page forms on which police officers briefly record their accounts of events surrounding alleged crimes; these forms also record salient administrative details, such as whether a statement was taken and whether the accused was held for a bail hearing. Occasionally, occurrence sheets were missing data relevant to the variables used here, either through an oversight by the recording officer or a lack of information at the time. In these instances, the missing information was coded as "d/k" (don't know). One thousand cases make up the sample. Each case involved a victim, and in each case an accused was charged. Accordingly, a great number of minor offinces (e.g., violations under the Highway Traffic Act, keeping a common bawdy house, liquor offences, etc.) are not represented in the sample.

Fifteen per cent of the offences in the sample are "against persons," while 85 per cent are "against property." Approximately 45 per cent of the charges involve theft. It should be noted that no charges of murder or other High Court offences listed in section 457.7(1), (2) are present. Such cases result in automatic detainment for a bail hearing by police, since release decisions in these cases must be made by Superior Court Judges.

Since this research is exploratory, a variety of independent variables are considered. These variables (listed in Table 1.1) are initially divided into two general categories: accused- and offence-related characteristics. (We will leave until later our designation of these variables as legal, quasi-legal or extra-legal in their influences.) Accused characteristics include marital status, sex, age, employment status, behaviour with police, prior convictions, and prior incarceration. Frequently it has been argued that such characteristics (or "societal attributes") may "facilitate or impede the individual's ability to avoid the imposition of a deviant label" (Gove, 1975: 5). Thus, a young, unmarried, unemployed male who is unco-operative with the police and has been previously convicted and/or incarcerated is ex-

Table 1.1: Variables and Codings

	Variable	*Coding*	
Accused Characteristics	Marital Status	Married, Widowed	(0)
		Single, Common law, Divorced	(1)
	Sex	Female	(0)
		Male	(1)
	Age	Under 23	(0)
		Over 24	(1)
	Employment Status	Employed	(0)
		Unemployed	(1)
	Behaviour with Police	Co-operative	(0)
		Unco-operative	(1)
	Prior Convictions	No	(0)
		Yes	(1)
	Prior Incarceration	No	(0)
		Yes	(1)
Offence Characteristics	Number of Current Charges	One	(0)
		More than one	(1)
	Offence Seriousness	Lower	(0)
		Higher	(1)
	Warrant Issued	No	(0)
		Yes	(1)
	Victim's Relationship to Accused	Some Relationship	(0)
		No Relationship	(1)
	Victim Type	Individual	(0)
		Organization	(1)
	Statement Taken	No	(0)
		Yes	(1)
	Accused's Condition at Arrest	Sober	(0)
		Not Sober	(1)
Dependent Variables	Held for Bail Hearing	No	(0)
		Yes	(1)
	Trial Outcome (Verdict)	Not Guilty, Dismissed	(0)
		Guilty	(1)
	Trial Outcome (Sentence)	Fine, Suspended Sentence, Probation	(0)
		Incarceration	(1)

pected to experience more punitive treatment within the criminal justice system than an individual who possesses the opposite attributes—quite apart from the nature of the offence. In terms of our present research, we expect similar patterns to emerge.

The second category, offence-related variables, includes number of current charges; seriousness of offence; whether the accused was arrested by warrant; the victim's relationship to the accused; whether the victim was an individual or an organization; whether a statement was given by the accused; and the condition of the accused at the time of arrest. These variables provide information regarding the amount of harm associated with the charge (number of charges, offence severity), plus a variety of factors relevant to the circumstances and evidence surrounding the offence. For example, if a warrant had been executed or a statement given, this may suggest the presence of a "strong case" and therefore a higher probability of conviction. It is assumed that these variables increase the likelihood of pre trial detainment. A similar effect is anticipated for offence severity, because presumably an accused with serious charges has a high motivation to abscond, and/or may pose a greater threat to the "public interest" if released (see Landes, 1974).

Notable among variables *not* incorporated into the analysis is the plea of the accused. This information was not available in the data, although it probably has an important effect on trial outcome (i.e., a guilty plea is synonymous with a verdict of guilt).

Each variable is dichotomized, with the presumed "disadvantaged" condition occupying the higher value. For example, with the employment status variable, "employed" is assigned the lower value (0) and "unemployed" is assigned the higher value (1). Where continuous variables, such as age, are involved, the dichotomization takes place at the mean (thus "under 23" = 0, "over 24" = 1; in this case the mean is also the median). Where information is unavailable (i.e., "d/k" on the occurrence sheet), the case is placed in the "advantaged" category. This is done so as to retain all cases for analysis, while at the same time not compromising the "disadvantaged," or more suspect, condition. While this procedure may introduce some ambiguity into the data, such a consequence is preferable to the possible biases involved in omitting cases altogether. In any event, as mentioned earlier, the incidence of "d/k" is slight.

Our objective is to develop a statistical model whereby both direct and indirect causal linkages can be determined between the predictor variables and the three binary dependent variables (i.e., decision to hold for a bail hearing, conviction, and sentence severity). Accordingly, four different multiple regressions are presented. The first regression generates path (or beta) coefficients between the 14 independent variables and the decision to hold for a bail hearing. The second regression considers the effects of our independent variables on the adjudication of the case, with conviction assigned the higher value. At this stage of the analysis, the result of the bail hearing is added as an independent variable. The third regression considers only the population that received a guilty verdict; otherwise, this analysis replicates the first. Among other things, this part of the analysis is included to allow a comparison between the "presumed innocent" pre-trial population and the "found guilty" population. Finally, sentence severity is used as the dependent variable for our last regression. Prison sentences are assigned the higher values in this analysis, and the bail hearing is again treated as an independent variable. Descriptive statistics for the independent and dependent variables considered in this paper are presented in Table 1.2.

Table 1.2: Descriptive Statistics

Variables	*Total Population (N= 1,000)*		*Total Population (N= 704)*	
	X	S	X	S
Marital Status	.588	.492	.605	.489
Sex	.732	.443	.707	.455
Age	.500	.500	.528	.500
Employed	.346	.476	.357	.479
Behaviour with Police	.084	.278	.090	.286
Prior Convictions	.430	.495	.406	.492
Prior Incarceration	.161	.368	.136	.343
Number of Current Charges	.176	.381	.126	.333
Severity of Offence	.221	.415	.220	.415
Warrant Issued	.090	.286	.070	.255
Victim's Relationship to Accused	.790	.408	.828	.378
Victim: Individual or Organization	.643	.479	.685	.465
Statement Taken	.228	.420	.254	.436
Accused's Condition at Arrest	.165	.371	.158	.365
Held for Bail Hearing	.150	.357	.155	.362
Trial Outcome: Conviction	.704	.457		
Trial Outcome: Incarceration			.185	.388

The Findings

The results of the first regression analysis are presented in Table 1.3. The dependent variable for this analysis is the police decision to hold an accused for a bail hearing. The following characteristics of the accused have significant effects on this decision: prior convictions (beta = .11), prior incarceration (.19), employment status (.10), and behaviour toward police (.08). Several offence characteristics also have significant effects: seriousness of offence (beta = .13), type of victim (– .08), whether a warrant was issued (.07), and whether a statement was taken (.06). Although all of these effects are consistent with the preceding discussion and/or prior research, two are of particular interest for our purposes.

Thus the finding that unemployed accused are more likely to be held for bail hearings is not surprising, but it *is* a cause for concern. The employment status of the accused falls within the criteria of the OCAA Manual (see discussion above). As well, this information may form the basis for more general conclusions about the accused by the police: police may interpret unemployment as an indication of flight risk (i.e., reflecting the absence of a community tie that employment is thought to establish); the likelihood of future arrests (i.e., generating an increased opportunity or motivation for criminal activity); or simply as a sign of bad character (i.e., providing additional evidence of the incorrigibility of the accused). However, there are several causes for concern here. First, consideration of employment status is an obvious way in which the poor can be penalized in our criminal justice system. Second, although the OCAA Manual lends quasi-legal authority to the consideration of employment status, there is little established evidence that employment status and bail abuse are closely related. Third, even though the use of employment status by police in the decision to detain an accused for a bail hearing may have a quasi-legal claim to legitimacy the influence of this variable directly or indirectly at conviction or sentencing is not justifiable by law. We will return to this last point shortly.

Accused persons who are unco-operative in their behaviour with police are also more likely to be held for bail hearings. We regard the influence of this variable as evidence of police deviance. Clearly, the B.R.A. does not intend that detainment for a bail hearing can be used as a means of making accused persons more co-operative, or as a means of punishing accused who are unco-operative. Indeed, as we noted earlier, Lundman (1980: 5) makes the consideration of suspect demeanour an explicit part of his definition of "police misconduct." Furthermore, if this variable has an indirect influence on conviction and sentencing through its impact on pre-trial detention, then that should be a cause for additional concern. The part of our analysis we turn to next addresses this, among other issues.

In the second stage of our analysis we are interested in the effects of our independent variables, which now include being held for a bail hearing, on the chances of being convicted. The results of this part of our analysis are presented in the second part of Table 1.3. The results indicate that of all the characteristics of the accused, the only one that significantly influences the chances of conviction is whether the accused had been incarcerated previously (beta = −.08). Of the offence-related characteristics, the following have significant effects: the type of victim (.11), the relationship between the victim and accused (.08), the number of charges involved (−.20), and whether a statement was taken (.14). Most significantly, however, these results indicate that being held for a bail hearing also increases the likelihood of conviction (.08). The importance of this last finding becomes apparent in Figure 1.1.

Table 1.3: Correlation and Regression Coefficients and F-Levels for Total Population (N = 1,000)

	Independent Variable	*Dependent Variable = Bail Hearing* r	RSQ Change	B	Beta	F	*Dependent Variable = Verdict* r	RSQ Change	B	Beta	F
Accused Characteristics	Marital Status	.10	.006	.027	.04	1.15	.05	.003	.038	.04	1.24
	Sex	.14	.051	.022	.03	0.73	-.09	.003	-.043	-.04	1.53
	Age	.07	.051	.001	.00	0.00	.09	.005	.052	.06	2.37
	Employment Status	.13	.076	.076	.10	11.33*	.03	.000	-.000	-.00	0.00
	Behaviour with Police	.13	.007	.102	.08	6.98*	.03	.002	.082	.05	2.49
	Prior Convictions	.30	.035	.077	.11	8.91*	-.07	.004	.006	.01	0.03
	Prior Incarceration	.32	.030	.184	.19	31.23*	-.10	.005	-.095	-.08	4.49**
Offence Characteristics	Number of Current Charges	.11	.012	.002	.00	0.00	-.20	.036	-.238	-.20	39.15*
	Offence Seriousness	.20	.014	.109	.13	16.89*	-.00	.001	-.021	-.02	0.35
	Warrant Issued	.15	.017	.087	.07	5.30**	-.11	.007	-.096	-.06	3.56
	Victim's Relationship to Accused	-.11	.001	-.037	-.04	1.63	.14	.007	.094	.08	6.01**
	Victim: Individual or Organization	-.17	.026	-.058	-.08	5.01**	.14	.020	.105	.11	9.13*
	Statement Taken	.15	.009	.055	.06	4.05**	.10	.014	.152	.14	17.40*
	Accused's Condition at Arrest	.08	.001	.017	.02	0.30	-.03	.000	-.003	-.00	0.01
	Held for Bail Hearing						.02	.000	.098	.08	5.22**

* P = .01
** P = .05

Figure 1.1: Path Diagram of Bail Hearing and Conviction for Total Population (N = 1,000)

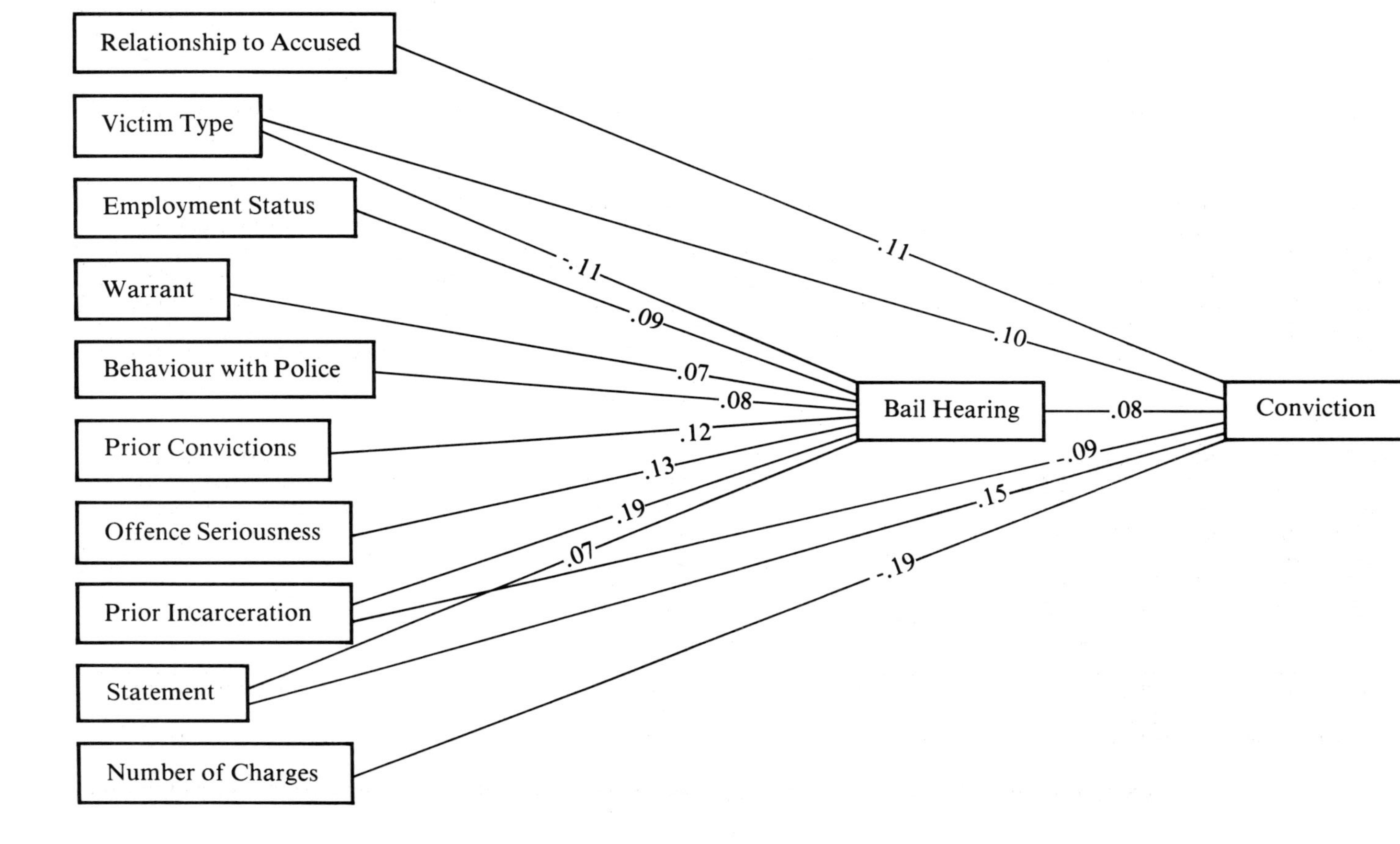

Figure 1.1 is based on a rewriting of the two regression equations we have already considered, with only the significant effects retained. What this figure conveniently illustrates is that although variables like employment status and the behaviour of the accused toward the police do not have direct effects on conviction, they do have indirect effects through the bail hearing variable. And, as we have emphasized earlier, both of these influences are extra-legal at the later stage. However, Bernstein et al. (1977: 752) offer a plausible explanation of why these influences may nonetheless persist: "If a prior set of societal reactors responded negatively to the defendant (i.e., the police) it might be organizationally functional to maintain consistency in decision-making."

In Table 1.4, we turn our attention exclusively to those cases that result in convictions (N = 704). The reason for this change in focus is to allow a separate analysis of those cases that are ultimately sentenced. The first part of Table 1.4 considers being detained for a bail hearing as the dependent variable. The findings here parallel those earlier, with the exception that type of victim is no longer significant. Employment status (.11) and behaviour toward police (.09) remain significant.

The second part of Table 1.4 presents the results of a regression analysis examining the independent effects of variables (including being held for a bail hearing) on sentences received by convicted offenders. Results presented in Table 1.4 indicate that offenders who have been previously incarcerated (.24) or previously convicted (.09) are more likely to be incarcerated. This is also the case for those who are convicted of serious offences (.19), who are convicted of more than one charge (.10), who are unemployed (.07), and, most significantly, who have been held for a bail hearing (.18).

The results of these two regressions are again summarized in the form of a path diagram. This diagram, presented in Figure 1.2, illustrates once more that variables like employment status and behaviour toward police have direct and indirect effects on sentence, with the police decision to detain for a bail hearing again serving as a mediating variable. It is interesting to note that the latter decision has a bigger impact on sentence than conviction, even though sentencing is further removed temporally from pre-trial detainment than is conviction. We turn now to an assessment of the significance of these findings.

Discussion and Conclusions

We began this paper with the concern that many more persons are imprisoned before trial than after. The research reported in this paper has focused on the role police play in detaining accused for bail hearings prior to trial. In doing this we have noted that Canadian police make pre-trial detention decisions with relatively little guidance from the law. Thus, while the Bail Reform Act instructs police to consider "reasonable and probable"

Table 1.4: Correlation and Regression Coefficients and F-Levels for Convicted Population (N = 704)

		Dependent Variable = Bail Hearing					*Dependent Variable = Sentence*				
	Independent Variable	r	RSQ Change	B	Beta	F	r	RSQ Change	B	Beta	F
Accused Characteristics	Marital Status	.11	.007	.038	.05	1.57	.15	.008	.028	.04	0.89
	Sex	.17	.011	.031	.04	1.04	.18	.008	.019	.02	0.38
	Age	.07	.000	.007	.01	0.06	.12	.001	.034	.04	1.33
	Employment Status	.14	.031	.087	.11	10.79*	.14	.012	.057	.07	4.68**
	Behaviour with Police	.14	.008	.111	.09	6.28**	.12	.002	.074	.06	2.84
	Prior Convictions	.32	.032	.067	.09	4.83**	.37	.042	.071	.09	5.37**
	Prior Incarceration	.32	.038	.220	.21	28.57*	.43	.051	.271	.24	41.99*
Offence Characteristics	Number of Current Charges	.11	.012	.006	.00	0.03	.22	.009	.117	.10	9.47*
	Offence Seriousness	.24	.010	.098	.11	9.27*	.34	.031	.181	.19	32.05*
	Warrant Issued	.19	.032	.148	.10	8.69*	.16	.009	.041	.03	0.66
	Victim's Relationship to Accused	-.13	.003	-.051	-.05	1.96	-.03	.004	.052	.05	2.07
	Victim: Individual or Organization	-.18	.030	-.053	-.07	2.78	-.14	.005	-.049	-.06	2.34
	Statement Taken	.21	.018	.079	.10	6.33**	.19	.007	.023	.03	0.51
	Accused's Condition at Arrest	.11	.002	.035	.04	0.87	.10	.000	.016	.02	0.18
	Held for Bail Hearing						.39	.155	.194	.18	26.29*

* P = .01
** P = .05

Figure 1.2: Path Diagram of Bail Hearing and Sentence for Convicted Population (N = 704)

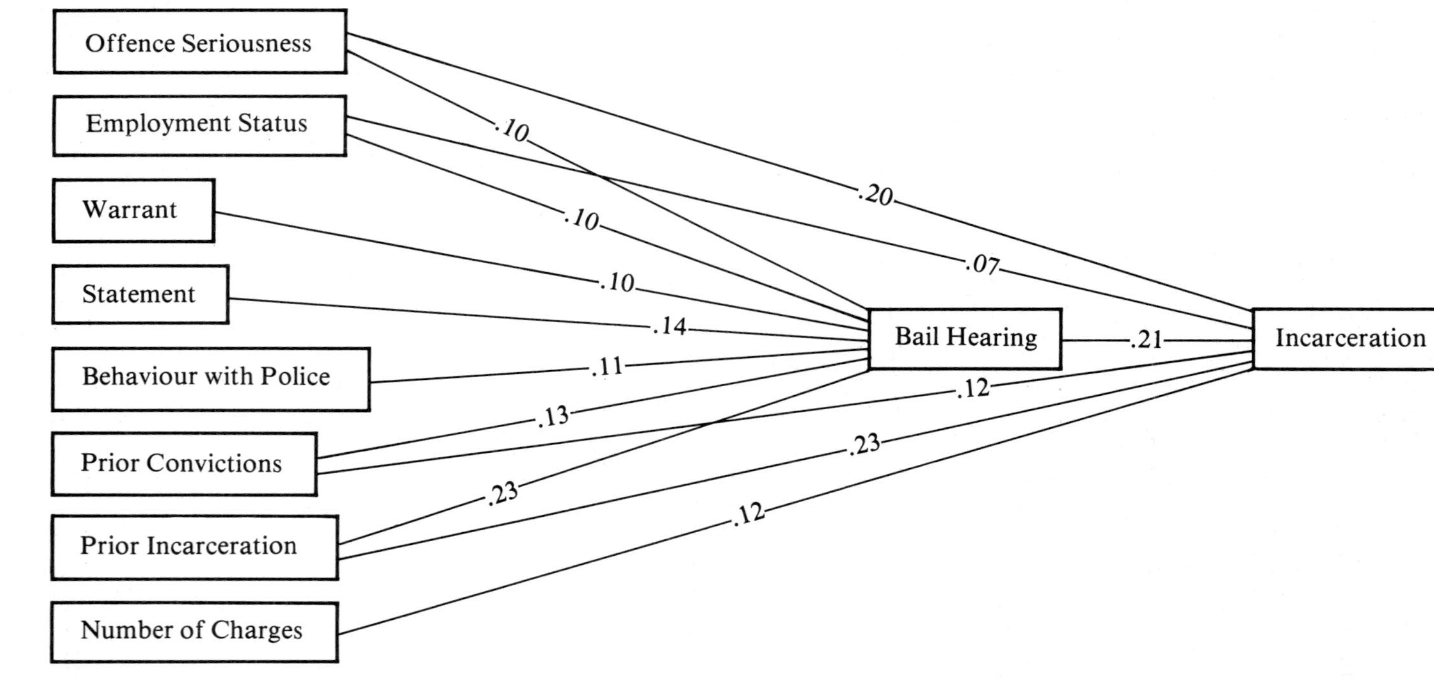

grounds of flight risk and the broader "public interest" in their decisions, it provides little indication as to the criteria to be used in doing so. This makes it impossible to draw a hard and fast line between legal and extra-legal criteria that influence pre-trial release decisions. For example, we know that consideration of the suspect's prior record (see s. 457.3) is legal under the Act, and that consideration of the suspect's behaviour or demeanour toward the police probably is extra-legal. However, there are a variety of considerations between these two that are ambiguous, or quasi-legal in character. Many of these considerations are given a quasi-legal legitimacy by virtue of their inclusion in the Ontario Crown Attorney Association's Manual, which lists a number of criteria for making pre-trial detention decisions.

The above manual's list of criteria follow from research done in the Vera Institute's Manhattan Bail Project. This research sought to establish a set of criteria that would rationalize the pre-trial release process by providing a way of identifying those suspects most and least likely to reoffend and evade trial. In this paper we have reviewed a number of studies that question the success of these criteria in accomplishing their intended goals. Added to this question of predictive validity is the concern that many of these criteria work against the poor and in favour of the more affluent. For example, employment status is taken as one measure of the suspect's likelihood of attending trial and reoffending. Indeed, we have found in our analysis that unemployed accused are more likely to be held for bail hearings. This disadvantaging of poor suspects has a quasi-legal legitimacy that derives from the Association's manual, yet it is a legitimization that has an uncertain grounding in prior research, and it would certainly seem to be in violation of democratic norms.

To the extent that the decision-making processes we have described do violate democratic norms, in spite of their quasi-legal status, they constitute a form of what we can call "structured police deviance." Our use of the word "structure" here is meant to indicate that the form of deviance involved does not so much derive from the motivations or actions of individual officers as from the legal and institutional structures in which they work; that is, it is these structures that encourage and even legitimate the violation of democratic norms. This point is given more significance by the role the bail decisions we have been considering play at conviction and sentencing.

In the current research, and in earlier work, it has been demonstrated that early bail decisions influence the likelihood of conviction and severe sentencing. For example, in our work it is found that those suspects who are held for a bail hearing are more likely to be convicted and severely sentenced. It is a cause for concern in itself that bail decisions have these lingering effects. However, what concerns us more, for the purposes of this essay, is that a consequence of the above situation is that all those variables (legal, quasi-legal and extra-legal) that directly influence bail decisions will indirectly influence conviction and sentencing. Thus, while being unemployed may have some quasi-legal claim to legitimacy at the bail stage, it clearly does not have a similar claim at later stages. Nonetheless, the influence prevails, with disadvantaging consequences for the poor and others.

The structured forms of police deviance we have discussed in this paper are not likely to be highly visible to the police themselves or to their public. Issues of police brutality and corruption, for example, are much more likely to attract public attention, at least in so far as they are exposed. However, we submit that the kinds of structured police deviance we have discussed in this paper have extremely important consequences for the suspects who experience them. A broader conception of police deviance may give these issues the attention they deserve.

REFERENCES

Ares, C. E.; Anne Rankin; and H. Sturz
1963. "The Manhattan Bail Project: An Interim Report on the Use of Pre-trial Release." *New York University Law Review* 38, no. 1: 67–95.

Baab, G. W., and W. R. Ferguson
1967. "Texas Sentencing Practices: A Statistical Study." *Texas Law Review* 45: 471–503.

Bernstein, I. N.; W. R. Kelly; and P. A. Doyle
1977. "Societal Reaction to Deviants: The Case of Criminal Defendants." *American Sociological Review* 42 (Oct.): 743–55.

Bernstein, Irene Nagel; Edward Kick; Jan Leung; and Barbara Schulz
1977. "Charge Reduction: An Intermediary Stage in the Process of Labeling Criminal Defendants." *Social Forces* 56, no. 2: 362–84.

Christenson, B. F.
1971. "Preventative Detention: An Empirical Analysis." *Harvard Civil Rights—Civil Liberties Law Review* 6 (March): 2.

Clarke, S. H.; J. L. Freeman; and G. C. Koch
1976. "Bail Risk: A Multivariate Analysis." *Journal of Legal Studies* 5, no. 3: 341–85.

Farrell, Ronald, and Victoria Swigert
1978. "Prior Offense as a Self-Fulfilling Prophesy." *Law and Society Review* 16, no. 2: 66–70.

Feeley, M.
1979. *The Process is the Punishment*. New York: Russell Sage Foundation.

Feeley, M. M., and J. McNaughton
1974. *The Pre-Trial Process in the Sixth Circuit: A Quantitative and Legal Analysis*. New Haven Pre-Trial Services.

Freed, Daniel
1973. "The Imbalance Ratio." *Beyond Time* 1: 25–34.

Friedland, Martin
1965. *Detention Before Trial*. Toronto: University of Toronto Press.

Gottfredson, Michael R.
1971. "An Empirical Analysis of Pre-Trial Release Decisions." *Journal of Criminal Justice* 2, no. 4: 287–304.

Gove, Walter R.
1975. *The Labeling of Deviance: Evaluation and Perspective.* New York: John Wiley and Sons.

Hann, Robert G.
1973. *Decision Making in the Canadian Criminal Court System: A Systems Analysis.* Vols. 1, 2. University of Toronto: Centre of Criminology.

Hart, H. L. A.
1961. *The Concept of Law.* London: Oxford University Press.

Kelly, W. H.
1976. "The Police" in W. T. McGrath (ed.) *Crime and Its Treatment in Canada.* 2nd ed. Toronto: Macmillan Co. of Canada.

Koza, Pamela
1974. "A Social Psychological Study of the Bail Reform Act." M.A. dissertation, Centre of Criminology, University of Toronto.

Koza, Pamela, and A. N. Doob
1975. "The Relationship of Pre-Trial Custody to the Outcome of a Trial." *Criminal Law Quarterly* 17: 391–400.

Lafave, Wayne R.
1965. *Arrest: The Decision to Take a Suspect into Custody.* Boston: Little, Brown and Co.

Landes, William M.
1974. "Legality and Reality: Some Evidence on Criminal Procedure." *Journal of Legal Studies* 3, no. 2: 287–337.

Lundman, Richard J.
1980. *Police Behavior.* New York: Oxford University Press.

MacKaay, E.
1976. *The Paths of Justice: A Study of the Operation of the Criminal Courts in Montreal.* Montreal: Groupe de Researche en Jurimetrie, Université de Montréal.

Mahaffy, Carol
1979. "Bail Verification and Supervision: An Overview." *The Community in Corrections Newsletter.* Toronto: Ontario Ministry of Correctional Services.

Ontario Crown Attorney Association
1976. *Bail Reform: A Manual for Law Enforcement Officers.* 2nd ed.

Ouimet, Roger (Chairman)
1969. *Report of the Canadian Committee on Corrections—Towards Unity: Criminal Justice and Corrections.* Ottawa: Information Canada.

Powell, Clay M.
1976. *Arrest and Bail in Canada: A Commentary on the Bail Reform Act.* 2nd ed. Toronto: Butterworths.

Rankin, Anne
1964. "The Effect of Pre-Trial Detention." *New York University Law Review* 39: 641–55.

Skolnick, Jerome
1967. "Social Control and the Adversary System." *Journal of Conflict Resolution* 11: 53–70.
Stanley, Paul
1977. *Prisoners Remanded in Custody*. Planning and Support Services Division, Ontario Ministry of Correctional Services.
Wice, Paul B.
1974. *Freedom for Sale: A National Study of Pre-Trial Release*. Lexington, Mass.: Lexington Books.

Chapter 2

Deviance and Conformity in the Reproduction of Order

Clifford D. Shearing

Recently, a number of theorists have directed attention to the problem of identifying the mechanisms through which the state acts to preserve "the hegemony of the dominant classes" (Burawoy, 1978: 59; see also Quinney, 1977: 80; Hall et al., 1978; Giddens, 1976; Beirne, 1979: 378). I have elsewhere (Shearing, 1981) sought to contribute to this discussion by elaborating upon Foucault's (1977) notion that social control has become increasingly diffuse, invisible and automatic through the identification of the subterranean mechanisms that direct and co-ordinate the activities of police officers in the maintenance of order.[1] The argument advanced was that the police subculture co-ordinates police action so as to reproduce structures of dominance in two ways. First, it encourages them to support the productive classes—referred to as "the public"—in their struggle with the unproductive "lumpen proletariat"—referred to by a variety of derogatory epithets such as "the dregs" or "the scum" (see Quinney, 1977: 136 and Silver, 1967). Secondly, it defines the formal values supposedly governing the police organization (both the legal system and departmental policy) as no more than a normative framework to be used in the legitimation of police action (see Bittner, 1967a; Katz, 1972; Manning, 1977).[2]

In this paper my purpose is to extend this analysis of the "mutual accommodation of power and norms in social interaction" (Giddens, 1976: 113) one step further by considering how individual police officers respond to the expectations of the police subculture as well as the formal values and rules governing the police organization. This analysis is directly relevant to Parson's attempt to develop a voluntaristic account of the manner in which normative expectations are translated into social action (see Giddens, 1976: chap. 3). I will accordingly examine its implication for the development of such a theory.

The Research

Both the analysis referred to above (Shearing, 1981) and the analysis to follow are based on research which took place within the Communications

Centre of a large Canadian municipal police department. Police officers working within the Centre received calls for police assistance from the public and responded to them by dispatching patrol officers to investigate. The officers in the Centre, like their colleagues in other parts of the department, were exposed both to the police subculture and to the values and expectations of the law and departmental policy. Within the Centre, however, it was departmental policy rather than the law that contributed most directly to this conflict. Accordingly, it will be the contrast between policy and the police subculture, rather than the similar contrast between the subculture and law, that will be the principal focus of attention in the analysis to follow. Nonetheless, as in both cases the individual police officer must respond both to formal rules about how the job should be done and to subcultural guidance as to the "reality" of police work, the analysis has a relevance to police work generally, and indeed to other organizational settings.

The data collection took place over a period of six months during the fall and winter of 1971. It involved the observation of over 60 shifts as well as the tape recording of several thousand telephone conversations, both between police officers in the Centre and citizens, and between police officers within the Centre and other officers within other parts of the police department (see Shearing, 1977, for a detailed description of the research). While the analysis to follow is based primarily on this research, it has inevitably been informed by my subsequent contacts with the police in a variety of capacities and in a number of other police departments.

The Police Subculture and Police Policy

I have elsewhere (Shearing, 1977; Shearing, 1981) discussed the nature of the police subculture and police policy as it was expressed within the context of the Communications Centre. In order to provide both an empirical and analytic context for the analysis to follow, it is necessary to summarize briefly the relevant arguments from these earlier discussions.

The police subculture is viewed by police officers as a source of direction and guidance—the "rules of thumb" of police work (Manning, 1977)—that rank-and-file police officers can turn to as they go about their work. It derives its authority and legitimacy from the fact that it is perceived by these officers as the embodiment of the collective wisdom of generations of police officers. It is viewed like tradition, as Anthony Burgess has recently written, "the voice of the past speaking to the Present" (1978: 79).

Police officers encounter the police subculture once they have completed their formal training and start work within the police organization. During this initial period more experienced police officers contrast the "book learning" of formal training with the "tried and true" advice of the subculture (see Niederhoffer, 1967; Harris, 1973; see also Becker and Geer, 1958). In the course of this contrast, new police officers are acquainted with the subcultural view of departmental policy, the law and the concerns of the senior police command.

The police subculture presents the senior police command as a group of police officers concerned primarily with legitimating police work to outside groups and political authorities by showing it to be governed by, and in accord with, liberal democratic ideals of egalitarian justice. This process of legitimation is viewed as involving the systematic denial of the "reality" of police work, as this is known to rank-and-file officers (Harris, 1973). That is, "the brass" is viewed as obscuring the fact that police participate in class conflict on behalf of the public by controlling the "dangerous classes" (Silver, 1967). This view of the role of the brass is reflected in the subcultural view of departmental policy. It is seen, like the law, not as a source of direction for police work but as a framework to be used in legitimating this work (c.f. Goffman's distinction between "front stage" and "back stage" (1959) and his concept of "evidential boundaries" (1974)). This conception of departmental policy and the brass's role in "enforcing" it is expressed in such subcultural maxims as "you can't do it by the book" (Wilson, 1968) and "cover your arse" (Manning, 1977: 140–42; see also Chatterton, 1973).

Although "the brass" were viewed as "officially" opposed to such hypocrisy, they were seen as tacitly supporting it by rewarding those who were successful in managing both their back-stage work and their front-stage appearances (for a revealing discussion of this process see Canada, 1976: 116-19; see also Mann and Lee, 1979).[3] Accordingly, while the legitimation of police work was viewed as primarily the responsibility of the brass, it was also regarded by the police subculture as a matter that rank-and-file police officers should be sensitive to. Indeed, the common view was that it was those who were most adept at sustaining the official hypocrisy of police work who had the best career prospects.

The Linkage Between Norms and Action

It is evident from the above that the normative structure within the Communications Centre was comprised of two interdependent subsystems, each of which promoted differing courses of action. The consequences these normative subsystems had for police action were a function of the manner in which individual officers responded to them. This response was by no means uniform. While all the officers within the Communications Centre recognized both the subculture and departmental policy, they responded to them in different ways. On the basis of these differences, the officers within the Centre identified a typology of role models that they used both in constructing their own actions and in identifying themselves and others within the police community. This social map provides a useful framework for describing the way in which the guidance of the police subculture was translated into action.

Wise Officers

> *Officer, after persuading a caller phoning about a landlord and tenant dispute to report his problem to the Landlord and Tenant Advisory Bureau on Monday morning, turns to the author and says: "Another buck successfully passed. Did you see that? Now here you have a glaring example of what can be done. You don't send a car [although this was required by formal policy], but you haven't done anything wrong now, have you?"*

The wise officers were individuals whose moral commitment was to the police subculture. They accepted the authority of this culture and in doing so accepted its view of the world in which the police operated. This included the subcultural view of the social structure and the police role within it as well as the subcultural view of the law and departmental policy as a legitimating framework. These officers expressed at an individual level the double standards of police work. They were directly concerned with controlling the unproductive classes while at the same time presenting appearances that could be used to affirm the egalitarian nature of police work (cf. Scott and Lyman, 1968).

These officers saw themselves as "world wise." Their wisdom, as they defined it, lay both in their appreciation of the knowledge of their predecessors, made available to them via the police subculture, and in the fact that they were "wise" to the Goffmanesque character of police work (Carlen, 1976).

The wise police officers in recognizing the brass's concern with legitimation believed that their ability to walk the "thin blue line" of control and legitimation was the single most important criterion for promotion within the police department. While wise officers differed in their ability to maintain these double standards (Bittner, 1967a; 1967b), they all shared a commitment to this goal and evaluated each other in terms of their success in achieving it.

Although the wise officers whole-heartedly embraced the values and expectations of the police subculture, not all the officers within the Communications Centre did. In addition to the wise officers, three other types of officers were identified by the officers within the Centre on the basis of their response to the police subculture.[4]

Real Officers

> *"The trouble with policemen today, I mean the new ones, is they're not policemen. Sure they know something, but they're scared. They pay us to do a job, and it's up to us, nobody else, to get it done."*

Despite the fact that it was the wise officers who accepted the values and perspectives of the police subculture most completely, they were not the heroes within the police department (cf. Klapp, 1962).[5] The heroes were the "real" police officers. These were individuals who accepted the view of the class structure and class conflict presented by the police subculture as well as the police role as participants in this struggle. However, they rejected the necessity of legitimation as degrading hypocrisy and wished to have nothing to do with it. In sticking to this principle they were prepared to risk the wrath of the brass if necessary. Because they wished to have no part of the hypocrisy of the wise police officers, they saw themselves as even more deeply committed to the "social theory," and associated expectations, of the police subculture. They wanted nothing to do with legitimating police action in egalitarian terms, believing that the obvious necessity of controlling the dangerous classes, who were after all "the scum" and "dregs" of society, was legitimation enough. They believed in calling a spade a spade and were admired by other officers for their forthrightness and courage, although the wise officers tended to scoff at their naivety.

The real officers saw themselves as "hard-nosed policemen" who had learned about policing from personal experience. They were tough. They presented themselves as "professionals" who made their own judgments about what should or should not be done and who went ahead and did what was right without reference to either the public or the brass. They were confident in their own abilities and unintimidated by either the public or the brass.

Good Officers

"Well, I'm responsible for this and I want to do it right."
"Sure, I take this seriously; if she dies it's my responsibility."

The good police officers lay at the opposite end of the ideological spectrum to the real officers. While the latter wished to have nothing to do with the legitimating framework of police policy, the good police officers, like Niederhoffer's (1967) "professional,"[6] rejected the values and expectations of the police subculture. Despite this ideological disparity, however, the good officers like the real officers rejected the hypocrisy that the management of appearances involves.

The good officers saw themselves as "good policemen" because while they recognized the police subculture they did not identify with it. Their commitment was to egalitarian values of liberal democracy expressed within departmental policy and the law. They believed that these were the values that ought to govern the operation of the police department and defined "police professionalism" as an attempt to bring police practice into line with these values. In support of this view of policing, good officers liked to believe that the brass, at least at the most senior levels, shared their commitment to "police professionalism" and issued directives that reflected a genuine commitment to egalitarian values. They regarded departmental policy as genuine instructions for action. The good officers believed that their responsibility as professionals was to implement, not undermine, departmental policy. They wanted to do a "good job" and believed that in this they had the support of the brass.

Given this view, it is not surprising to find that the good officers included within their number some officers who Reed et al. (1977) have identified as "doormen."[7] In their desire to see that policy was "properly" implemented, and to identify themselves as "good policemen" to the brass, these officers would sometimes pass on information about their fellow police officers to the brass. It is this identification with the brass which doormen express that gives meaning to the term "good policemen" when it is used by others within the Commmunications Centre. The most flattering comment the "good officers" were likely to receive from these other officers was a sarcastic "Mr. Perfect." Doormen, however, were more likely to be referred to as "brown nosers" and "arse creepers."

Cautious Officers

> *"This job's really boring, but some of us don't have much choice. It's either the radio room or out. It's going to be just what you make of it, and it can be fun because most of the men are nice guys to work with. It's just a job. All I do is get a name and address and send a car off. I don't argue with people, it doesn't make sense. There are a lot of guys here that argue over every car they send out. I can't be bothered."*

Unlike the types of police officers we have already discussed, for the cautious officer police work had ceased to be a vocation. These officers responded neither positively nor negatively to the police subculture. They were indifferent to it, and indeed, to the entire police world. For the cautious officers, each shift was something they wanted to get through with a minimum of difficulty. They did not want to be "hassled" by either their colleagues or the brass. They took account of both of these groups, but they were committed to the values of neither. Nor did they wish to secure the approval of either. They wished simply to avoid their disapproval. Above all, they wanted to avoid trouble, and this made them cautious. They had "dropped out." They were in the police world but not of it. Some cautious police officers were what they were because they felt they had been hurt once too often at the hands of the brass. Others were simply near retirement and had lost interest in police work. They had already turned their attention away from policing and focused it on the world outside.

This analysis of police types is at variance with the tendency to treat the police as a homogeneous community distinguishable from outsiders but relatively indistinguishable from each other. A notable exception to this is Niederhoffer's (1967) attempt to develop a typology of police identities and to relate this to police career development. While his typology is in many ways not unlike the one presented here, it is flawed because it is essentially an evaluative framework developed from the perspective of the good police officer. One consequence of this is that Niederhoffer treats the police subculture as a destructive cancer within the police community that must be resisted, and he looks forward to the day when this fight will have been won and the police subculture's influence, if not eradicated, will have been greatly diminished. Despite this important limitation, however, it is significant to note that Niederhoffer's typology (which defines a career progression from the idealistic good police officer to the cynical cautious one) is, like the one presented here, premised on the notion that police identify themselves and their fellows in terms of their response to the normative structures of the police world.

Another exception is Muir's (1977) discussion of four different categories of police officers. While Muir is not explicitly concerned with police officers' responses to subcultural guidelines, the two dimensions he focuses on—the view of human nature officers hold and their attitude toward coercion—relate directly to the conception of the police culture presented here. Muir reported that two of the four police officers he focused upon as exemplars of different orientations to police work made a distinction in their perception of the public between "workingmen" whom they served and the villains who were their enemies (1977: 22). This is obviously strikingly similar to the distinction between "the public" and "the scum" referred to above. The other two officers, like our good officers, rejected this dichotomy (1977: 28). In a similar manner, two of the officers Muir discussed regarded coercion as an appropriate means for dealing with trouble, and one of them in particular felt it was necessary to go beyond the limits of the law and departmental policy in its use (1977: 25–26). These officers were not unlike our wise and real officers. The two officers who did not share this view of coercion were in their turn not unlike the good officers both in their reluctance to use force and in their refusal to go beyond legal and departmental restraints in its use.

The Consequences of Differing Interpretations

The question the above analysis poses is this: How is it possible to at once argue, as I did at the beginning of the paper, that the police subculture coordinates police action in the production of order, and at the same time contend, as I have in the foregoing, that there are three categories of police officers who reject its guidance? As only the wise officers appear to actively target the "dangerous classes" and at the same time legitimate police action in egalitarian terms, it would seem that far from contributing to the police role in the reproduction of order, the real, good and cautious officers detract from it by introducing a disruptive element into the police organization. The theoretical problem this raises is precisely the problem that

Parsons came face to face with very early on in his quest for a voluntaristic theory of social order (see Parsons, 1935). Parsons, following Durkheim, identified the normative structure as the critical mechanism in the maintenance of social order.[8] He argued, in a Hobbesian vein, that to serve this function it had to be an extraordinarily powerful mechanism because the forces at work within the individual (both biologically and psychologically based) would, if left unrestrained, create chaos. As a result, Parsons was reluctant to conceive of this mechanism in terms which would permit individuals any leeway in their response to the normative restraints which produced order (this reluctance and the reasons for it are particularly clear in Parsons, 1935). He also recognized, however, that without allowing individuals some elbow room with respect to their normative environment it would be impossible to conceive of them theoretically as "active, creative, evaluating creatures" (Parsons, 1935) who respond rather than simply react to their social world (Blumer, 1969).

Parsons thus found himself on the horns of a theoretical dilemma. If he was to construct an adequate theory of social order, he believed he would have to introduce theoretical postulates antithetical to a voluntaristic conception of man. On the other hand, if he retained a voluntaristic conception he would not, he believed, be able to account for social order (Parsons, 1935). As this dilemma is essentially the dilemma the argument above poses, the question posed above is ultimately the problem of the possibility of voluntaristic theory of social order. That is, is it possible to acknowledge that different police officers interpret and respond to their social world differently and still be able to argue that the normative structure within the police community constitutes an essential mechanism in the production of order?

Although Parsons wrestled with this dilemma for some time (see Parsons, 1937), he ultimately abandoned voluntarism in favour of developing a theory which would satisfactorily account for social order, namely, a position of normative determinism.[9] This choice is clearly evident in this development of his theoretically central concept "institutionalization" (see Parsons, 1951: 249–325). Parsons conceives of the actor as doing "what he does as a result of values 'internalized' as need-dispositions of personality (in conjunction with the non-normative conditions of action): he is portrayed as an unthinking dupe of his culture [cf. Garfinkel, 1967] and his interaction with others as the enactment of such need-disposition rather than as, as it truly is, a series of skilled performances" (Giddens, 1976: 113). Although this criticism of Parsons is now well established, the dilemma Parsons confronted remains unresolved (Giddens, 1976: chap. 3). While contributions to its resolution have been made by both ethnomethodologists and conflict theorists, neither of these theoretical perspectives provides the basis for its resolution (Giddens, 1976: 113). The Parsonian question thus remains unanswered. How are we to develop a theory of the production and reproduction of social order that is not based on assumptions of normative determinism?

In considering Parsons' theory of institutionalization it is evident that despite the Durkheimian acknowledgement that deviance has positive functions, Parsons equated deviance with disorder and conformity with order. As a result the only organizational response to deviance Parsons acknowledged in his theory of institutionalization was a system of rewards and punishment which acted to encourage conformity and discourage deviance (Parsons, 1951). This position, however, fails to take into account the now well-established findings that deviance can and does contribute to social order and that organizations do not simply respond to deviance by discouraging it, but facilitate its use in the fulfilment of organizational requirements (Sutherland, 1940; Dentler and Erikson, 1959; Bensman and Gerver, 1963; Coser, 1965; Erikson, 1966; Katz, 1972; Reed et al., 1977; Mann and Lee, 1979). Once the possibility of functional deviance as a *routine* feature of the reproduction of social order is acknowledged (see especially, Bensman and Gerver, 1963), the equation of conformity with social order and deviance with disorder can no longer be sustained.[10] The Parsonian assumption that normative orders function to produce social order only when their expectations are followed (that is, only when there is a positive commitment to them) becomes untenable. Once this assumption is abandoned, however, one is left with the theoretical problem that Parsons concluded was insolvable, namely, accounting for social order without insisting on the equation of conformity with order and deviance with disorder. It is on the solution to this problem that the possibility of a voluntaristic theory of action depends; for if this equation is insisted upon, as Parsons believed it had to be, one is led inextricably to a position of normative determinism. In suggesting how one might avoid this equation, it is useful to examine the organizational response to the three "deviant" categories of officers I have identified and the contribution they made to the police enterprise.

Good Officers

While the good officers did not contribute to the operation of the police department in the same way that wise officers did, they nonetheless had an essential and useful part to play. One relatively marginal way in which they did this, as Reed et al. (1977) have noted, was as an information conduit to senior levels in the police command structure. However, they made a much more important and pervasive contribution to the reproduction of order than their occasional role as "informers" suggests. In these more general roles, although the good officers tended to be viewed as outsiders by the real and wise officers, they were not despised.

Good officers were inclined to seek out and to be assigned to public relations positions and divisions within the police organization where their genuine commitment to egalitarian values and their belief in departmental policy and the law as the proper sources of guidance for police action made them fine salesmen for the police department. One such division was the Communications Centre. The Centre was a showpiece for citizen tours of the police department. Visitors were usually impressed with the idea that this was the control centre of the police department and with the general atmosphere of "hustle and bustle." On tours of the Centre, good officers were invariably selected as guides. During these tours their commitment to the values used in legitimating police work enabled them to do an outstanding job of presenting the department in a good light.

As a researcher I was directly exposed to good officers as legitimators of police work. When I began my research it was one of the good officers who was assigned to introduce me to the Centre. When I began listening to telephone calls within the Centre, I was initially assigned exclusively to good officers, and it was only once I insisted on using randomly generated numbers to select officers that I was able to observe other officers at work within the Centre. The good officers, both in their work and in their descriptions of it, portrayed an image of police work that was entirely consistent with egalitarian expectations.

In addition to the Communications Centre, there were several other areas within the police department to which good officers were routinely assigned. Two of the most obvious were the Research and Planning Bureau, which was used to prepare annual reports, and major statements to the press, and the Safety Bureau, which was involved principally in public relations work in schools.

This tendency for good officers to be located in positions in which their perspective on police work could be used to contribute to the operation of the police organization was possible because the good officers co-operated with both their immediate supervisors and senior officers in facilitating this. They felt comfortable in positions in which they could fully express their view of police work and consequently tended to encourage initiatives which would locate them in such positions. At the same time, their supervisors and more senior officers who were concerned with staffing the various positions within the police organization were anxious to ensure that officers worked in positions in which their orientation to police work could be fully exploited.

One of the prices good officers paid for their commitment to the egalitarian values explicitly expressed in the law and policy was that they were unlikely to be promoted beyond the supervisory level. Good officers were just not regarded as "wise" enough to be promoted to the key positions of authority within the police department. Such positions were viewed as the preserve of wise officers.

Real Officers

As folk heroes within police departments, the real officers were living expressions of the "social theory" of the police subculture. As such, they were useful to have scattered sparingly around the police department in positions where they could act as visible symbols of this culture. The real officers highlighted, particularly for recruits, the subcultural view of the class structure and the police role within it. Within the Communications Centre, where there were always a handful of trainees, there was one real officer.

Although the real officers contributed to the symbolic affirmation of the police subculture, they also made a much more direct contribution to policing. There are certain areas of police work in which considerable toughness is regarded as an asset and in which the legal niceties of due process are regarded by the police as an unaffordable luxury if social control is to proceed properly.[11] One such area prevalent in Canada at present is the police response to motorcycle gangs (see Ontario, 1978). Another is the police response to "drug pushers." Yet another is organized crime. These are all relatively low-visibility areas of police work in which the public is regarded as being more tolerant of, and indeed as demanding, greater toughness than might otherwise be the case. Real police officers are fine candidates for squads that specialize in such work. They feel comfortable with physical force and they are more willing than wise officers to take the risks this involves (Muir, 1977: 25–26). Real officers in accepting such roles are typically under no illusions about the attitude the senior command is likely to take if ever their toughness becomes public, despite their tacit approval of it. They expect to be "weeded out" as "bad apples."

Like good officers, the real officers have very limited career prospects and remain within the specialized and low-visibility areas of police work for which they are most suited.

Cautious Officers

Cautious officers find their niche in those boring, less palatable areas of police work where what is required is tortoise-like plodding. Such glamourless, uninteresting jobs occur in most organizations and the police organization is no exception. While other police officers find such work unattractive, for the cautious officers it provides a welcome oasis away from the limelight. These positions require little commitment and thus allow them to "do their time" with a minimum of interference. For instance, cautious officers make fine record clerks—a job that requires patience and accuracy but little commitment to the goals of police work. Here one can daydream about other worlds and while away one's time (see Goffman's discussion of "the away" and other similar strategies, 1959). Within the Communications Centre there was much to be done that many police officers found unattractive. To the cautious police officers, however, these boring areas of police work provided opportunities for a quiet desk job where they could carve out a place for themselves with little responsibility.

What this discussion of the police department's response to real, good and cautious officers indicates is that the activities of these "deviant" police types are co-ordinated with the activities of the "conformists"—the wise police officers—so that together they work to produce the institutional hypocrisy of police work and thereby contribute to the reproduction of order. This co-ordination is such that even those individuals who, in one way or another, reject this hypocrisy, nonetheless contribute to it. Indeed, their rejection is an important and essential feature of their contribution. So long as these individuals operate within the police organization, they become "willy-nilly," via the process of placement to which they themselves contribute, part of "the system."[12] In short, police officers were located in positions where their inclinations were aligned with organizational objectives.

This process of alignment provides the basis for suggesting how it may be possible to forge the theoretical link necessary to permit the inclusion of a voluntaristic conception of man with a normative account of the production and reproduction of social order.[13] What it suggests is that a normative solution to the problem of order must embody a more complex model of the relationship between norms and actions than the Parsonian theory of institutionalization permits. More specifically, it suggests that there are two critical "complications" which must be included within an adequate account of the relationship between norms, order and action. First, it is necessary to conceive of normative systems not simply as embodying directions for action but as including both a directional and legitimating component. Further, our analysis suggests that the norms guiding action are likely to be subterranean in character, while those used in legitimating action are likely to be more visible (Homans, 1950). This suggestion serves to introduce into a normative account of social order the Marxist position that formal rules are essentially superstructural (Lockwood, 1956; Quinney, 1977).

Secondly, it is necessary to acknowledge that a variety of different orientations to any normative structure can contribute to the production of order. This flexibility can be introduced if "organizational position" is recognized as a critical variable in considering the relationship between norms, action and order. Once organizational position is acknowledged it becomes possible to demonstrate how organizations are not only able to accommodate individual choice but also how "deviance," together with "conformity," contributes to the production of social order. This recognition of the role of both "deviant" and "conformist" responses in the production of order makes it possible to transcend the Parsonian impasse, thereby reconciling social order with voluntarism.

Whether it is possible to use the analysis we have offered as the basis for developing a *general* voluntaristic theory of social action is, of course, an empirical question. There is, however, already considerable empirical evidence on "functional deviance" to suggest that this can be done (Dentler and Erikson, 1959; Erikson, 1966; Reed et al., 1977, to cite but a few). The nature of this support can be illustrated by considering the conclusions reached by Bensman and Gerver (1963) in their classic analysis of organizational deviance within an aircraft factory. Although these authors did not explicitly consider the question of the development of a voluntaristic theory of action, the conclusions that may be drawn from their analyses are remarkably similar to the ones above.

Bensman and Gerver found that both deviance and confirmity with respect to formal organizational policy contributed to the operation of the aircraft factory and concluded that "the 'deviant' action may be as central to the system as is the norm it deviates from" (1963: 595). In disputing the conventional structural-functional equation of deviance with disorder and conformity with order, these authors went on not only to describe a normative system comprised of conflicting formal and informal components but, as I have done, identified organizational differentiation as the critical variable in the integration of these components into patterns of voluntaristic action in which both "deviance" and "conformity" contributed to the production of aircrafts (1963: 596).

Summary

The empirical question addressed in this paper was, how is it possible for the police to participate in class conflict by targetting the "problem populations" when they work within an environment of official rules which appear to encourage egalitarian law enforcement? In short, how is the hypocrisy of police work possible?

In answering this question I drew upon Foucault's (1977) analysis of the subterranean character of political power by identifying the police subculture as the normative mechanism directing police participation in class conflict. In examining how the conflict between the egalitarian ideals of the formal rules and the non-egalitarian premises of the police subculture were translated into action, I considered two more specific questions. First, how do police officers respond to the two sets of values which constitute their normative environment? In response I argued that police officers themselves recognize four ideal-type responses which they use as role models in terms of which they define themselves and others.

Second, I asked how the senior echelons of police organization responded to these four types of responses. This analysis was used to examine the problem of developing a voluntaristic theory of social order. The argument advanced was that by recognizing the manner in which organizational requirements are aligned to individual inclinations it is possible to provide a voluntaristic account of action at the microscopic level while at the same time demonstrating how such activity contributes to the maintenance of stable social structures.

NOTES

1. This is similar to the structural Marxists' notion that "state apparatuses exercise a 'relative' autonomy in their relationship with the capitalist class" (Beirne, 1979: 379). See also Balbus (1973).
2. This view of the police subculture presented by Shearing (1981) differs significantly from the traditional view. For a review of the literature on the police subculture, see Wexler (1974).
3. Jacobs and Britt point to the wider social context in which this hypocrisy takes place when they observe in relation to police violence "that for inequality to lead to more lethal violence by the police it is not necessary to assume that elites make direct demands for harsh methods. All that is required is that elites be more willing to overlook the violent short cuts taken by the 'dirty workers' in the interests of order" (1979: 406).
4. These types can be related to Riesman's distinction between traditional-directed, inner-directed and outer-directed men (Riesman, 1950), to Thomas's bohemians, philistines and creative men (Volkart, 1951), and to Klapp's heroes, villains and fools (Klapp, 1962). More specific and less systematic distinctions can also be related to this typology. The "rate buster" of the Hawthorne experiments (Homans, 1950) is, for instance, reminiscent of the good officer discussed below.
5. For an interesting general discussion of the hero as the courageous yet naive man, dedicated to principles he believes in, see Steinbeck (1976).
6. Niederhoffer refers to the "professional police officer" on numerous occasions. Perhaps the most relevant reference from the point of view of the argument being developed here is the following:

   > The new patrol man must resolve the dilemma of choosing between the professional idea of police work he has learned at the Academy and the pragmatic precinct approach. In the Academy, where professionalism is accented, the orientation is toward that of the social sciences and opposed to the "lock-them-up" philosophy. [1967: 56]

7. The types of police officers identified by Reed et al. (1977) represent marginal roles that are found within the police organization. These types do not provide a systematic base for classification which includes all officers. Consequently, while interesting as features of the police world, these types are not particularly helpful with respect to the problem of concern here.
8. Parsons' conception of the normative structure is simpler than the conception presented here in that it does not differentiate between legitimating the directing normative systems. The conception of the normative structure in this essay takes into account the ethnomethodological notion that a formal system constitutes a legitimating surface structure (Cicourel, 1973; Wieder, 1974), as well as the similar Marxian notion that the formal normative system constitutes a superstructural framework which serves ideological purposes (Lockwood, 1956; Carlen, 1976; Hall et al., 1978). At the same time, it introduces at the substructural level a conception of a normative structure similar in many respects to the Parsonian notion of a normative system which directs action. The equivalent

notion within the ethnomethodological perspective is that of a constitutive grammar (Garfinkel, 1967; Garfinkel and Sacks, 1970) which forms part of a "deep structure" (Cicourel, 1973; cf. Chomsky, 1972). There is no obvious equivalent within the Marxian perspective, as the substratum level tends to be viewed in non-normative terms thus suggesting that normative phenomena are entirely superstructural (Lockwood, 1956; Taylor et al., 1973; Quinney, 1977).

9. This statement requires some elaboration. What Parsons in fact did was to modify his definition of "voluntarism" until it was compatible with what he regarded as the requirements of a theory of social order. The net result of this was that eventually, for Parsons, voluntarism came to mean no more than the requirement that action be conceived analytically as taking place within a "means-end scheme." Within this framework Parsons proceeded to reduce individual discretion to zero, believing that it was only under these circumstances that social order was possible. Parsons begins moving toward this definition of "voluntarism" in Parsons (1935) and develops this definition more fully in Parsons (1937) and Parsons (1951). Giddens discusses this shift in Parsons' thinking in the following terms:

> Parsons' early work was directed towards reconciling . . . voluntarism . . . with the idea of the functional exigency of moral consensus. For Parsons the very same values that compose the *consensus universal*, as "introjected" by actors, are the motivating elements of personality. If these are the "same" values, however, what leverage can there possibly be for the creative character of human action as nominally presupposed by the term "voluntarism"? Parsons interprets the latter concept as referring simply to "elements of a normative character", *the "freedom of the acting subject" then becomes reduced—and very clearly so in Parsons' mature theory—to the need-dispositions of personality.* In the "action frame of reference"; action itself enters the picture only within the context or the emphasis that sociological accounts of conduct need to be complemented with psychological accounts of "the mechanisms of personality"; the system is a wholly deterministic one . . . there is no room here for the creative capacity of the subject on the level of the individual actor. . . . [1976: 95–96]

10. The now well-established research tradition concerned with the functions of deviance has to date unfortunately had a limited effect on the influence of this Parsonian assumption because of the tendency of persons working within this area to accord the notion of "functional deviance" and relate notions like "structured deviance" (Mann and Lee, 1979) an ironic status. This sense of irony serves to define "functional deviance" as something special, something unusual. By placing it in the category of the unusual, the implications of this concept for the equation of conformity with social order are blunted. At best, this equation is treated as something which, though generally true, is not always true. Work on functional deviance thus serves to identify the exceptions which prove the rule and does not become a challenge to it.
11. As the public response to the findings by the McDonald Commission of wrongdoing by the Royal Canadian Mounted Police suggests, this attitude toward certain aspects of police work is not limited to the police community (see Mann and Lee, 1979).
12. For a discussion of this process in a broader social setting, see Steve Biko's discussion of the contribution white liberals make to the political system in South Africa (1978).
13. For an earlier suggestion as to how this problem might be resolved, see Shearing (1973).

REFERENCES

Balbus, I. D.

1973. *The Dialectics of Legal Repression: Black Rebels Before the American Courts.* New York: Russell Sage Foundation.

Becker, Howard S., and Blanche Geer

1958. "The Fate of Idealism in Medical School." *American Sociological Review* 23 (Feb.): 50–56.

Beirne, Piers

1979. "Empiricism and the Critique of Marxism on Law and Crime." *Social Problems* 26, no. 4: 373–85.

Bensman, Joseph, and Israel Gerver

1963. "Crime and Punishment in the Factory: The Function of Deviancy in Maintaining the Social System." *American Sociological Review* 28 (Aug.): 588–98.

Biko, Steve

1978. *I Write What I Like.* London: Bowerdean Press.

Bittner, Egon

1967a. "Police Discretion in Emergency Apprehension of Mentally Ill Persons." *Social Problems* 14, no. 3: 278–92.

1967b. "The Police on Skid Row: A Study of Peace Keeping." *American Sociological Review* 32, no. 6: 699–715.

Blumer, H.

1969. *Symbolic Interactionism.* Englewood Cliffs, N.J.: Prentice-Hall.

Burawoy, Michael

1978. "Contemporary Currents in Marxist Theory." *The American Sociologist* 13, no. 1: 50–64.

Burgess, Anthony

1978. *1985.* Boston: Little, Brown and Company.

Canada

1976. *The Report of the Commission of Inquiry Relating to Public Complaints, Internal Discipline and Grievance Procedure within the Royal Canadian Mounted Police.* Ottawa: Department of Supply and Services.

Carlen, Pat

1976. *Magistrates' Justice.* London: Martin Robertson.

Chatterton, M.

1973. "A Working Paper on the Use of Resource-Charges and Practical Decision-making in Peace-keeping." Paper presented to the 2nd Bristol Seminar on the Sociology of the Police, Bristol, England (April).

Chomsky, N.

1972. *Language and Mind.* Enl. ed. New York: Harcourt Brace Jovanovich Inc.

Cicourel, Aaron V.

1973. *Cognitive Sociology: Language and Meaning in Social Interaction.* Harmandsworth: Penguin.

Coser, Lewis A.

1965. *The Functions of Social Conflict.* London: Routledge and Kegan Paul.

Dentler, Robert, and Kai Erikson

1959. "The Functions of Deviance in Groups." *Social Problems* 7 (Fall): 94–197.

Erikson, Kai T.
1966. *Wayward Puritans: A Study in the Sociology of Deviance*. New York: John Wiley and Sons Inc.
Foucault, Michel
1977. *Discipline and Punish: The Birth of the Prison*. New York: Pantheon Books.
Garfinkel, Harold
1967. *Studies in Ethnomethodology*. Englewood Cliffs, New Jersey: Prentice-Hall.
Garfinkel, Harold, and Harvey Sacks
1970. "Formal Structures of Practical Action." In J. C. McKinney and E. A. Tiryakian (eds.) *Theoretical Sociology: Perspectives and Development*. New York: Appleton-Century-Crofts.
Giddens, Anthony
1976. *New Rules of the Sociological Method*. London: Hutchinson.
Goffman, Erving
1959. *The Presentation of Self in Everyday Life*. Garden City, New York: Doubleday.
1974. *Frame Analysis: An Essay on the Organization of Experience*. Cambridge, Mass.: Harvard University Press.
Hall, Stuart; C. Critcher; T. Jefferson; J. Clark; and Brian Roberts
1978. *Policing the Crisis: Mugging, the State and Law and Order*. London: Macmillan.
Harris, R.
1973. *The Police Academy: An Inside View*. New York: John Wiley and Sons Inc.
Homans, George C.
1950. *The Human Group*. New York: Harcourt Brace and World.
Hughes, Everett C.
1971. *The Sociological Eye: Selected Papers on Work, Self and Study of Society*. Chicago and New York: Aldine-Atherton.
Jacobs, David, and Davit Britt
1979. "Inequality and Police Use of Deadly Force: An Empirical Assessment of a Conflict Hypothesis." *Social Problems* 26, no. 4: 403–12.
Katz, Jack
1972. "Deviance, Charisma and Rule-Defined Behavior." *Social Problems* 20, no. 2: 186–202.
Klapp, Orrin E.
1962. *Heroes, Villains and Fools: The Changing American Character*. Englewood Cliffs, New Jersey: Prentice-Hall.
Lockwood, David
1956. "Some Remarks on 'The Social System.' " *The British Journal of Sociology* 7: 134–46.
Mann, Edward, and John A. Lee
1979. *RCMP vs The People*. Don Mills, Ontario: General Publishing.
Manning, Peter K.
1977. *Police Work: The Social Organization of Policing*. Cambridge, Mass.: MIT Press.

Muir, William K., Jr.
1977. *Police: Street Corner Politicans*. Chicago: University of Chicago Press.
Niederhoffer, Arthur
1967. *Behind the Shield: The Police in Urban Society*. Garden City, New York: Doubleday.
Ontario Police Commission, Inquiry into Police Practices in the Waterloo Regional Police Force
1978. *Report* (including recommendations). Toronto.
Parsons, Talcott
1935. "The Place of Ultimate Values in Sociological Theory." *International Journal of Ethics* 45, no. 3: 282–316.
1937. *The Structure of Social Action*. New York: McGraw-Hill.
1951. *The Social System*. Glencoe, Illinois: Free Press.
Quinney, Richard
1977. *Class, State and Crime*. New York: David McKay Co.
Reed, Meyer A., Jerry Burnette, and Richard R. Troiden
1977. "Wayward Cops: The Function of Deviance in Groups Reconsidered." *Social Problems* 24, no. 5 (June): 565–75.
Riesman, David
1950. *The Lonely Crowd: A Study of the Changing American Character*. New Haven: Yale University Press.
Scott, Marvin B., and Standford M. Lyman
1968. "Accounts." *American Sociological Review* 33, no. 1: 46–62.
Shearing, Clifford D.
1973. "Towards a Phenomenological Sociology." *Catalyst* 7 (Winter): 9–14.
1977. "Real Men, Good Men, Wise Men and Cautious Men." Ph.D. dissertation, University of Toronto.
1981. "Subterranean Processes in the Maintenance of Power: An Examination of the Mechanisms Coordinating Police Action." *Canadian Review of Sociology and Anthropology* 18, no. 3 (Aug.): 283-98.
Silver, Allan
1967. "The Demand for Order in Civil Society: A Review of Some Themes in the History of Urban Crime, Police, and Riot" in D. J. Bordua (ed.) *The Police: Six Sociological Essays:* at 1–24. New York: John Wiley and Sons Inc.
Steinbeck, John
1976. *The Acts of King Arthur and His Noble Knights*. Garden City, New York: Farrar, Straus and Giroux.
Sutherland, Edwin
1940. "White Collar Criminality." *American Sociological Review* 5: 1–21.
Taylor, Ian; Paul Walton; and Jock Young
1973. *The New Criminology*. London: Routledge and Kegan Paul.
Volkart, E. H.
1951. *Social Behaviour and Personality: Contributions of W. I. Thomas to Theory and Social Research*. New York: Social Science Research Council.
Wexler, Mark N.
1974. "Police Culture: A Response to Ambiguous Employment" in C. L. Boydell, C. F. Grindstaff, and P. C. Whitehead (eds.) *The Administration of Criminal Justice in Canada*. Toronto: Holt, Rinehart and Winston.

Wieder, D. Lawrence
1974. *Language and Social Reality*. The Hague: Mouton.
Wilson, J. Q.
1968. *Varieties of Police Behavior: The Management of Law and Order in Eight Communities*. New York: Atheneum Publications.

Chapter 3

Some Structural Aspects of Police Deviance in Relations with Minority Groups

John Alan Lee

There is already a considerable literature on the behaviour of police forces in relation to minority groups (see References at the end of this paper). Much of this literature, however, has developed in response to crisis situations: ghetto riots, civil rights demonstrations, the Black Panthers, and so forth. There is also a considerable literature on police deviance (see References), but much of this has concerned itself with police violation of the civil liberties of the dominant sector of society: white, older, male, middle-class citizens of Anglo-Saxon background. These are the citizens with the most power to complain effectively against police misbehaviour and wrongdoing.

However, the emergence of organized social movements of change and protest among North American minorities (a distinctive feature of our society during the past two decades) has brought increasing attention to police activity which previously was taken for granted. As Wilson (1968: 170) reports an Albany policeman: "In the old days any Negro who talked back was hammered on the head . . . and nobody thought twice about it." But the rise of civil rights and political movements among blacks, Hispanic Americans, native peoples, and even homosexuals has profoundly altered police-minority relations. As Chevigny (1969) notes, the individual member of a minority is generally ineffective in complaining about police misdemeanours, but a citizen backed by an organization is likely to be heard. An isolated incident may quickly be converted into a "last straw" of "police harassment" against an outraged minority. Conversely, police frustration in the face of minority defiance has produced a relatively new phenomenon of police deviance, the "police riot."

In short, the study of police-minority relations has hitherto consisted largely of ad hoc responses to traumatic interactions, especially those attracting media attention (e.g., police riots, race riots). This paper proposes a more fundamental or "structural" approach. We will view incidents of deviant behaviour in police-minority relations as symptoms of relatively long-lasting and basic ("structured") relations between *organized groups*. We will not allow ourselves to be distracted by extreme events or individuals. For example, we will eschew explanations of trouble between police and minorities which lay the cause at the door of "bigots" in the police or "extremists" among the minority. History has shown that the replacement of a few "bad apples" in the police or the minority will not resolve more fundamental, structural conflict between the two groups.

The meaning of the term "deviance" as used here will be clear enough when applied to citizens in a minority group; the deviant behaviour of oppressed groups has received more than its share of sociological analysis. But the concept of "police deviance" may be new to the reader. How can the very people entrusted and empowered to enforce the law, act illegally? Do we not even refer to the cops as "the Law"? But the police must also be bound, both by the Criminal Code and by the various Police Acts that dictate correct police methods in enforcing the Criminal Code. Police deviance, then, is behaviour that violates the Criminal Code or the formal rules of police forces. In our case, we are especially concerned with police violations of laws defining the "civil rights" of minorities.

Emergence of a Structural Analysis of the Police

Recent literature on the police has paid increasing attention to the structure of the police organization: the policeman's job as an occupational role, the policeman's work as a subcultural context, the police bureaucracy as a source of official deviance and bureaucratic propaganda (e.g. Wilson, 1968/78; Vincent, 1979; Douglas and Johnson, 1977; Altheide and Johnson, 1980). There is correspondingly less interest in analysing the "police personality," especially in psychological terms of "reaction formation" (e.g., Kirkham, 1975) or "authoritarian personality" (Muir, 1977).

This shift in emphasis follows upon studies showing that the typical policeman is no more authoritarian in outlook than the typical citizen in the community the police serve (Bent, 1974: 105; Bayley and Mendelsohn, 1969: 18; McNamara, 1967: 195). Niederhoffer, a policeman before he became a social scientist, concludes (1967: 160) that "police authoritarianism does not come into the force along with the recruits, but rather is inculcated in the men through strenuous socialization. The police occupational system is geared to manufacture the 'take charge guy.' " Police authoritarianism is not a personality orientation that attracts recruits to the force; it is a form of behaviour that the police organization demands of its members. Individual policemen may feel a profound ambivalence and anxiety about the "authority" they are expected to assert (Kirkham, 1974; Muir, 1977).

Our society increasingly calls upon the police to maintain social order in situations where the citizens abdicate any personal responsibility to act, even to ask a neighbour to quiet his party. The police must "take charge" most frequently in contexts that they did not initiate or invite. The officer is under strain to achieve rapid and effective control of the situation, while at the same time respecting the "civil liberties" of the citizen(s) involved.

Taking charge efficiently may seem to call for minor and sometimes major shortcuts in legal niceties. The officer may bluff or bully, mislead or lie, verbally abuse, or physically "rough up" the alleged offender. Senior officers are not concerned to eliminate such short-cuts, but merely to manage them, so as to keep citizen complaints (especially from politically powerful citizens) at a minimum while getting the day's work done. The most important learning required of the rookie in his first six months is the ability to keep his/her mouth shut about the deviance from law and police regulations which veteran officers consider necessary if the police are not to be "hamstrung" in their control of social order (cf. Fink and Sealy, 1974: 10ff). The rookie who survives on the force learns to look at the world through the needs of his/her occupation (Vincent, 1979: 92ff; Bayley and Mendelsohn, 1969: 106).

Some students of police behaviour (eg., Reiss, 1968) have even suggested that the police themselves have become a sort of "minority." Bayley and Mendelsohn (1969: 54) note these similarities of the police subculture to minority status: stereotyping by outsiders, stigmatization based on visible signs (eg., uniform), a feeling of being collectively misunderstood, and a tendency to band together against outsiders. Police deviance may even be attributed to collective solidarity. A Toronto police inspector noted that incidents of alleged "police brutality" increase when police are in pairs or groups (*Toronto Star*, August 3, 1976).

In the present author's opinion, a minority group model is not very useful in understanding the structural sources of police deviance. The police may suffer from an "Us against Them" feeling, but they are not a *minority* in the generally accepted sociological use of that concept. When the sociologist speaks of a minority, he/she refers not to relative size or number of persons, but to power status. It is entirely possible for a numerically larger number of people to be in the minority status vis-à-vis a small but dominant "majority." This has been the situation of blacks in the American South for generations. It is the situation of Canadian Eskimos in the northern regions.

Sociologically, a minority is an identifiable category of stigmatized persons existing in a subject relationship to a more powerful, identifiable category (Bierstedt, 1968). The minority may not suffer from this situation. There are a variety of Canadian minorities who may be stereotyped and occasionally made the butt of humour, but who are not "oppressed" by the dominant sector of the population (e.g., Irish, Scottish, or Scandinavian Canadians). Thus, in focusing on police relations with minorities, we need to refine the concept of minority still further. Makielski (1973) suggests the term "beleaguered minorities."

Beleaguered minorities may be contrasted to older minorities in North

American society who, while still identified with a distinctive cultural heritage, have been largely assimilated into the institutions, and particularly the power structure, of society. Irish, Jewish or German Canadians are no longer "beleaguered." Italian Canadians are in a transitional stage of assimilation. A decade ago, police relations with this minority were a major problem in Toronto, and led to the formation of a police "ethnic squad" (discussed in detail below). Today the Italian community is not a major concern of this squad. At present, the beleaguered minorities include blacks, Indians, gays and lesbians, and long-haired, drug-using youth. There are indications that "militant women" (radical feminists) may soon be added to the list.

Is a Stigma or a Social Class the Real Issue?

Some sociologists have argued that the crux of police-minority relations is not a visible stigma (especially race, but possibly including sex, sexual orientation, or age) but the social class typical of most members of the minority (Fein, 1968). "If all Negroes were turned white tomorrow, [police] hostility, only slightly abated, would continue . . ." Wilson argues (1978: 297). Reiss (1968: 147ff) found that social class was a better predictor of police treatment of citizens than race. Gandy (1979: 46) notes that members of police-minority committees in Toronto felt that "the real problem is one of class, and if you are a member of a visible minority and in a lower class, race is merely one of the factors in unequal treatment by the police."

There is indeed a correlation between membership in certain beleaguered minorities and socio-economic status. American blacks, Indians and Hispanics are among the most economically deprived sectors of the population, with unemployment rates at least double those of comparable white age groups. Among beleaguered (long-haired, drug-using) youth, the lower-class youth is much more likely to be criminalized. However, class is not always the *governing* factor. Gay men often enjoy a middle- or professional-class standing, but may readily become targets of police harassment. Social class does remain an important consideration. In recent Toronto instances, a city council member, a member of the board of education, and others of high social standing who were arrested and charged for sexual offences, received politer treatment than was accorded less prestigious citizens.

The "class or race?" debate (like certain other classic debates, such as "nature or nurture?") is probably a futile contest. Social power is not one-dimensional, but made up of a variety of factors, of which class may often be the apparently predominant factor. Any well-dressed, high-status black who has been called "boy" by a cop, or university professor who has been called "faggot," knows that social class need not be the *determining* factor.

To the extent that social class is a major consideration for the policeman in relating to a member of a beleaguered minority, it is a doubly complicating factor because of the typical social class background of the *policeman*. Police are most often recruited from the lower- or working-class strata (McNamara, 1967: 193; Preiss and Ehrlich, 1968: 12; Niederhoffer, 1967: 36; Bayley and Mendelsohn, 1969: 6). Thus the typical police officer suffers status anxiety in dealing with those of a higher social class. This anxiety is compounded by desire to think of him/herself as a "professional" of at least middle-class status, while at the same time doing the sort of "dirty work" for society (Hughes, 1962) which is most often assigned to workers of low status (cf. Radelet, 1973: 267ff; Hongisto, 1980: 39; Banton, 1964: 11). Senior officers, more distant from the dirty work, become more comfortable about their own status and their dealings with upper-status citizens. The author has noticed that senior police officers have little difficulty in being at ease among publicly self-proclaimed gay men and lesbians or militant black lawyers.

Police Targetting of Minority Problems

Modern police forces emerged out of the need to protect dominant communities from "riotous and dangerous classes" (Marx, 1977). Police rookies soon learn to distinguish the "public" they are supposed to serve and protect, from the public they are supposed to control and punish (Westley, 1970: 96ff; Shearing, 1981). The latter may be variously designated as "scum" or "animals," while the former may be divided into the "helpless" and "the better class of people." When the socio-economic status of a minority member puts him or her among the better class of people, but a visible social stigma puts him or her among the scum, the police are often baffled. The prestigious but homosexual lawyer, the black member of city council, the pot-smoking professor, pose a difficult problem for the police. At the very least, the police demand that such high-status members of beleaguered minorities not "flaunt" their status or become "militant." Such behaviour is an invitation to the police to find some grounds for treating the minority member as "scum" (Adam, 1978: 43).

The scum are those under the power of the police, supported by an apparent social consensus to "let the police handle these people." Cray suggests the concept of "police property" (1972: 11). Ownership, as Clark and Lewis note (1977: 114) is simply "the assertion of superior power." Any category of citizens who lack power in the major institutions of their society (institutions in the economy, polity, education, media, etc.) are liable to become police property. At one time or another, such diverse categories as winos, hobos, unemployed drifters, labour union organizers, Japanese, blacks, long-haired youth, and homosexuals have been appropriated by the police as their property; that is, categories of people over whom the police successfully exert superior power.

A category becomes police property when the dominant powers of society (in the economy, polity, etc.) leave the problems of social control of that category to the police. "Let the police deal with these (niggers, queers, hippies . . .)." So long as the police demonstrate their expertise in controlling the minority without attracting "media flack," the title to that minority is ceded to the police. In a society such as ours, where there is a strong need by powerful officials to assert title and property control over some jurisdiction, it is not surprising that the police should want power over some property. After all, the businessman has "my company" even though the production is carried out by others; the politician speaks of "my ward"; the professor refers to "my class" or "my course"; and the social worker has "my clients."

Any holder of a property title ("owner") is likely to become bellicose when denied access to, or control over, "my property." For example, landlords become angry when tenants use tenants' rights laws to prevent eviction. Cray (1972) notes the same sort of anger among the police when social change, or militant action by the minority, begins to deny the police title and control over "their property." This is especially true when members of the controlled minority get "out of place." So long as the black stays in his ghetto, the gay in his closet, the Indian on his reservation, the police may be content to let them alone. Clark and Lewis (1977: 114) note the same pattern with male property over women. Women who are out of place (not at home with their husbands, but alone, late at night, on the street) "deserve what they get" from the mugger or rapist. Likewise, the militant black, gay, Indian, or long-haired youth who is in a public place where he should not be is often considered by the police—and by the dominant sector of the public—to "deserve what he gets" in the way of police violation of his civil rights.

When the general responsibility of the police to "take charge" in an interaction with citizens (of whatever status and background) is combined with the police imperative to "take possession" because the particular citizens in question are perceived as members of a minority which is "police property," then a volatile police-citizen interaction is probable. The task of the police officer is not merely to take charge, but to "keep the lid on" this particular minority, as concretely represented by the citizen(s) before him.

Actual implementation of this enterprise often begins by labelling the citizen as police property. The long-haired youth is hailed "hey punk," the black becomes "boy" and the gay, "faggot." As a former New York City police official notes (Black, 1968: 190):

> When children play and fight, they say "Sticks and stones will break my bones but names can never hurt me." But . . . the words of the police have the badge of authority behind them . . . a club, a gun, or a pair of handcuffs, and the power to arrest.

Police use of verbal abuse asserts the "superior power" that is the nature of property ownership. The punk, nigger or faggot becomes "ours to deal with."

Should a citizen object to a verbal taunt, and perhaps go so far as to ask for, or note, the constable's badge number, the policeman is quite likely to reply, "What are you, a wise guy?" Where minorities are unorganized, the police may openly admit verbal taunts. At a time when Toronto's blacks were leaderless, police detectives boasted to a *Toronto Star* reporter that they were bigoted and did not like "niggers, or have any use for them" (August 20, 1972). The detectives, incidentally, were at the same Division 14 where subsequent harassment led to black organization, and in turn, to the shooting of Albert Johnson. Police racist attitudes were also exposed by city council in the police association staff publication, *News and Views* (December 1978 and March 1979 issues).

Skolnick (1966: 82) observed (in an otherwise hard-hitting and critical analysis of legal processes in America) that the police use of racial epithets did not necessarily reflect racist attitudes. The words were simply "street language" reflecting the working-class background of many constables. The same argument was made by police witnesses in 1980 at a hearing of the Ontario Human Rights Commission. The OHRC was investigating a complaint by a Pakistani police recruit that he had been unfairly dismissed. When he presented evidence of fellow officers taunting him with various racial epithets, the police defence provided witnesses to testify that such words were meant harmlessly. One officer told the hearing, "Paki means peace or love or something like that, and you hear spook, nigger, Frenchie and Newfie as common terms of friendship among constables" (*Globe and Mail*, May 30, 1980).

Others remain unconvinced. Rafsky (1973) studied a sample of police by first assessing their attitudes to various racial questions, especially the black civil rights movement. He then observed their use of racial labels. He reports a highly significant correlation between the constables' preferred terms of reference to racial minorities and assessed attitudes to minority movements. Police opposed to black liberation liked to refer to blacks as *nigger, spade*, or *coloured;* middle-of-the-road police tended to use *Negro*, and pro-civil-rights police used *black*.

In 1979, police-minority confrontations in Toronto eventually led to the appointment of Cardinal Emmett Carter as a one-man board of inquiry. He reported:

> The use of verbal taunts is far too prevalent. When a person is called a nigger, a queer, a faggot, a chink, a paki, usually with the appropriate accompanying adjectives, he has been attacked as surely as if he were struck.

The Cardinal's recommendation that police be instructed to refrain from use of such language was adopted by the police commission. However, there is little evidence at the time of writing that the "constable on the beat" has changed his practice. For example, in the largest mass arrest in Canada since the War Measures Act (1970), the Toronto police raided four gay baths on February 5, 1980. The 286 men arrested were repeatedly mocked.

According to the press, police even suggested, while arresting men in the showers, "it's too bad these showers don't use gas" (a reference to gas chambers fitted out as apparent showers in Nazi death camps (*Globe and Mail*, February 6, 1981).

The Utility of Identifiable Property

In an increasingly pluralistic and polyglot society, the police task of social control becomes inevitably more difficult. The apprehension of criminals requires both a sophisticated array of identification methods and a set of elaborate screening processes for estimating the potential suspiciousness of citizens. Thus the police are constantly on the alert for identifying tags—the citizen's age, race, sex, class, language, and stigmata. Police attention to "incongruity" of behaviour and characteristics tends to discriminate against minority persons. It greatly simplifies the search for a thief or rapist who is known to be black, in a community where only ten per cent of the population is black. Indeed, the higher visibility of minorities may be one of the factors accounting for their higher arrest rates.

From the point of view of the minority, such methods of identification may appear stereotyped and stigmatizing. In 1979, Toronto police conducted a public relations program in the schools. In this "Cop Shop" program, one activity called on the students to view a film, then identify possible suspects according to the police "codified designations" (Hartjen, 1972: 71). The materials used soon came into the hands of minority-group leaders, who for the first time discovered the contents of Toronto police identification sheets. Among the designations were such entries as "Sex: Male, Female, Homosexual, Lesbian"; "Complexion: Light Negro, Negro, Chocolate Black"; "Amputations and Deformities: Left-handed, Thick lipped"; "Speech: British accent, Refined, Vulgar, Deaf and Dumb"; "Apparent Nationality: French Canadian, Jewish, Foreign, European, Gypsy, USA, Asia, South America." An untitled category included designations such as "Hippie, Motorcycle club, Demonstrators."

Angry protests at police commission meetings finally persuaded the police to survey comparable identification sheets in other cities. It was discovered that Toronto police were the only force in Canada recognizing four sexes rather than the usual two (male and female). Other designations were also revised; "chocolate" disappeared, and "deaf and dumb" became "mute."

The Demand for Deference

Once a citizen has been identified as a member of a beleaguered minority, and thus potential police property, the stage is set for a special demand for deference to police authority. The police-citizen encounter is exactly that in most cases; an encounter, not a relationship. Such encounters form a large part of the policeman's day, but are only occasional events in the life of the typical citizen. Thus the role to be played by the constable is more likely to be "embraced" than is the case with the citizen. Most citizens have little practice in playing the role of interaction with police (Sykes and Clark, 1975: 587).

Citizens with high self-esteem built upon high social standing are least likely to be embarrassed by police. "You don't have any feeling of guilt with the upper classes," a detective told Banton (1964: 211). In symbolic interactions for the exchange of services and obligations, high self-esteem motivates less deference (Goffman, 1956). At the other extreme, those of low standing are expected to defer submissively to the police, and generally know this. If they do not, the demand is soon made clear by the policeman:

> You would ask a kid who was loitering what he was doing and he would say "I don't even have to tell you my name." The kid was right—He didn't. But it was hard on the cop. . . . It wasn't surprising to me that . . . some policeman would take the kid into an alley and slap him on the mouth. . . . I didn't condone it, but it worked. [Toronto constable to *Toronto Star*, October 26, 1974]

Chevigny (1969: 70ff) cites many examples of police demands for submissive deference, not merely civility, from minority-group members. Reiss (1971: 144ff) notes that even in encounters where both citizen and policeman behave with civility, "neither is satisfied. . . . The officers want more than civility; they want deference. . . ." Citizens want more than formal politeness from police; they want individual attention. Reiss (1971: 144) found that where the citizen acts other than civilly, the alternative is most commonly deference, but when a policeman acts other than civilly, the alternative is usually hostility. Citizen hostility appears most often when the charge is a minor one for which the citizen feels he or she has been singled out, while similar offences on the part of others are ignored (Reiss, 1971: 53).

Fink and Sealy (1974: 16) confirm that when a citizen shows a lack of deference, the typical police interpretation is that the citizen is challenging authority. The usual response is to "put the wise ass in his place" by verbal abuse, rough handling, or worse. Westley (1956/1970) found that 37 per cent of his police sample felt that simply showing disrespect for an officer was reasonable grounds for the use of force. A significant number of citizens have been found to agree with this opinion; at least ten per cent of the author's university students, surveyed annually, feel that an officer is justified in using physical force to compel respect from a citizen.

Reiss (1971: 147) observes that "excessive force is used when it becomes unclear as to 'who is in charge'. The police subculture demands that the officer show *he or she is in charge*. The police code prohibits 'backing down.' " But the amount of deference a constable expects, and thus the amount of force he feels justified in using in the absence of deference, depends largely on the constable's estimate of the citizen's social status. The lower the status, the more deference expected. But in applying the various codified designations that the police use to estimate social standing (sex, age, race, apparent income, minority-group membership, and so forth), the police often make errors (Hartjen, 1972: 71). In such cases, the officer must either proceed anyway, "toughing it out" and perhaps provoking a "crime" on the part of the citizen (resistance to arrest, obstructing the police, etc.), or else back down. Interestingly, those who have studied the police demand for deference have failed to examine the available mechanisms for backing down (cf. especially Sykes and Clark, 1975).

This author's admittedly unrepresentative observations indicate that when a policeman discovers he has made an error in estimating the citizen's social standing, and thus the appropriate amount of deference, he rarely apologizes, since he must still stay "in charge." However, he is likely to shift the focus of interaction in such a way as to justify more civility on his part; for example, by commenting approvingly on the profession of the citizen after learning that this profession is not what the appearance of the citizen would have suggested.

Ironically, police expect more than the usual deference from low-status minority-group members, but these citizens are often inclined to show less deference to the police than a high-status dominant citizen! The latter can psychologically afford the exchange cost of being more polite to the policeman than his station requires. The excess politeness can always be self-assessed as "noblesse oblige." But the member of a beleaguered minority resents being expected to submit, and may insist on his or her "right" to polite treatment by the police. This insistence may take the form of sarcasm or abruptness, or it may be verbalized as outright criticism of the way the policeman is doing his job.

Criticism of the police almost inevitably evokes hostility from the officer (Chevigny, 1969: 99), especially when it comes from a person with no apparent claim to high social standing. If the critic can be justifiably categorized among the "troublemakers" or "scum" of society, the hostility is likely to be expressed in physical force. Hopefully, from the police point of view, such force will provoke a physical response from the critic, who can then be charged with assaulting a police officer. Even where the citizen refrains from physical response, the police may seize on any obvious excuse. In one instance observed by the author, two long-haired youths criticized a constable for roughly handling a citizen on the sidewalk. Once the police had the citizen in the patrol car, they turned on their critics. One constable suddenly threw the "lippy kid" to the ground, frisked him, and found a metal comb with a long handle. He was charged with "carrying an offensive weapon."

When criticism of the police comes from organized and militant members of a beleaguered minority, the police reaction is likely to be even more hostile. Now it is not simply a question of individual "scum" attacking individual actions of the police; the issue has become one of police property in revolt against authority and social control. As Lofland notes (1969: 36), the better organized the threat to legitimate control, the greater the determination to "put the scum back in their place." (Other terms may be substituted for "scum," of course: "niggers," "faggots," "punks," etc). Minority criticism of the police may thus take on the features of "class war," with the police acting on the part of the powerful classes (cf. Shearing, 1981).

Accepting criticism or apologizing for errors are not easy options in the police subculture. Those who take leadership roles in expressing criticism on the part of a beleaguered minority are those most resented by the police (Bayley and Mendelsohn, 1969: 152; Chevigny, 1969: 61). Thus the use of deviant methods is often targetted against the "spokespersons" of the minority. For example, the efforts of the FBI to ruin Martin Luther King are well documented (cf. Watters and Gillers, 1973).

A chain reaction may build up, in which relatively minor and routine acts of incivility by the police lead to complaints by the minority, which in turn cause resentful police to harass minority members, who then organize in protest, provoking further police deviance, sometimes culminating in a "police riot." Sykes and Clark (1975: 589) note the difficulty of the "good cop" in breaking through such structures of confrontation and conflict. A completely unprejudiced and even sympathetic policeman may expect no more than formal civility from a minority-group member, realizing that to demand more is to put himself into the perceived role of "tough cop" (cf. Banton, 1973: 35ff). The minority citizen, however, may feel that assertion of his "rights" requires him to be less than civil to the police, who are viewed as part of "the system" or "the establishment." Unable to abdicate his occupational responsibility to take charge, the "good cop" may find himself compelled to play the role of "tough cop."

These social dynamics help to explain why minority groups sometimes complain of "police brutality," even when no physical violence has occurred. Members of the dominant population tend to restrict the term "brutality" to physical injury (Bayley and Mendelsohn, 1969: 125). But minority members are aware of the close relationship between police demands for deference and the potential for rough treatment, and are likely to slide over fine distinctions between verbal abuse and physical force. "Police brutality" becomes a generic term for a range of incivil actions by the police (Glenn and Bonjean, 1969: 498).

Minority Response to Police Targetting

Generalizations are dangerous. There are obviously policemen who tolerate and even enjoy the diversity of the public. There are minority-group members who welcome and appreciate the presence of the police in their community. A few members of most minorities *are* police. However, the overall relationship of police and minority community is structured by the social status of the minority. Members of a minority who are "exceptional" because of education, income, artistic skill or whatever, nevertheless tend to be lumped into the stereotype of that minority, especially during times of militant minority activism. As a senior police officer told Wilson (1978: 43): "Pretty soon you decide they're all just niggers."

Minority-group members return the favour by stereotyping police. The best-intentioned constable becomes little more than a uniform and a gun during periods of angry confrontation between police and a militant community. Leaders of the minority community who talk and react too "reasonably" to the police are disowned by their own community as "Uncle Toms." As confrontation escalates, high-status members of the minority community, who previously considered themselves immune from police harassment, now become targets and are polarized and politicized in turn.

For example, there have long been numerous members of the Toronto gay community who enjoyed a high social status in the city. They could pass easily as heterosexuals at work or in politics, and did so. They tended to share the general consensus of citizens that "Toronto's cops are tops." In the 1970s, civic authorities and the police reacted to a sudden influx of heterosexual "massage parlours" and "body rubs" which turned Yonge Street, the city's "main drag," into a "sin strip." A special task force of patrols and intelligence units was established to "clean up Yonge Street" (Report of Toronto Police Commission, January 1978). Within a year Yonge Street was clean; not a single body rub remained open (Toronto Police Commission, January 1979). However, the special police task force was not dismantled. A series of events soon suggested that it simply perpetuated itself by finding a new target, the gay community (Right to Privacy Committee brief, Toronto Police Commission, June 1979).

Until this time, several gay "baths" had operated unmolested by the police for many years. The morality squad took the attitude (expressed to the author) that "at least it's better than having them on the streets." Gay men also advertised for sexual partners in various gay periodicals, in much the same way as heterosexuals (and gays) advertise openly for "Companions" in the major Toronto daily newspapers (cf. Lee, 1978).

Now these gay men found themselves the target of highly organized police intelligence and harassment. Even teachers and lawyers advertising in American gay periodicals (for contact with gay Americans visiting Toronto) were caught up in the police activity. After the intelligence unit located the target male, a regular constable (carefully chosen for personality and appearance) would contact the target, suggesting that he was interested in sexual activity. In short, the cop posed as a gay person.

It is not illegal in Canada for two adults (over 21) to engage in homosexual acts in private. The police therefore converted a law directed against heterosexual brothels to a new use. The "bawdy house" section of the Criminal Code may be used against anyone "keeping a place to which resort is had for prostitution . . . or for indecent acts." On the grounds that the gay men targetted were advertising for sexual partners, they were charged with keeping a bawdy house *in their own homes*.

A second line of police activity against gay men was developed by well-prepared raids on the previously unmolested gay baths. (These are steam baths where men may rent rooms, much as in a hotel, for sexual encounters with other customers first met in the steam room (cf. Lee, 1978).) After weeks of advance work posing as gay customers, police raided gay baths and laid charges of keeping, or being found in, a bawdy house.

In one such raid (December 1978), police arrested 23 found-ins, of whom six were school teachers. Nine days later, a staff sergeant in the police intelligence unit telephoned the boards of education employing these men, to inform school administrators of the fact that some of their teachers (who were named) had been arrested in a bawdy house. This action directly violated police regulations (Toronto Police Commission minutes, June 28, 1979).

Despite critical press reaction, the police chief took no action against the sergeant. However, one of the teachers involved, after assurances from his superiors that there was no need to fear for his job simply because he was gay, publicly condemned the sergeant's action. Supported by gay-community organizations, demands were made to the police commission for disciplinary action. Eventually the sergeant was "reprimanded," but only after the police chief observed that "some of the men want to give him a medal."

In a series of events unlikely to be coincidence, the protesting gay teacher soon received a visit from a policeman posing as a gay man interested in sex. When the gay teacher manifested interest in the caller, he was charged with using his home as a bawdy house. Since this case is still before the courts, no further comment can be made except to observe that gay militancy and political action, both at the police commission and in city council, increased dramatically. This, in turn, escalated police harassment, leading to the mass arrest of 286 men at gay baths in 1980.

Similar phenomena have been widely observed in police–black relationships. A moderate observer of the police–black-community relationship in the United States has noted:

> Coloured people inevitably came to feel that, for them, the country was ruled by men, not by laws. . . . Threats are usually as effective as the use of violence because coloured workers realize that the threats . . . are supported by the system. [Fox, 1976: 57]

The belief that the police enforce the law differently for blacks than for whites is widespread among blacks (Goldstein, 1977: 104ff). Blacks in America and Indians in Canada are likely to enter into an encounter with the police with a predisposition to expect discrimination. The greater the experience and contact with the police, the more critical the black citizen is of the police (Bayley and Mendelsohn, 1969: 120).

Even when policemen are charged as a result of deviant acts such as harassment, injury or killing of minority-group members, the likelihood that they will be criminally punished is extremely small, and this is known by minority-group members. When a Miami court freed police accused of killing a black salesman, a riot followed. Subsequent analysis of the prosecution's procedure raised grave doubts that convictions were seriously sought after (Williams, 1980).

Two policemen who shot and killed a Toronto black for creating a disturbance (in his own home) were eventually found not guilty of manslaughter by an all-white jury. *Toronto Star* reporter Christie Blatchford (1980) published an analysis "What the Jury Didn't Hear in the Johnson Case," which indicated that the Crown prosecutor was the policemen's best defence. She found that the Crown knew of, but did not introduce, evidence that the black victim had complained of police harassment to the Ontario Human Rights Commission, and OHRC records noted the man's "increased desperation. . . . His biggest fear was that the police would shoot him down." The strangest feature of the trial was evidence that the victim had been shot from above, at an angle corroborating the testimony of the victim's child (of nine years) that the police made her father kneel, then shot him. After a police officer testified that he had observed "an adult woman coaching the child" to testify accordingly, the judge instructed the jury to place little reliance on the child's testimony. What the jury was to make of the forensic evidence of the angle of shooting was left unclear. But strangest of all, the jury was not told that the child had given the same story (of her father being forced to kneel) to the press *on the day of the killing*, long before any alleged "coaching" for the trial by an alleged, but unnamed, adult woman.

Statistics seem to suggest that blacks cannot expect the same "justice" as whites. Blacks form about one-tenth of the American population but about one-third of the prison inmates. They are considerably more likely to be imprisoned for serious offences, and have a higher recidivism rate, than whites (Forslund, 1970; Johnson, 1970). Some sociologists argue the need for a special theory of criminality for blacks, since their rates of crime are higher, even after allowing for socio-economic deprivation (Savitz, 1970; Moses, 1970). Other sociologists would reply that any special theory of black criminality is simply "blaming the victim."

The Canadian "equivalent" of the black minority in the United States is the Canadian Indian. The proportion of native people arrested and imprisoned in the four western provinces far exceeds their share of the total population. Nettler (1978: 144) reported that the percentage of native inmates in western prisons ranged from ten per cent in some jails to 100 per cent in two women's prisons, at Oakalla, B.C., and The Pas, Manitoba.

Despite the fact that the median proportion of native inmates in western Canadian prisons is two-thirds of the total prison population, Hagan (1974) has argued that "when legal variables are held constant, differences in sentences are minimal." Likewise, Bienvenue and Latif (1975), in a study of 6,000 arrests and sentences in Winnipeg, found that while Indians were significantly overrepresented, and more likely to be arrested for minor offences, the evidence did not prove legal and police discrimination against Indians. If Indians land in jail for weaker reasons than whites, it may be, the authors suggest, because Indians prefer to go to jail. Indians are said to consider jail a "shared experience, a chance to rest . . . get better food and meet old friends." Thus, the authors conclude, "it is impossible to ascertain whether [incarceration rates] are the consequence of poverty or a reflection of attitudinal differences." In the opinion of the present author, such sociological "research" merely substantiates minority convictions that much social science is simply an intellectual apology for oppression, or at the very least, another way of "blaming the victim."

When young people seem rebellious to adult authority, police often target them as police property, much like blacks, Indians and gays. Police deviance often occurs in the social control of young people identifiable with countercultural movements and subcultures—in more recent times, those symbolized by long hair, drug use, and loud music. During the 1960s and 1970s Canadian police were particularly active against visible youth minorities. A survey of Quebec police found a greater tolerance for convicted criminals (25 per cent of the sample) than for beatnik youths (24 per cent of the sample) (*The Varsity*, December 10, 1969).

In Ontario, the provincial police assigned officers to the full-time task of sabotaging youth efforts to arrange sites for rock concerts. A staff sergeant described his work to the *Globe and Mail* (July 12, 1970). He visited local municipal councils considering applications for rock concerts. He showed an American film made by police at Woodstock and Altamont (sites of two of the largest youth rock concerts). He described the traffic chaos, litter, noise, disorder, drug abuse and death which local councillors would be responsible for if they approved a rock concert application.

The best-known acts of police deviance against youth minorities were directed at Toronto's Rochdale College. This residential educational facility was developed by the student co-operative movement at the University of Toronto. It soon attracted rebellious and nonconforming youth from across Canada. Thus, it soon attracted more than its share of police harassment. In fact, harassment reached such a scale that the famous Canadian author, Pierre Berton, was moved to write a detailed, angry letter of protest to the

Globe and Mail (June 2, 1971). After interviewing police, college residents and security staff, and university faculty witnesses to the events, he described a raid by 88 Toronto police.

The police allegedly arrived in search of several drug pushers said to be resident in the college. Why 88 police were necessary was never explained. Despite offers of co-operation from college security staff, including the supply of passkeys to open any door, the police used axes to smash their way into residents' rooms, ransacked the contents, then departed without making any arrests for drug offences. However, they did charge several college security guards with "obstructing the police" when the guards tried to open with keys doors which the police preferred to smash down. This is a favourite form of deviance by police. It has been used several times in police raids on gay steam baths in Montreal and Toronto, despite willingness of attendants to open any door the police requested.

Discretion and the Necessity for Targetting

Some authors, and even some police commissioners (including members of the Toronto police commission in conversation with the author) insist that the responsibility of the police is to enforce all the laws equitably on all citizens. Some police statutes are written in the same terms. But any realistic analysis of the police cannot avoid the conclusion that there are not enough resources to enforce every law on the books and arrest every offender. Instead, the police use "discretion" about whether to arrest a woman who may be soliciting, or to raid an illegal gambling party. If all offenders against our laws were arrested, the jails could not hold them. The President's Commission on Law Enforcement (1967: 106) put it this way:

> The police should openly acknowledge that quite properly, they do not arrest all, or even most, offenders they know of. Among the factors accounting for this exercise in discretion are the volume of offences and the limited resources of the police, the ambiguity of the public desire for the nonenforcement of many statutes, the reluctance of many victims to complain, and most important, an entirely proper conviction by policemen that the invocation of criminal sanctions is too drastic a response to many offences.

The structural fact is that police discretion is not used only in response to these factors; it is also a function of the minority status of the offender (Skolnick, 1966: 85; Wald, 1967: 139; Bayley and Mendelsohn, 1969: 60). The arrest rate for black males in America is much higher than that for whites, and a much higher proportion of blacks have at some time been arrested (Boesel and Rossi, 1971: 321; Wilson, 1978: 190). The National Minority Advisory Council (NMAC; Washington) reports the following arrest rates per 100,000 population age 14 and over (selected years: NMAC, 1980: 112):

	Whites	*Blacks*	*Indians*
1960	572	1,957	3,492
1965	1,301	4,856	17,158
1970	2,324	9,225	24,309
1975	2,860	11,225	34,785
1978	3,271	12,256	36,584

While it might be argued that these rate differences do not reflect discrimination in the use of police discretion to arrest, but a higher rate of criminality among blacks, and an astronomical rate of criminality among Indians, there is little convincing evidence for this explanation. Even if it were partly conceded, this would not account for the further fact that in the course of making an arrest, police are much more likely to use deadly force on blacks than on whites. Tagaki (1979) found that, state by state in the years 1960–70, blacks were 15 to 30 times more likely to be killed by police making arrests, than whites (cf. also NMAC statistics on deadly force [NMAC, 1980: 11]).

Cray (1972: 169) concludes from his study of police deviance that many "crimes," especially those of minority-group members, occur only after the police-citizen encounter:

> Some word or action on the part of the law enforcement officer transforms a routine stop or minor disorderly conduct into an assault, provoking a crime where no arrest was even contemplated.

Whatever the "truth" of the matter, there can be no doubting that many minority-group members believe this to be the case (Harding, 1971; Bayley and Mendelsohn, 1969; Banton, 1973). This perception of discriminatory use of police discretion and deviant provocation to arrest extends to minorities far from North America. New Zealand, for example, has long enjoyed an external reputation for unusual integration of Maori and white peoples in a single society. However, upsurges of police-minority confrontation occasionally tarnish the legend.

In 1974 a special police "task force" was established in Auckland, New Zealand, to clean up certain "trouble spots" in the city, all of which happened to have high concentrations of Polynesian population. About 1,500 arrests were made in six months, and most seem to fit Cray's thesis; the charges were largely for disorderly behaviour, "obscene language," and "obstructing police" (*New Zealand Herald*, August 22, 1974). After six months, newspapers reported that the number of muggings and other assault crimes had not changed in these trouble spots. The rate of these crimes was already very low (about one-thirtieth of the rate in San Francisco, for example), but, as Acord (1975) noted, the press continued to emphasize the "crime wave" among Maoris, using the higher arrest rates of the task force as their evidence!

The police capacity to use the discretion to arrest as a means of manufacturing a "crime wave" among a minority population is equally illustrated by a series of raids on gay bars and baths in Montreal prior to the 1976 Olympics. Montreal police arrested over 300 gay men and lesbians in a clean-up campaign (*Body Politic*, August, 1976). Blacks, Indians, Maoris, gays and other minorities serve as a residual pool of arrest potential when the police feel the need to generate evidence (especially for the media) of zealous activity in the defence of public order.

We have already referred to the intelligence unit of the Toronto police force. In 1981, this unit of more than 165 personnel faced the threat of severe budget cuts, as a result of the expected publication, for the first time, of a detailed accounting of the police budget at city council. The foremost responsibility of the unit was gathering information to control syndicated and organized crime (the most sophisticated sector of the "criminal world"). The unit had accomplished remarkably little in this direction. Thus it was not surprising that it should choose one of the currently favourite targets in the city as police property: male homosexuals. Massive raids involving at least 150 police officers were carried out, and the justification given to the press was that the gay baths were connected to American crime syndicates (*Globe and Mail*, February 6, 7, 1981). These same baths had operated without police intervention for 18 years in Toronto.

The intelligence unit's need to explain the sudden use of discretionary arrest power over alleged sexual offences in gay steam baths was made more compelling by the fact that sexual behaviour (and police enforcement of laws concerning it) was properly the jurisdiction of the *morality* squad, not the intelligence unit. The morality squad was not involved in the raids, and its members, by and large, have for many years regarded the gay baths as socially harmless and legally insignificant.

Another example of the manner in which police may arbitrarily choose to exert power over their "property" by discretionary use of powers of arrest is provided by an RCMP raid on a Sikh family. Four RCMP officers burst into the family's home at four o'clock in the morning, allegedly in search of illegal immigrants hiding there. During the 90-minute search, they entered the family's "holy room." Not only did they refuse to remove their shoes according to Sikh custom; they insisted on handling the Sikh holy book, which must never be touched. When the family protested that no one could be hiding under the book, the police retorted, "We are not under your instructions. We can do anything we want" (*Globe and Mail*, December 1, 1980). However, in this case the police assertion of superior power to take possession went beyond the acceptable limits and produced "media flak." The Solicitor General of Canada issued a formal letter of apology to the family.

"They Made Me Like This"

When police deviate from the legal and organizational rules governing their behaviour in reaction to perceived "provocation" by a minority, they are likely to argue that the scum made them tough or brutal. "The punks made me brutal," a former policeman told the *Toronto Star* (November 9, 1977). "I earned my name 'Mad Dog' in the streets. Criminals expect cops to be tough. You're dealing with the garbage of society. There are heavies on every city force and they're needed." Boesel and Rossi (1971: 323) report similar attitudes in their study of American police. Even the use of deadly force may be neutralized as a justifiable response, though the "punk" may only be running away from police apprehension (Tagaki, 1979).

In response to criticism of "brutality" and misuse of force, the police also argue the great danger of their jobs. Officers from distant cities will gather in elaborate funeral rites any time a policeman is killed (NMAC, 1980: 72; Posner, 1978). Yet police work is far from being the most dangerous occupation. The fireman, miner and construction worker all face much higher probabilities of death on the job. The 1978 rate of deaths per 100,000 employees was 25 per year in American police forces, but 94 per year in mining, 76 in construction, 55 in agriculture and 44 in transportation (Tagaki, 1979; cf. also Sykes and Clark, 1975: 585).

While the rate of police killed by civilians is higher than that of civilians killed by police in most West European countries, the reverse is true in Canada and the United States, where police kill several citizens for every policeman killed by a civilian (U.S. Commission, 1980; NMAC, 1980). Tagaki (1979) found that while American blacks were 28 per cent of all citizens arrested, they constituted 51 per cent of all citizens killed by the police in the same year. Most citizens in the dominant population are ready to excuse police killing of beleaguered minority members and will exonerate them when acting on a jury, if the policeman is charged and tried (Kohler, 1975, using a sample of 1,500 police killings). In the decade ending in 1979, Philadelphia police killed 63 civilians, while only nine police were killed. Only six of the police who killed civilians were charged, and none was punished (NMAC, 1980: 166).

Police officers may go further in justifying their deviance by arguing that they are "all on their own" in law enforcement and cannot expect law-abiding citizens to come to their aid, for example, when struggling with a violent suspect. In short, the police may tend to view the public as their enemy. Sociological study of this phenomenon dates at least from Westley's work (1956/70). His view has often been unfairly oversimplified; he argued that police distinguish between five sectors of the public: children, decent people, the better class of people, the scum, and blacks. Subsequent work on police forces suggests other divisions (e.g., Shearing, 1981). It has been observed that when the police do not view the public(s) with hostility, they generally underestimate the amount of public support for the police (Wilson, 1978: 28; Bayley and Mendelsohn, 1969: 51; McNamara, 1967: 180).

Hartjen (1972: 71) prefers to analyse police-public relations in terms of variables of encounter rather than sectors of population. He suggests that police approach citizens with five variables to be estimated in each situation: danger, hostility, authority, suspicion, and efficiency. In encounters with visible minorities, police often expect a higher risk of danger and hostility, a greater need to exert authority, and a lack of co-operation to achieve efficient action (in terms of time and resources required). Minorities are also more suspect as offenders.

At the same time, the police are aware that in recent years minorities have organized to demand their "rights." The notion that some of these minorities deserve any rights is difficult for many police to accept. A typical reaction to minority demands is "Next thing you know, criminals and prostitutes will be demanding their rights too!" There is some justice to this view—prisoners and prostitutes *have* organized rights groups, as have drug users and former mental patients. None of these groups falls into the ordinary policeman's category of "decent people." As Fink and Sealy conclude (1974: 24):

> During the past decade a number of publics have been . . . verbalizing their claims. Among these publics are blacks . . . women, youth, students, poor people, prison inmates and homosexuals. Most policemen resent having to respond to all that input.

The police further resent losing certain classes of people whom they have traditionally considered police property. For a period of time after a minority group succeeds in gaining public support and legal recognition of its rights, the police are likely to harass members of the minority more, rather than less. This is especially the case where the police have actively lobbied to prevent the minority from gaining legitimacy (cf. *Globe and Mail*, September 7, 1968, for an example: opposition of the Canadian Association of Police Chiefs to decriminalization of homosexuality. The association argued that the homosexuals' search for sex partners "often leads to assaults, thefts, male prostitution and murder.")

The police have shown special determination, in certain cases, to keep members of beleaguered minorities out of the police force. In 1980 the International Association of Chiefs of Police reaffirmed its 1958 resolution abhorring the hiring of homosexuals by police forces. A new urgency was felt because the San Francisco force had just graduated its first contingent of gay police officers (Hongisto, 1980). The Ontario Provincial Police force has strenuously resisted the reinstatement of a gay policeman whose exemplary record of service did not compensate for the discovery of his sexual orientation (*Toronto Star*, April 1, 1980).

The police bureaucracy may use indirect means to achieve goals in relations with beleaguered minorities when legal means are unavailable. For example, the Toronto force for many years used a height restriction to effectively exclude Asian recruits, while arguing that the restriction had no discriminatory intent but was based simply on the "fact" that tall men command more authority. Indeed, it was argued that tall police were less likely to deviate from police rules for the treatment of civilians. Smaller officers would have to resort to use of their billy clubs more often, it was claimed (*Toronto Star*, October 19, 1979; statement of police commissioner).

The Toronto force maintained its opposition to recruits under five feet ten inches, in spite of the fact that the International Association of Chiefs of Police had found that shorter officers showed no disadvantage (IACP, 1975). Several of the more difficult cities to police, such as New York, New Orleans and Chicago, all managed with officers only five feet four inches tall. Though expert Ontario studies (Clement, 1980) led to recommendation for relaxation of the height rule, it was only after a major confrontation with minority groups that the police commission finally conceded.

Containment versus Seduction

Police forces are paramilitary organizations with the important function of serving as occupation forces in the areas of the city inhabited by economically deprived classes and certain beleaguered minorities. Bordua (1968) argues that the police must serve as the "front line" in relationships between the dominant population and the minority "ghettos." He notes that other social forces representing the dominant society—teachers, priests, social workers—generally return to their middle-class residential areas at night, leaving the police as the only social control agency in 24-hour contact with the minority. In this argument Bordua simply gives sociological legitimacy to a feeling rather common among police working in the ghettos: they "know" the minority better than the general population (cf. Skolnick, 1966: 82; Bent, 1974: 56).

However, Bordua went further than dispassionate observation to argue that the police must exploit their contact and knowledge for the management of social change. He called on police forces to develop better public relations to "explain their role" to the minority communities. They should co-opt the support and assistance of other professional agencies in the ghetto, along with business interests serving the ghetto. The police should organize "ethnic squads" to reduce friction between the minority and the regular police units. Perhaps most important, the police should enforce the laws as much as possible, but try to avoid enforcement which would fuel the hostility and potential militancy of the ghetto.

An opposite approach is recommended by sociologists Fink and Sealy (1974). After analysing the unsuccessful efforts of the New York City police force to recruit more members of minorities, especially blacks and Puerto

Ricans, they conclude: "The ultimate solution to the problem [of police-minority relations] does not lie within the recruitment program, but within the police operation itself" (1974: 129). These authors found that most white (dominant) police already on the force do not want minority recruits. They believe that blacks and other minorities in uniform will lower the standards of police work, impair the drive to professional status for the police, and burden the force with an internal "fifth column" of men who are more loyal to their own minority than to fellow police officers. Most important, the image of the police held by "the better class of people" will be tarnished (Fink and Sealy, 1974: 132; cf. also Goldstein, 1977: 270).

At the same time, few minority members want to join the police, despite aggressive advertising campaigns, offers of steady employment at good wages, and a host of fringe benefits. The authors found that "the stereotype of police officers as a repressive and abusive maintainer of the status quo proves again and again to be stronger than potential economic and social gains" (1974: 129). They conclude that the only means of drawing more minority members into the police force is to "make it clear that Black recruits are wanted, not to fit into the existing system, but to help change the system" (1974: 134). Needless to say, neither the New York police force nor very many others have been prepared to offer this sort of inducement to "the scum."

The Canadian preference has been for the Bordua solution: the police must improve their image, manipulate the minority, and contain the ghetto militancy. In Toronto, the first ethnic squad was formed in 1973 to serve the Italian community. Later, several Asians and West Indians were added. In 1980 the squad was still only a token force of 16 constables (in a police force of more than 5,000). It sees its role as "interpreting the police to the ethnic community" (*Toronto Star* interview with ethnic squad officers, August 5, 1979). In the language of Erving Goffman, their role is to "cool out" minority dissatisfaction with the police. As the *Toronto Star* put it:

> Ethnics sometimes think that a policeman can just come over and put a man away just like that [i.e., arrest an offender against the minority community]. We tell them what they can do. We tell them who they should see. We even make some calls for them, to help them out. But the men are police officers first, and if they discover any violation of the law, they must perform their duty. If for example it turns out that a man they're talking to is an illegal immigrant they must turn him over to immigration. That man's broken the law. We can't close our eyes to that.
>
> We make it quite clear: If you're good and you're right, we're on your side. Or else we'll be the first to arrest you. If there are some bad apples in the [ethnic] community, we want to weed them out. [*Toronto Star*, August 5, 1979]

The irony of this officer's explanation is obvious. Knowing that his words will be read both by the dominant classes (who employ him to *Serve and Protect* their interests) and by some of the ethnic community, he must tread a delicate line between social control and social work. The ethnic squad members, in fact, are not considered "real cops" by their fellow police, and companions in the force often tease the ethnic squad members about "when you're going to be a cop again" (personal interview by the author).

Despite some small successes in easing police-minority tension (particularly with the Sikh community in Toronto), the ethnic squad has not significantly reduced the belief among several minorities that the police deliberately deviate from lawful and legitimate methods in order to control the minority through "harassment" and "brutality." In 1975, following an unusually nasty series of police-minority encounters including several deaths, a group of moderate and professional citizens formed the Toronto Urban Alliance on Race Relations. Acting with the city's Social Planning Council, they organized a conference with the police, which gave rise to the Liaison Group on Law Enforcement. This group in turn undertook a "pilot program" of local police-minority committees, with funding from the solicitor general and the provincial attorney general. It was made very clear to the group that this funding was intended to support only work for better police-minority relations; it was not to be used to study or propose changes in the police structure (personal interviews).

Four pilot committees survived long enough to be evaluated in 1979 by a professor of social work (Gandy, 1979). His report clearly indicates that the function of the committees was to contain and cool out minority complaints about the police. Gandy observed that the police tended to control the issues discussed by the committees, as well as the available information on those issues. A prime police objective was to avoid any unpleasant exposure of police "dirty laundry" to outsiders (Gandy, 1979: 58, 63, 68). Police on the committee were especially concerned to remind citizen members that only "general concerns" should be discussed, never specific cases of police abuse of individuals (Gandy, 1979: 45). Specific complaints would have to continue to go to the Citizens Complaint Bureau of the police department. There they would be safely processed by the police themselves.

Under such circumstances it is not surprising that Gandy found the committees were able to attract very few individuals from beleaguered minorities in the city. Indeed, the committees were unable to persuade many citizens with complaints to talk about them to committee members. "When a citizen appears before such a group he loses his anonymity which is a traditional safeguard against the actions of bureaucrats" (Gandy, 1979: 66).

Needless to say, minorities are rarely satisfied with processing of their complaints against police deviance by the deviant's fellow policemen in a "Complaints Bureau." In Toronto, as in several other cities, this discontent has risen to the level of angry and organized protest on several occasions. Minorities have descended on police commission meetings in large numbers to demand an independent investigation and adjudication of citizen complaints against the police.

The Toronto police commission has used a variety of tactics to divert and defuse such protest. Several expert inquiries have been appointed. After a series of charges, highlighted by both major newspapers, of police brutality directed at the drug-using youth minority and racial minorities, Judge Donald Morand was appointed to investigate. The Morand report, far from whitewashing the police, condemned both deviant police practices and their internal investigation:

> One of the most disturbing things which came out in the hearings was the extent to which I found the evidence of police officers mistaken, shaded, deliberately misleading, changed to suit the circumstances, and sometimes entirely and deliberately false. . . . [There was] a willingness of police officers to alter their notebooks and evidence in order to buttress their case. [Morand, 1976: 123, 132]

On the police internal investigation of some of the more serious citizen complaints of brutality, he noted:

> The allegations were of the most serious nature. They demanded swift, complete and impartial investigation. . . . [The] investigation which was done was totally and hopelessly inadequate . . . an effort was made to dissuade [the complaining civilian] from pursuing the complaint. [Morand, 1976: 174–76]

Judge Morand noted that citizens had few alternatives to the police complaint bureau: "Civil actions are lengthy, expensive, and in many, perhaps most, cases the damages awarded are very small (1976: 181).

In Vancouver, allegations of police brutality against a youth demonstration in support of decriminalization of marijuana led to an inquiry by Justice Thomas Dohm (August, 1971). His report found that the young demonstrators were no threat to peace and order, but when the police decided to use mounted officers to disperse the crowd, "The arrival of the mounted police caused panic, terror and resentment. The violence erupted only after the police intervened" (*Globe and Mail*, October 8, 1971).

In short, beleaguered minorities face a Catch–22: very often the "offences" with which they are charged take place *after* the intervention of police in ways which the minority members interpret as deliberate and provocative harassment (Chevigny, 1969; Glenn and Bonjean, 1969). Citizens who wish to complain about such police deviance must take their complaints to a police bureaucrat. Not only is the complaint unlikely to lead to redress for the citizen; it is likely to serve as the pretext for further police retaliation.

In the Toronto case, not only Judge Morand but also the Ontario ombudsman, Arthur Maloney, and the former attorney general, John Clement, as well as Cardinal Emmett Carter, have all, in independent inquiries into police activity, recommended a processing of citizen complaints which is independent of the police themselves (Morand, 1976; Maloney,

1975; Carter, 1979; Clement, 1980). In 1980 the provincial government finally introduced a bill which would provide Toronto (alone among all cities in the province) with a board for civilian *review* of complaints against the police. However, the investigation of evidence would continue to be carried out by the police, and any complaint against the final decision of the review board would go to the commissioner appointed by the attorney general, who also, as solicitor general, oversees the police forces in the province. Alleging that there was more of facade than substance in such arrangements, opposition parties defeated the bill.

During these confrontations, efforts have been made to severely limit the scope of the definition of "minority." The term "visible minority" has been used consistently by both the police and the attorney general's department. One effect of this is to exclude minorities which the established order fervently wish would remain invisible, and especially, unorganized and non-militant. These include gays and lesbians, former mental patients, and prisoners (who are visible only to their guards, not to society in general) (Foucault, 1977). Radical feminists would argue that theirs constitutes the largest such "minority" of all.

Conclusions

The perspective of conflict sociology (which is the approach of the present author) would suggest that community relations programs, campaigns to recruit more minority members to the police, and even independent investigation of citizen complaints against police deviance are likely to be merely cosmetic changes in a system of social interactions where police dominance and control will continue to struggle with the militancy of beleaguered minorities. Police organizations have successfully resisted or defeated most efforts to seriously contain their power (Black, 1968; Galliher, 1972; Goldstein, 1977). Little success has been achieved in recruiting minorities to police work (Task Force, 1974; United States Commission, 1980); this process is unlikely to serve minority interests in any case. Where minority recruits are successfully integrated into the police organization and subculture, they simply become typical policemen (Alex, 1969: 51; Niederhoffer, 1969: 193). The self-effacing, uncomplaining minority recruit may be accepted by his fellow officers "if he tacitly shares the norms of conduct, beliefs and values of the police world as defined by the white majority" (Alex, 1969: 96). Minority police may even feel more pressure to be "tough cops" with their own kind, than dominant policemen (Banton, 1973: 172). The police subculture is a powerful "subterranean process" for the maintenance and reproduction of "relations of dominance" (Shearing, 1981: 21).

Minorities remain profoundly suspicious of dominant manipulations to co-opt their leadership and spokespersons into "liaison" arrangements, and properly so, in the view of the conflict theorist. One minority group told the Toronto Law Enforcement Liaison committees that:

> A forum such as this which deals with specific law-community problems is not an effective vehicle for dealing with pervasive racism. . . . It is an establishment thing and not relevant to our lives. [Gandy, 1979: 53]

"Liaison" is viewed by some as an unreliable and tentative arrangement, easily rescinded by the real powers of the establishment, of which the police are only servants:

> The police are agents of oppression . . . not the source. . . . Until those laws have been repealed, any accord can be rescinded, any liaison can be broken. . . . The existence of good cops and bad cops is a bogus issue. On the whole police reflect the attitudes of [the establishment]. [*Vancouver Gay Tide*, June 1977]

Militant minorities view liaison much as militant trade unions view "improved labour relations" and "personnel work" by corporations. From the establishment side there is always the fear that the co-opted minority may "turn against" the co-opters. Black police who have formed their own Afro-American police associations may discover that "before, we were the good mercenaries in a colonial situation. Now we're saying we're black men first and policemen second" (Fink and Sealy, 1974: 134–139).

The well-intentioned white policeman may find himself caught up in the structured conflict of police and minority, with little opportunity to reduce the confrontation or even direct it away from his own territory. George Kirkham, a white professor of criminology, took up a student's challenge to find out what a cop's life was like. He enrolled in police academy. After 100 tours of duty as a constable, he wrote:

> I quickly found that my badge and uniform, rather than serving to shield me from such things as disrespect and violence, only acted as a magnet which drew me toward many individuals who hated what I represented. [Kirkham, 1974]

The National Minority Advisory Council summed up the paradox in its 1980 report:

> America stands as a distinctive example of ethnic, religious and linguistic pluralism but it is also a classic example of the heavy-handed use of state and private power to control minorities and suppress their opposition to the continued hegemony of white racist ideology. [P. 1]

The structural conflict is regarded by some sociologists as extending to the very foundations of police functions in a democratic society. Berkley (1969: 2) argues that "the police, more than any other institution, exhibit an antagonism, both in concept and practice, to some of the basic precepts of a democratic society." In particular he notes the paradox of a pluralistic democracy in conflict with police action based on assumed consensus of legitimacy, and the paradox of democratic freedom which requires participation in power, in conflict with police forces which, by the very nature of their organization, resist participation by outsiders. Ralph Nader has argued that if power in a democracy is to be responsible, it must be kept insecure, but if police power is insecure, how is it to maintain social order for the establishment?

The treatment of police deviance in minority relations provided in this paper obviously rejects the proposed remedies of those such as Long (1975) who call for a change in the "style" of police behaviour and law enforcement. Long argues for a shift of emphasis from Wilson's (1968/78) "legalistic" style of policing to his "service" style. That is, police would be trained to act more as peace officers than as law officers. They would be less concerned with apprehending offenders than with resolving social conflict. Even if it were possible to train modern, urban police to act more like the legendary village bobby of nineteenth-century England, and abolish the enormous investment of modern North American police in technology, "tactical squads," two-man car patrols, and so forth, there is no reason to believe that the personal "cop on the beat" so frequently called for in recent inquiries into police-minority relations (e.g., Carter, 1979) would really change the nature of police-minority conflict.

A hard, structural fact which continually obtrudes itself into any discussion of remedies is the sheer cost of modern policing. On resigning as provincial police commissioner and intended reformer of police systems in British Columbia, sociologist John Hogarth concluded "we can't keep throwing more bodies at [social] problems" (*Globe and Mail*, December 21, 1977). He noted that each additional policeman on patrol 24 hours a day actually means five men (sharing the 168 hours of the week in shifts), a car, radio backup, computer technology, and other services which make the total cost of that single additional police body $160,000 a year.

Another hard, structural fact is the resistance of the policemen's associations to any significant alteration in present working arrangements which would reduce their income, organizational power, and working conditions. For example, police organizations have strenuously resisted not only civilian review boards, but also the assignment of "police" duties to other personnel. There are grave doubts about the necessity of armed, trained, $27,000-a-year constables to direct traffic, or operate speeding traps, or make a variety of innocuous domestic calls about noisy dogs. There is even doubt about the advantages of such personnel to photograph the scene after a traffic accident or to collect data after a burglary. In some European countries, many of these tasks are assigned to civilians (20 per cent of Sweden's "police" work is done by civilians). Wilson (1978: 285) has argued for central police bureaus to deal with serious crime, complemented by local precinct stations, staffed by a mixture of trained police and citizens.

Another hard, structural fact blocking the way to fundamental police reform is the increasing professionalization of the police occupation, and indeed the active desire of many police and police chiefs for "more professional standards." A variety of inquiries into the police have called for a more professional force (e.g., Morand, 1976). But one of the perquisites of professions in our society is self-administration, and self-investigation of complaints by clients. (For example, the College of Physicians assesses patient complaints against doctors; the Law Society, client complaints against lawyers). Police opposition to civilian review of civilian complaints often takes the form of a reminder that police are professionals and should not be subject to such review any more than doctors or lawyers (Radelet, 1973: 57ff). The notion of a professional police includes a norm of *secrecy*—just as does the code of other professionals, who are expected not to denounce each other in public (Johnson, 1972).

But perhaps the most troublesome stumbling block in the path of reform is ideology. The consensus view of our legal system holds that the police are servants of all the citizens; that laws and not men govern social order. "The police are the public and the public are the police" (Task Force, 1974). It follows that failure of the legal system to provide justice for minority groups, especially for their complaints against police deviance, is essentially a misfiring of an otherwise suitable engine. The remedy is a little fine tuning. To put it into the common language of typical inquiries by consensus theorists, the injustices are essentially *misunderstandings*.

For example, Judge Donald Morand, in spite of severe criticism of the police cited above, concludes that public criticism of the police, and police lying, harassment and brutality in dealing with some sections of the public, are simply the two sides of a mutual misunderstanding, a "misunderstanding which has led to conflict between the police and the public which has resulted in the use of force which might have been avoided" (Morand, 1976: 145). The elements of this misunderstanding are a police belief that the public wants offenders controlled and punished, at whatever cost, while individual citizens want respect for their democratic rights at the same time as they want fast police action for individual complaints against offenders.

Conflict theorists deeply distrust explanations of "misunderstandings," and instead argue that very often the two sides in a conflict understand each other all too well but have fundamentally different and conflicting interests and ideologies. Improving the police "understanding" of public wishes, especially those of minority groups, while leaving the police organization in place as the paramount agency of social control, would simply make the police "more efficient oppressors" (Galliher, 1972: 316).

In conflict analysis of labour-management relations, fundamental contradictions can be resolved through fundamental reorganization of the system (for example, through "workers' control" on one hand, or "managerial revolution" on the other), or they can continue in a state of unstable equilibriums with "working compromises" negotiated as temporary truces by the conflicting parties (for example, labour contracts). Since fundamental reorganization of the police function in North American society is not in the cards for the foreseeable future, what kinds of working compromises might alter the existing structure of police-minority relations to provide better control of police deviance, and better redress of minority complaints?

Civilianization of some police functions offers no sure guarantees, since much depends on whether the civilians merely become vigilante appendages of the police, or a check on police secrecy and professionalized self-regulation. Judge Morand notes, and suggests for further study, an experiment in management of local police stations by "boards of governors" in which civilians would have significant representation (Morand, 1976: 156). He rightly observes that such experiments are likely to meet "strong opposition" from the police force itself. They might also prove no more useful to minorities than the pilot committees assessed by Gandy. These committees generally underrepresented minorities in the community, and were sometimes "lily white."

Any effective minority representation must include a hand on the purse strings of the police. In most North American cities, civic councils rubber-stamp immense police budgets annually, with little information on how the money is spent. Until 1976, even the meetings of the Toronto police commission were secret and closed to the public. The Toronto police budget until 1979 consisted of two portions. One section broke down (in minute detail) the spending of the force on furniture, the horses, and other trivia, for which the total spending amounted to about five per cent of the budget. The other section consisted of one line, "Salaries and Benefits," and accounted for the other 95 per cent of the budget. A similar situation is found in most North American cities.

Several years ago, minority groups in Los Angeles (especially blacks and gays) combined to pressure the police and the city council for a detailed budget. This is now available, and has had a considerable effect on police treatment of minorities. The budget revealed, for example, that the police spent more each year on "vice squad" activity than on *all* crimes against persons (assault, rape, etc.). The vice squad, needless to say, was one of the major police instruments for harassment of minority citizens. In Toronto, the 1980 budget provided a better breakdown of police spending, as a result of repeated demands by a Working Group on Police-Minority Relations, which brought together for political action the leaders of 20 black, gay, Asian, and other minority groups. The data on the intelligence unit (165 men, far more than in the ethnic squad) and its activities was one of the outcomes of new budget information.

Reiss (1971) makes several imaginative proposals for turning the increasingly technological, bureaucratic and expensive facilities of the police to better protection of citizens' rights. For example, he proposes that each time a constable interacts on duty with a citizen, a written "receipt" be provided to the citizen. This receipt would require the policeman's badge number (thus removing the hesitation of citizens to ask for this information if dissatisfied, because they know it will provoke police hostility); the date, time, and place; and the nature of the encounter, briefly stated (for example, "John Doe was stopped for questioning for five minutes at the corner of Yonge and Bloor at 2 a.m. because he was carrying what looked to be a set of burglar's tools"). Reiss notes that the computer facilities of police departments could be easily adapted to run random checks on individual constables, to search for patterns of deviance in issuing receipts (for example, stopping blacks for questioning far more often than whites, in proportion to population). Citizen complaints about a constable could be quickly compared with existing patterns for that constable.

Such proposals are examples of the sociologist at his or her best—not merely describing, analysing and theorizing about social conflict, but also contributing imaginatively to the discussion of means for improving the quality of human life in a democratic society. Perhaps the student-reader, after considering the structural features of police-minority relations discussed in this article, will think of some additional means by which our society, and especially the beleaguered minorities in pursuit of social justice, may achieve a police force which more truly Serves and Protects every one of us.

REFERENCES

Acord (Auckland Committee Against Racism and Discrimination)
1975. *A Disaster in Community Relations*. Auckland: Wamganui Press.

Adam, Barry
1978. *The Survival of Domination*. New York: Elsevier.

Alex, N.
1969. *Black in Blue: The Negro Policeman*. New York: Appleton.

Altheide, D., and J. Johnson
1980. *Bureaucratic Propaganda*. Toronto: Allyn and Bacon.

Banton, Michael
1964. *The Policeman in the Community*. London: Tavistock.
1973. *Police-Community Relations*. London: Collins.

Bayley, David, and H. Mendelsohn
1969. *Minorities and the Police*. New York: Free Press.

Bent, Alan
1974. *The Politics of Law Enforcement*. Toronto: Lexington.

Berkley, George
1969. *The Democratic Policeman*. Boston: Beacon.

Bienvenue, R., and A. H. Latif
1975. "Arrests, Dispositions and Recidivism: A Comparison of Indians and Whites" in R. A. Silverman and J. J. Teevan (eds.) *Crime in Canadian Society*. Toronto: Butterworths.

Bierstedt, Robert
1968. "The Sociology of Majorities" in R. Mack (ed.) *Race, Class and Power*: at 29–42. New York: Van Nostrand.

Black, A. D.
1968. *The People and the Police*. New York: McGraw Hill.
Black, D. J., and A. J. Reiss
1967. "Patterns of Behaviour in Police and Citizen Transactions," *Studies in Crime and Law Enforcement*, vol. 2, sec. 1. Washington: U.S. Government Printing Office.
Blatchford, Christie
1980. "What the Jury Didn't Hear in the Johnson Case." *Toronto Star*, Nov. 14: at A10.
Boesel, David, and Peter Rossi
1971. *Cities Under Seige, Anatomy of the Ghetto Riots, 1964–68*. New York: Basic Books.
Bordua, David
1968. "Comments on Police-Community Relations." *Connecticut Law Review* 1, no. 2 (Dec.).
Carter, Emmett
1979. Report to the Toronto Police Commission. (Text: *Toronto Star*, Oct. 30).
Chevigny, Paul
1969. *Police Power*. New York: Pantheon.
Clark, Lorenne, and D. Lewis
1977. *Rape: The Price of Coercive Sexuality*. Toronto: Women's Press.
Clement, John
1980. Report to the Toronto Police Commission. (March.)
Cray, Ed
1972. *The Enemy in the Streets*. New York: Anchor.
Douglas, Jack, and John Johnson (eds.)
1977. *Official Deviance*. New York: Lippincott.
Fein, Rashi
1968. "An Economic and Social Profile of the American Negro" in R. Mack (ed.) *Race, Class and Power*. New York: Van Nostrand.
Fink, J., and L. G. Sealy
1974. *The Community and the Police*. New York: Wiley.
Forslund, M. A.
1970. "Comparison of Negro and White Crime Rates," *Journal of Criminal Law, Criminology and Police Science* 61: 214–17.
Foucault, Michel
1977. *Discipline and Punish: The Birth of the Prison*. New York: Pantheon.
Fox, Oliver
1976. *Race Relations*. Detroit: Wayne State University Press.
Galliher, J. F.
1972. "Explanations of Police Behaviour." *Sociological Quarterly* 12: 308–18.
Gandy, John
1979. *Law Enforcement and Race Relations Committees in Metro Toronto*. Toronto: Social Planning Council.
Glenn, N. D., and C. M. Bonjean
1969. *Blacks in the United States*. San Francisco: Chandler.
Goffman, Erving
1956. "The Nature of Deference and Demeanor." *American Anthropologist* 53, no. 3: 473–502.

Goldstein, H.
1977. *Policing and Free Society*. Cambridge, Mass: Ballinger.

Green, E.
1970. "Race, Social Status and Criminal Arrest." *American Sociological Review* 35: 476–90.

Hagan, John
1974. "Criminal Justice in a Canadian Province. Ph.D. thesis, University of Alberta.

Harding, James
1971. "Canada's Indians, A Powerless Minority" in J. Harp and J. Hofley (eds.) *Poverty in Canada*. Toronto: Prentice Hall.

Hartjen, C. A.
1972. "Police-Citizen Encounters; Social Order in Interpersonal Interaction." *Criminology* 10: 61–84 (May).

Hongisto, Richard
1980. "Why Are There No Gay Choir Boys?" *Perspectives Civil Rights Quarterly* 12, no. 2: 39–43.

Hughes, E. C.
1962. "Good People and Dirty Work." *Social Problems* 10: 3–12.

International Association of Chiefs of Police
1975. *Police Height and Selected Aspects of Performance*. Washington: IACP.

Johnson, J. B.
1970. "The Negro and Crime" in W. E. Wolfgang (ed.) *Sociology of Crime and Delinquency*: at 419–30. New York: John Wiley.

Johnson, Terence
1972. *Professions and Power*. London: Macmillan.

Kirkham, George
1974. "Bitter Lessons for a Scholar." *Toronto Globe and Mail*, May 15.
1975. "On the Etiology of Police Aggression in Black Communities" in J. Kinton (ed.) *Police Roles in the Seventies*. Aurora, Ill.: Social Science and Sociological Resources.

Kohler, Arthur
1975. "Police Homicide in a Democracy," *Journal of Social Issues* 31: 163–67.

Lee, John Alan
1978. *Getting Sex*. Toronto: General Publishing.

Levy, Burton
1968. "Cops in the Ghetto," *American Behavioural Scientist* 2 (April): 31–34.

Lieberson, S., and A. Silverman
1965. "The Precipitants and Underlying Conditions of Race Riots." *American Sociological Review* 30: 887–98.

Lofland, John
1969. *Deviance and Identity*. New York: Prentice Hall.

Long, E.
1975. *American Minorities: The Justice Issue*. New York: Prentice Hall.

Lundman, R.
1979. Police Misconduct as Organizational Deviance." *Law and Policy Quarterly* 1, no. 1: 81–100.

Makielski, S. J.
1973. *Beleaguered Minorities*. San Francisco: Freeman.
Maloney, Arthur
1975. *Report to the Toronto Police Commission; Review of Civilian Complaint Procedures*. Toronto: Police Commission.
Marx, Gary
1977. "Riot Control" in Jack Douglas and John Johnson (eds.) *Official Deviance*: at 197. New York: Lippincott.
McNamara, J. H.
1967. "Uncertainties in Police Work" in D. J. Bordua (ed.) *The Police*: at 163–252. New York: John Wiley.
Morand, Donald
1976. *Royal Commission into Toronto Police Practices*. Toronto: Queen's Printer.
Moses, E. R.
1970. "Negro and White Crime Rates" in M. E. Wolfgang (ed.) *Sociology of Crime and Delinquency*: at 430–39. New York: John Wiley.
Muir, W. K.
1977. *Police, Steet-corner Politicians*. Chicago: University of Chicago Press.
National Minority Advisory Council
1980. *The Inequality of Justice*. Washington: NMAC.
Nettler, G.
1978. *Explaining Crime*. Toronto: McGraw-Hill.
Niederhoffer, A.
1969. *Behind the Shield: The Police in Urban Society*. New York: Doubleday.
Posner, Michael
1978. "Law and Order on the March." *Maclean's Magazine*, Oct. 2: 26–30.
Preiss, J. J., and H. J. Ehrlich
1966. *An Examination of Role Theory: The Case of the State Police*. Lincoln: University of Nebraska Press.
President's Commission on Law Enforcement and Administration of Justice
1967. *Report of the Task Force on the Police*. Washington: U.S. Government Printing Office.
Quinney, R.
1977. "Police and Minority" in Quinney, *Class, State and Crime*. New York: McKay.
Radelet, Louis
1973. *The Police and the Community*. Beverly Hills: Glencoe Press.
Rafsky, D. M.
1973. "Police Race Attitudes and Labelling." *Journal of Political Science and Administration* 1, no. 1: 65–86.
Reiss, Albert
1968. "Police Brutality: Answers to Key Questions." *Transaction* 5 (July): 10–19.
1971. *The Police and the Public*. New Haven: Yale University Press.
Savitz, L.
1970. "The Dimensions of Police Loyalty." *American Behavioural Scientist* 5 (Aug.): 693–95.

Shearing, Clifford
1981. "Subterranean Processes in the Maintenance of Power." *Canadian Review of Sociology and Anthropology* 18, no. 3 (Aug.): 283–98.
Skolnick, Jerome
1966. *Justice Without Trial.* New York: John Wiley.
Stoddard, E. R.
1968. "The Informal Code of Police Deviancy." *Criminal Law, Criminology and Police Science* 59 (June): 201–13.
Sykes, Richard, and John Clark
1975. "A Theory of Deference Exchange in Police-Citizen Encounters." *American Journal of Sociology* 81: 584–600.
Tagaki, Paul
1979. "Death by Police Intervention" in U.S. Department of Justice, *A Community Concern.*
Task Force on Policing in Ontario
1974. *Report to the Solicitor General of Ontario*. Toronto: Queen's Printer.
United States Commission on Civil Rights
1970. *Mexican American and the Administration of Justice*. Washington.
1980. *Police Practices and the Preservation of Civil Rights.* Washington.
U.S. Department of Justice
1979. *A Community Concern: Police Use of Deadly Force*. Washington: U.S. Department of Justice (Jan.).
Vincent, C. L.
1979. *Policeman*. Toronto: Gage.
Wald, P. M.
1967. *Poverty and Criminal Justice*. Washington: President's Commission on Law Enforcement and Criminal Justice.
Watters, P., and S. Gillers
1973. *Investigating the F.B.I.* New York: Doubleday.
Westley, William
1970. *Violence and the Police*. Cambridge, Mass: MIT Press. (Revised from 1956.)
Williams, Verne
1980. "No Trust in the Courts." *Toronto Globe and Mail*, May 21.
Wilson, J.
1968. *Varieties of Police Behaviour*. Harvard University Press. (Revised 1978.)

Chapter 4

Rules *For* Police Deviance

Richard V. Ericson

Deviance, Rules, and Discretion

Sociologically, the tools for analysing police deviance are no different from those used to study deviance within any other occupational group or social sphere.

One line of inquiry has treated the police as a social problem, conceiving their deviance as a pathology either individually or socially induced (for reviews see Sherman, 1974; Lundman, 1980: esp. 163–80). Studies of this type follow the criminological tradition of searching for the causes of crime and other forms of deviance as if it was possible, or worthwhile, to separate human beings into distinctive groupings of the normal and the pathological.

Another approach, the one we utilize in this paper, is to understand deviance in terms of social rules as used to construct social order (Douglas, 1971). Deviance is not given in the rules themselves nor in the behaviour of individuals, but in transactions where particular rules might be employed to ascribe deviance in order to achieve particular interests. Rule usage and enforcement is a matter of negotiation, worked out in terms of the interests of the parties involved (Manning, 1977: esp. 247, 248; Strauss, 1978). "The important sociological problem is not to decide *a priori* which phenomena are deviant and which ones are not but rather to discover why this property is conferred upon a person when it is" (Scott, 1972: 14).

Within this framework, one must understand the nature of social rules in order to appreciate how something or someone is constituted as deviant. The police are an important substantive subject for this inquiry because they are highly rule conscious and rule oriented (Manning, 1977b: 47). Examining their use of rules in the context of their organizational activity can shed light upon the properties of rule usage in organizational and social life in general.

Rules are important power tools in the reproduction of order. They have two interconnected functions, as weapons of social conflict (Turk, 1976) and as justifications for action (Scott, 1972).

Social conflict comes about when parties differ about the interests at stake in their transactions. In order to resolve the conflicts, they may bring to bear power resources, including the important resource of rules (e.g., law, administrative rules of an organization, social norms). As a power tool, rules are used tactically to induce a party to conform with actions that will serve particular interests. In most situations the rules remain tacit, making salient the features of an encounter which participants must take into account in terms of their respective roles. Thus, the power of the rules does not come into being only when they are overtly "exercised." Indeed, one means of obtaining routine compliance is to exercise discretion (power) by not invoking a rule to its letter, thus sustaining a relationship on the basis of exchange. As Ignatieff (1979: 445) observes, this type of "tacit contract" was a primary tool employed by the early police in establishing their legitimacy in the community.

Another powerful aspect of rules is their use in providing a framework of accounts that serve to rationalize, justify, and legitimate actions taken. The normative order of rules made applicable and the meanings applied to a situation are closely related (Giddens, 1976: esp. 109, 110). The powerful nature of rules is not gleaned in "perceptible determination of behaviour," but rather in how they "constrain people to *account* for their rule-invocations, rule violations and rule applications" (Carlen, 1976, referring to Durkheim, 1964).

This has become a focal point of study among socio-legal scholars. For example, Feeley (1973: esp. 420–21) seeks to understand how "facts" and "rules" are related to construct a criminal case whereby "the interpretation and use of the rules themselves are viewed as instruments of rationalization, not application." Kadish and Kadish (1973: 4) set out to explore how "legal systems affect people's decisions not only by threatening violators with sanctions, but also by offering people a framework for justifying their actions." Chambliss and Seidman (1971) and Balbus (1973), among others, have portrayed the entire order of formal legal rationality as a means of reproducing the state's legitimacy in face of demands for order and in the context of organizational imperatives within control bureaucracies which necessarily belie it. These themes have been taken up by sociologists studying the police on both the micro-level of how police take rules into account in formulating their accounts (e.g., Chatterton, 1976; Sanders, 1977; Manning, 1980; Ericson, 1981a, 1981b; McBarnet, 1981), and the macro-level of how the law serves as a canopy of mystification to cover police actions (e.g., Manning, 1977a). Within this framework, justice is seen primarily in terms of justifications, and police undercover work becomes understood in terms of police officers' use of legitimate organizational accounts as covers that allow them to get the job done while appearing to be rule-abiding.

To the extent that there is a wide range of rules that can be made to "fit" the account of particular circumstances, enormous latitude is introduced for using rules to one's advantage. As McBarnet (1976, 1979, 1981) points out, no matter what interests provide the motive for police actions, the law and other organizational rules of the legal system provide the opportunity to achieve those interests. Rules and practice interrelate, as rules are taken into account both prospectively and retrospectively. Thus, contrary to Wilson's view (1968: 31), the law and other rules in the organization of crime control do guide the police officer's actions, although of course the rules used to retrospectively account for action taken may not be the rules used to constitute the action at the time (cf. Rawls, 1955).

This conception of deviance and rules is incorporated in the widely used and abused concept of discretion. Davis (1969: 4) states, "A public officer has discretion whenever the effective limits on his power leave him free to make a choice among courses of action or inaction." The other side of this definition in terms of influences on an official's actions is contained in Black's (1968) definition of "discretion" as simply "autonomy in decision-making." In either case, the question of influence and autonomy is the question of power, and any talk about the control of discretion is essentially talk about the reallocation of power.

While discretion may in some instances be "lawless" (Packer, 1968: 290) in the sense that it is without reference to legal rules, it is never "ruleless." That is, discretionary decisions always relate to rules (cf. Thomas, 1974: 140), whether these rules are legal or non-legal, formal or informal, more visible or less visible, and so forth. The particular rule that is used in an action, and/or that is later used to justify it, may be entirely outside of the law itself even though the action is apparently in terms of the law. Thus, a police force may have an administrative rule, or a recipe rule among line officers, that directs officers not to lay charges in domestic conflict situations even though there is apparent evidence available to justify a charge. What could be constituted as "assault occasioning bodily harm," "indecent assault," "common assault," and so forth, is either handled via the private information route, or simply reported as a "domestic" without charges being laid. On the other hand, when officers perceive that serious conflict might ensue if they do not separate the domestic combatants, they may use laws which depend only on their own evidence to justify an arrest (e.g., breach of the peace, obstruct police, assault police, causing a disturbance, liquor violations, or whatever other one can be made justifiable). In any case their decisions are always rule based, with reference to the recipe rules by which they get the job done, and the criminal law rules which may be helpful in the process.

The rule of law or principle of legality is supposed to operate to reduce the arbitrariness of action by the police and other officials. The ideal is embodied in the phrase "Ours is a government of laws, not men," but the reality is that ours is a government of men who use laws. Moreover, as Rothman (1980) has recently documented in detail regarding the United States, the twentieth century has been characterized by a perpetually increasing number of laws and administrative rules that are selectively translated and used in the interests of control agents. The entire control apparatus has become characterized by individualization, which means that a wide range of rules can be used to justify any particular disposition an official deems appropriate for his organizational interests. What some have characterized as "extra-legal" rules turn out to be not extra-legal at all, but are built right into the law to legitimate particular decisions (e.g., the residence and criminal record criteria under the Canadian Bail Reform Act). What some have characterized as due process protections in the interests of the accused over and against the interests of crime control turn out to serve the interests of crime control (McBarnet, 1976, 1979, 1981; Ericson, 1981a, 1981b). Deviation from the standards of legality (as well as from the moral standards of particular groups in society) is institutionalized in the law itself (McBarnet, 1979: esp. 28; Kadish and Kadish, 1973; Freedman and Stenning, 1977). Legal rules, as well as other organizational rules, enable an enormous range of practices. The rules are *for* police deviance.

Rules in Organizational Context

The truism that rules can best be understood in the contexts of their use has led sociologists studying the police and other organizations to favour observational research techniques and to emphasize the informal system of control. As McBarnet (1976, 1979, 1981) has advised and shown, there is a need to pay more attention to the formal rules that provide the framework for the actions of organizational members. Doing so allows one to appreciate that much of what might at first appear to be informal or extra-legal practice is actually built into the legal rules. Furthermore, it reveals the complex interaction among rules in use from a variety of sources: the substantive and procedural law, disciplinary and administrative rules, and the operating or recipe rules as developed and put to use by practitioners. Sociologically, attention to the formal rules as they articulate with other rules in use can further our knowledge about the dialectic between the levels of social structure and social interaction.

Max Weber states: "The modern capitalist concern is based inwardly above all on calculation. It requires for its survival a system of justice whose workings can be *rationally calculated*, at least in principle, according to fixed general laws, just as the probable performance of a *machine* can be calculated . . ." (quoted in Lukacs, 1971: 96; see generally Fine et al., 1979). In the case of criminal law and its product of order, the machinery is that of crime control, especially as practised by its primary agents, the police. As we shall document in detail in the next section, substantive and procedural laws are enabling for the police to help them with their crime control and wider public order efforts. Their enabling power resources, especially the law, allow them to secure compliance routinely. Of course, these structural advantages are characteristic of other occupations that are part of the order business, such as bailiffs (McMullan, 1980), unemployment insurance and other welfare enforcers (Hasson, forthcoming), and prison guards (MacGuigan, 1977). In general we should expect to find relatively few officially designated violations of legal rules by police officers, because the laws typically give them sufficient resources to produce what they want, and sufficient covers.

On the other hand, laws and administrative rules exist to reproduce an internal order within the police organization. These rules, such as the Ontario Police Act, are created to make police officers appear orderly as they go about their business of reproducing order in the community. The fact that these rules, similar to the substantive criminal law rules in the community at large, are inevitably violated en masse on a daily basis does not detract from the appearance of orderliness.[1] Instead, it suggests that the formal laws and other rules are not necessarily controlling except as a threat to be selectively used, often for reasons other than those evident in the particular rule being invoked to justify sanction.

In sum, just as criminal law can be viewed as one vehicle for keeping the population at large in working order, so the internal rules of the police organization are there to be selectively used in ordering workers. One should not expect full compliance nor full enforcement, for that is not how order is put together and maintained.[2]

> An analogy can be made with the framework of rules regulating business practices in the society at large. The legal controls are loose or non-existent as they pertain to the expansion of capital. Where the law proliferates and the controls tighten is in relation to the productivity of the masses who labour for capital. A complex system of laws, enforcement, and corrections exists to put back into working order those who have thrown a spanner in the works (cf. Foucault, 1977). Comparing the police force, we can appreciate that controls are not designed to regulate the productive expansion of the crime making business itself, but only the workers who through minor indiscretions, threaten the productivity potential of the police economy. [Ericson, 1981: 65]

As in any occupation, the police develop working recipe rules which provide them with the basis for action (e.g., Manning, 1971, 1977a, 1980). Line officers see these rules as the real or valid basis for what they do, although usually this is with reference, and occasionally with deference, to the law.

> In a sense, the freedom of the patrolman to enforce or not to enforce has the effect of creating rules. His rules are not the administrative rules, which derive substantially from the criminal code or municipal regulations, but are those "rules of thumb" that mediate between the departmental regulations, legal codes, and the actual events he witnesses on the street. . . . No one argues that policing is random or uncertain, only that the pattern that is produced can be called "rule-guided" only in the sense that one can infer the meaning of events by applying the term "rule-guided" to instances observed. It is unlikely that there is a written "policy", for example, on how to deal with multiple-charge situations. . . . The ways in which policemen, usually in concert with immediate supervisors, resolve these multiple-charge situations is in effect the nexus of generating rules. [Manning, 1977a: 162–63]

In most cases these effective recipe rules remain known only to police organizational participants, and sometimes only to a particular subgroup within the organization. Of course, this means that predictability, a characteristic benefit of any rule system, is not available to all the parties who are affected by the rules (e.g., citizens, and other control agents). This is a crucial aspect of police power: the rules of operation are effectively in their hands, while the rules that are supposed to affect their operations (e.g., the law) serve as covers, rationalizations, and justifications of their actions.

A dominant rule among police officers is to keep these working rules submerged. As elaborated later, the fact that these rules constantly threaten to surface is one reason why the draconian law and rules with respect to internal discipline are kept in place. The officer who violates recipe rules invites sanctions from within the force, and one obvious source of sanction is a disciplinary rule, even though it may relate to quite a different matter. Since the disciplinary code provides almost unlimited opportunity to bring disciplinary charges against an officer, the wise officer comes to appreciate that part of his discipline includes silence on matters that count organizationally, especially the recipe rules.[3]

Thus, "The most powerful constraints on formally constituted organizations are of course the least obvious or invisible ones built into social structure and perceptions of social structure . . ." (Manning, 1979: 41–42). Police officers orient their actions in terms of rules that are not typically visible to anyone but themselves, using the formal rules to justify what they want to accomplish according to their working rules. They are constrained to do this because of the *threat* of disciplinary action against them if they do not conform in matters that count. Their compliance in matters that count is exchanged for a degree of licence in matters that do not count, although they are always subject to having this licence revoked. Although the entire organization is implicated in this structure of rules for deviance, when deviance becomes public it is the individual who is sacrificed for the sake of the perpetuation of the structure.

An apparent complication in police organizations regarding the use of rules is the constitutional position of the individual constable having an original, ministerial authority in law and not a delegated authority (Williams, 1974; Gillance and Khan, 1975; Oliver, 1975).[4] Of course, this authority is belied by the constable's subordinate rank in the police force. In law in Canada (where there is no statutory duty to full enforcement) the individual officer can make choices in individual cases concerning whether or not he might invoke the law. Organizationally, the constable is subject to supervision and review of his decisions, and is frequently ordered by a senior officer to change his decisions regarding invocation of the law (for examples see *Toronto Globe and Mail*, December 13, 1980; Ericson, 1981a, 1981b). The legal position leads one to ask whether lawful orders from more senior officers can relate only to internal discipline, or whether they can also relate to law enforcement decisions. What happens to the constable who disagrees with the senior officer's decision regarding law enforcement?[5]

One obvious answer is that an officer who fails to follow a senior officer's orders regarding invocation of the criminal law may be subject to discipline under the Police Act for "Neglect of Duty," or for any other violation that the administration might find handy; or, he might be even more summarily dealt with via, for example, an unfavourable transfer. However, to the extent that police officers come to believe that internal rules of the police organization override all other rules, including the criminal law,[6] it is unlikely that this situation will arise with any frequency.

Similar to members of delinquent subcultures as discussed by criminologists in the tradition of Cohen (1955) and Cloward and Ohlin (1960), police officers appeal to higher loyalties (interests) in ignoring or breaking or selectively using the criminal law. "There are systematic pressures on police officers to break certain kinds of rules in the interest of conforming to other standards" (Skolnick, 1966: 109). Sir Robert Mark, former head of the Metropolitan London Police, admits that police officers come to believe "there is some moral justification for getting around the rules if it increases the likelihood of getting men convicted whom they believe to be guilty" (interview in *The Observer*, May 16, 1975, quoted by Chibnall, 1979: 141–42). And, former RCMP Commissioner William Higgit expressed the opinion that RCMP officers should be able to break the law in pursuit of a "noble purpose" (cited in *Toronto Globe and Mail*, November 9, 1978, quoted by Mann and Lee, 1979: 234).

The only rule to keep in mind when bending others is that one should take every precaution to avoid being found out. When such a discovery is made, "the little white god" in uniform becomes the big black sheep, thrown to the wolves to preserve the order of things.

> It was as though there were two police forces. One was real, the one which caught criminals, and the other one that existed in some high up's office in the Yard. The real police force was there to catch criminals the best way it knew how; and if you couldn't get them down according to Judges Rules, you got them down in your own way. The real police force worked in and around police stations; the real police force worked.
>
> The other one was the one the Press wrote about, the one the taxpayers believed in. It was full of unsung heroes with blue eyes and honest English faces . . . that police force helped old ladies across the road, in between spells of taking finger prints and running four-minute miles. That police force gave you a pain in the arse. Not only didn't it exist, it couldn't. If it did, the prisons would be empty. And the senior officers knew all about the real police force. . . . But for some reason, once you got up that end of the ladder you started forgetting what it was like. Police duty as it was done became a dirty word. And let some poor sod get caught out in something—whether it was a bit of exaggeration in a magistrate's court, or laying someone else's old woman—and they all raised their clean little hands in horror. "But this is terri-

> ble'', they would say, their own dirty skeletons locked out of sight, ''to think a policeman could do a thing like this''. When what they really meant was, ''Some bloody reporter's going to get hold of this and splash it on the front page''. [Brock, 1968]

Line police officers must keep up the appearances, even while engaging in practices that would belie them. It is arguable that the increasing emphasis upon professionalism functions to make this task easier, because professionalism is essentially an ideology, ''a set of rationalizations about the worth and necessity of certain areas of work, which, when internalized, gives the practitioners a moral justification for privilege, if not license'' (Habenstein, 1963: 297). Most professional programs give organizational legitimation to what was previously practiced informally, or they provide a cover for traditional practices. Indeed, specific measures aimed at professionalization serve to solidify practices they were ostensibly designed to alter, increasing the autonomy of line officers (for examples, see Chatterton, 1979; James, 1979).

In sum, police officers operate with several sets of rules from different sources. They develop recipe rules for getting the job done, in conjunction with the enabling procedural and substantive rules of the criminal law. They are structurally able to innovate with these rules and use them for deviance, limited only by a consideration of the implications for the appearances code of the police organization. They know that if they violate the appearances code, the administration has an array of disciplinary rules that can be selectively used against them in the same way that they use laws as all-purpose control devices in relation to certain segments of the citizenry. They know that if they fall from official grace they will be out on a limb on their own, or treated as a rotten apple fallen from the tree. Since most prefer to mature in some branch of the force, with the hope of eventually being hand-picked for something special, they remain committed to keeping up appearances.

Police Use of Criminal Law Rules

In accomplishing their mandate of reproducing order (Ericson, 1981b) the police have as one key tool the criminal law. Regardless of the recipe rules guiding police actions, and regardless of their motives vis-à-vis the interests at stake, the criminal law rules provide the police with the opportunity to accomplish what they want. The police do not conceive of the criminal law as something that should make their task more difficult. Instead they campaign for enabling procedural law, and for a range of substantive laws that may be situationally useful in handling troublesome people.[7]

Police officers use the substantive law as an all-purpose control device that comes in handy either on a systematic basis or situationally (Bittner, 1967a, 1967b, 1970). This is particularly the case in their public-order work, where the criminal law is variously used, threatened, or ignored according to the perceived local standards of morality (cf. Banton, 1964: esp. 146–47).

When faced with a person who is apparently incapable of caring for himself because he is drunk, high on other drugs, suffering from some mental disorder, and so forth; or, when faced with a boisterous youth who challenges police authority by refusing to disperse along with his friends; or, when faced with a husband who continues to menace his spouse in a "domestic" conflict; or, when faced with a traffic violator who has not heeded previous warnings, the police officer may decide that an arrest and charge is the only effective means left to order the person and/or reproduce order in the situation. The law becomes a residual resource used in the absence of, or after the extinguishing of, other alternatives. As Bittner (1967b: 710) expresses it:

> Patrolmen do not really enforce the law, even when they do invoke it, but merely use it as a resource to solve certain pressing practical problems in keeping the peace. . . . The problem patrolmen confront is not which drunks, beggars, or disturbers of the peace should be arrested and which can be let go as exceptions to the rule. Rather, the problem is whether, when someone "needs" to be arrested, he should be charged with drunkenness, begging, or disturbing the peace.

The substantive criminal law does not in any sense determine apprehension, but simply makes it possible. Many substantive laws are written broadly enough, and with sufficient ambiguity, that they can be applied across a range of circumstances. Causing a disturbance, a breach of the peace, obstructing police, and many others serve as a pretext for making the arrest, while the "real reason" for the arrest lies elsewhere.[8]

Substantive laws of this type are situationally used as "aspirins" (cf. Wilson, 1968: 121) to suspend the symptoms of public ills and to preserve the order of public decorum. Other substantive laws are selectively used on a more systematic basis to preserve the order of things. For the sake of "street cosmetics" (Schur, 1980: 115, quoting a chief of police), prostitutes may be arrested on a regular, predefined basis and fined ("taxed"). For the sake of order on the highways, traffic violations may be enforced by quota up to an administratively acceptable level, while many violators are not stopped or are not summonsed for identical detected acts. Interestingly, in an area such as traffic violation where it is most possible to be legalistic in terms of the objective features of the situation, there is still substantial variation in decisions to charge. In *the* area in which law can be used for order, it is only selectively used. Again there is a recognition that order can be sustained by various means, and the law is only one of them.

The substantive criminal law is also a useful vehicle in circumventing apparent procedural impediments. For example, in order to arrest (detain) someone, the police officer must have reasonable and probable grounds to believe that the person has committed an indictable offence.[9] However, this requirement can be negated by arresting the person for something else and using this as a pretext for in-custody interrogation regarding the matter of concern. For example, the usual practice in Ontario is to issue an appearance notice to a suspect stopped on suspicion who is in possession of a small amount of marijuana. However, a person suspected of break, enter and theft who is found in possession of one marijuana cigarette may be arrested and held in for a bail hearing in relation to the marijuana in order to facilitate questioning in custody regarding the break, enter and theft (cf. Ericson, 1981b). As McBarnet (1979: 37) documents, "Holding charge practices do not then require abuse but simply use of the law. They are not informal subversions of due process: they are due process as defined by common law and statute." From the police viewpoint, the more laws available for such purposes, the more able they are to do their job as they see "fit." This may be one reason why the police are resistant to legal change even with respect to behaviours that are regarded as commonplace and normal.

Another use of the substantive law is as a threat to obtain valued commodities, especially information, from a citizen. As Skolnick (1966: 138) discovered, the threat of conviction and punishment "are the capital assets of the informer system." The police regularly threaten charges, or charge and then offer to withdraw the charges, in exchange for information about matters they regard as more important. Furthermore, the ambiguity of the law and the citizen's inadequate knowledge of it (cf. Ericson and Baranek, 1981), usually allow the police officer to say that he could charge but is giving the person a "break" in exchange for information, when there is no basis for a charge in the first place (for examples, see Ericson, 1981a: chaps. 5 and 6).

The substantive law also serves as a tool to coerce the accused into pleading guilty in court without a trial. Again the ambiguity of the substantive law allows the police leeway, for they can justify charging with higher categories as a lever to induce a guilty plea to a lower category even though they predict they can only sustain evidence for the lower category in the first place. Similarly, the law allows multiple charging, even when convictions cannot be sustained on more than one count because they arise out of the same fact situation (e.g., *Kienapple v. The Queen* (1974), 15 C.C.C. (2d) 524; *R. v. Houchen* (1976), 31 C.C.C. (2d) 274, 71 D.L.R. (3d) 739; 5 W.W.R. 182). Recent studies on police charging practices in a Canadian jurisdiction reveal the general practice of charging everyone possible with everything possible as a means of starting from a maximal position for plea bargaining purposes, even though there is no hope and no intention of sustaining convictions on all of the charges (Ericson, 1981a, 1981b; Ericson and Baranek, forthcoming).

Turning our attention to the procedural criminal law, we also find that the rules are *for* the police rather than impediments to them. As McBarnet (1976, 1979, 1981) has argued, Packer's (1968) dichotomy between a due process model of procedural protections for the accused and a crime control model of expedient law enforcement turns out not to be a dichotomy at all. In the law as written, as well as in the law in action, "due process is *for* crime control." That is, the rules of procedure as written and used explicitly serve the expedient ends of law enforcement. Indeed, especially in countries like England and Canada where the suspect and accused have no entrenched rights, one is hard pressed to find any direct evidence of due process. Even in the United States, where rights are entrenched, there is frequently no empirical referent for ideals such as the rule of law or due process (Black, 1972). As Thurman Arnold ([1962], cited by Carlen, 1976: 95) states, "When a great government treats the lowliest of criminals as an equal antagonist . . . we have a gesture of recognition to the dignity of the individual which has an extraordinary dramatic appeal. It's claim is to our emotions, rather than on our common sense."

As pragmatic professionals whose theory and practice is based on common sense, the police can usually work within the procedural law to achieve the outcomes they want. As McBarnet (1976, 1979, 1981) in Britain, and Freedman and Stenning (1977) in Canada show, an examination of the procedural law itself tells us much about why this is the case.

First of all, any apparent procedural protections for the citizen from undue interference or restraint by the police may be circumvented by gaining the "consent" of the citizen for the action taken. Thus, if the police officer can show that a person has consented to an action such as a search, detention or confession, the interference is legally justified. "Consent to such security activities, furthermore, may be expressed or implied, and may be obtained in a number of ways" (ibid: 68). This is a frequently used technique, made easy by the fact that the vast majority of citizens defer to the authority of the police officer (Ericson, 1981a, 1981b). Moreover, the broad definition of what constitutes consent, and the legal resource costs for the citizen who might challenge it, are arguably prohibitive enough to deter citizens from taking legal action in this regard.

Taking the example of searches we find that without consent, searches of a building, receptacle or place can be undertaken with the authority of a search warrant issued by a justice (Criminal Code, sections 443 to 447). Since a justice typically has no means to independently check the police officer's "reasonable grounds" for a search, he ordinarily issues a warrant.[10] Where narcotics are allegedly involved, RCMP officers with writs of assistance for searches may be called upon and used without the bother of obtaining a warrant issued by a justice. Furthermore, searches of person and property may be undertaken incident to arrest. Vehicles may be searched under various provisions of the Narcotic Control Act, the Liquor Licensing Act (Ontario) and the Highway Traffic Act (Ontario) (Freedman and Stenning, 1977: 119ff; Ericson, 1981b: chap. 6). Persons may be searched under the Narcotic Control Act, and under section 103(1) of the Criminal Code, "whenever a peace officer . . . believes on reasonable grounds that an offence is being committed or has been committed against any of the provisions of this Act relating to prohibited weapons or restricted weapons." Furthermore, if the police officer is so incompetent that he somehow fails to fit his actions within one or more of this array of enabling provisions, or at least fails to successfully convince others that he has done so, he may still have any illegally obtained material admitted for evidence in court because there is no exclusionary rule in Canada.[11]

With respect to the arrest (detention) of a suspect and the questioning of a suspect, there is also an array of enabling rules for the police. Arrests may be made with a warrant, although this is not as common as arrests without a warrant (Ericson, 1981a, 1981b). A warrant is issued by a justice, upon the laying of an information by a police officer. There is every reason to believe that arrest warrants are issued on the same "rubber stamp" basis as search warrants.[12] Arrests without warrant (Criminal Code, section 450) may be made in relation to a range of indictable offences that the officer believes on "reasonable and probable grounds" the person is about to commit, is committing, or has committed; and in relation to selected indictable and hybrid offences, as well as summary offences, that he believes on "reasonable and probable grounds" the person is committing.

Among other things, one must ask what is meant by "reasonable and probable grounds." McBarnet (1979: 32) comments that ". . . the common law merely offers a post hoc check on the 'reasonableness' of the policeman's *belief* that arrest was justified. The law also accepts the belief that people ought to be taken into custody if they have a past record . . . or are jobless or homeless." Furthermore, the courts have introduced enabling interpretations of what it means to have reasonable and probable grounds to find a person committing an offence. In *R. v. Biron* (1975), 23 C.C.C. (2d) 513, the Supreme Court of Canada, following *Wiltshire v. Barrett* (1965), 2 All E.R. 271, held that the words "finds committing" must be interpreted as "finds apparently committing," thus enabling an arrest of a person allegedly engaging in a criminal act to be deemed lawful even if the person is subsequently not convicted.

Along with the vagueness in the definition of arrest, there is an array of sanctions for resisting or escaping lawful arrest, for example, up to two years' imprisonment for obstructing a police officer in the execution of his duty (Criminal Code, section 118); up to two years' imprisonment for escaping from lawful custody (Criminal Code, section 133); up to five years' imprisonment for assaulting a police officer (Criminal Code, section 246); and ultimately, being subject to whatever force, up to and including deadly force, is necessary to effect the arrest (Criminal Code, section 25(4)).[13] Furthermore, a police officer, as someone "who is required or authorized by law to do anything in the administration or enforcement of the law . . . is, if he acts on reasonable and probable grounds, justified in doing what he is required or authorized to do and in using as much force as is necessary for that purpose (Criminal Code, section 25(1)). As Freedman and Stenning (1977: 95) observe, this provision can be used to protect police officers making arrests from criminal and civil liablility, and to remove from accused persons in some cases the defence that the arresting person was acting unlawfully.

Similar observations can be made regarding interrogations and the right to silence. The law allows the police to employ a variety of techniques of trickery and deceit (Kaufman, 1974; Freedman and Stenning, 1977), and even if a judge rules that a statement has not been voluntarily obtained, that part of the statement which is supported by subsequently discovered facts is admissible. Faced with this barrage of enabling rules for dentention and questioning, along with isolation (low visibility) and the intimidating aura of the police office, it is little wonder that suspects routinely comply and talk (for evidence on compliance and the routine nature of confessions, see Softley, 1980; Great Britain Royal Commission on Criminal Procedure, 1980; Ericson, 1981a, 1981b; Ericson and Baranek, forthcoming).

In sum, the rules themselves provide the police with what they need to accomplish their tasks in a routine manner. Deviation from principles of legality is part of the law as written by legislatures and interpreted by the courts.

> Legality requires equality; the law discriminates against the homeless and jobless. Legality requires that officials be governed by law; the law is based on post hoc decisions. Legality requires each case be judged on its own facts; the law makes previous convictions grounds for defining behaviour as an offence. Legality requires incriminating evidence as the basis for arrest and search; the law allows arrest, and search in order to establish it. Legality embodies individual civil rights against public or state interests; the law makes state and the public interest a justification for ignoring civil rights. . . . Deviation from legality is institutionalized in the law itself. The law does not need to change to remove hamstrings on the police: they exist only in the unrealized rhetoric. [McBarnet, 1979: 39]

Both the substantive and procedural criminal law are also useful to the police as a discourse. They allow a conflict with a colourful kaleidoscope of complexities to be transformed into a black and white "still" of factual/legal discourse. Rules and accounts are bound together as police officers prospectively decide what to do with a case, following the maxim, "Unless you have a good story, don't do it" (Chatterton, 1979: 94). In formulating the story along with the taking of action, and in reformulating it in written documents for the consumption of senior officers and the courts, the police officer keeps in mind the rules of the game. The rules become embedded in the formulations used to make the case (Sanders, 1977: esp. 98–99), so that it is difficult to distinguish between the generation of fact, its provision to senior officers and the court, and the use of rules for its accomplishment.

The structure of the criminal process is very enabling for the police in this regard. They have fundamental control over the construction of "facts" for a case, and all other actors (the prosecutor, the judge, the defence lawyer) must work from the framework of facts as constructed by the police. As Carlen (1976: 112) observes, the police (in prosecution) "frame their accounts in the language of the *fact* when everybody else is invited to give *evidence*." For example, information that is no more than the unverified account of an informant is presented as if it were factual (Rubinstein, 1973: 385). Police documents, including their notebooks with times, places, names, and dates, come to stand for the reality of what happened.[14]

While prosecutors, lawyers and judges may know that this is the case, they routinely defer to the police accounts because the system depends upon mutual trust and co-operation among these persons who have recurrent and regular contact (Blumberg, 1967; Ericson and Baranek, forthcoming). A defence lawyer who regularly challenges police accounts may find himself ostracized, and perhaps excluded from things important to his case, such as pre-trial discovery. Indeed, most cases result in guilty pleas, with no inquiry in open court as to how the cases were constructed. Accused persons regularly defer to this order of things (ibid.). As Balbus (1973: esp. 258–59) discovered, even accused persons with political motives tend to defer to a court's actions to serve their short-term interest of a lenient penalty, rather than engage formal legal discourse in a long-term political struggle in court.

Of course, in saying that the police are able to construct the facts of the case we are not saying that they are fabrications. Indeed, the ways in which the factual accounts and rules are intertwined make it very difficult to distinguish what is fabrication, or perjury, and what is not. However, several accounts do point out that what may amount to fabrication and perjury is not uncommon. For example, James (1979: 79) refers to the practice of inventing verbal evidence among British police officers, who refer to it as "verbling to work the oracle." Morris (1978: 29) cites an English barrister writing in the *Criminal Law Review*, who observed that the Judges' Rules (regarding the right to silence and admissibility of confessions) actually "*result in* police officers committing perjury." Ontario Justice Morand, in the *Report of the Royal Commission into Metropolitan Toronto Police Practices* (1976: 123), comments:

> Judges know that a good deal of perjury is committed in the Courts. . . . There is a natural tendency among Judges, as among the public generally, to accept the sworn testimony of a police officer, particularly when it contradicts the words of a person whose credibility is suspect. . . . It is with considerable regret that I am bound to report that one of the most disturbing things which came out in the hearings was the extent to which I found the evidence of police officers mistaken, shaded, deliberately misleading, changed to suit the circumstances and sometimes entirely and deliberately false.[15]

The police have an array of legal resources to use, along with other structural resources of the organizations within which they operate, to accomplish the crime and criminal aspects of their mandate. As mentioned in previous sections, just as they have rules to use to accomplish this task, there are also rules to be used against them to sustain internal order within the police department. We now turn to an examination of these rules and their uses.

Police Uses of Internal Disciplinary Rules

Police organizations are faced with the dilemma that the rules by which the job gets done are rarely articulated clearly and still more rarely written down as policies. Indeed, given the great variety of human beings and troubles the police confront, it is unlikely that rules of adequate performance could be written down, short of what would amount to a compendium on all the manners of society (Laurie, 1972: 111; see generally Wilson, 1968: esp. 66; Manning, 1979). The constant reference by police officers to the necessity of using common sense and playing it by ear reflects this situation. If it is the case that police work is so multifaceted that it cannot be systematized or generalized, then of course it is difficult to conceive of how the individual officer's discretion can be organizationally constrained.

As many researchers and commentators have pointed out, one response has been to professionalize the police in a way that gives the appearance of control. Emphasis is placed upon particular measures of output (e.g., charge quotas, clearance rates), and on conformity to disciplinary standards which are designed to make the organization appear impeccably in order. Of course, as we stated previously, this type of professionalization serves to strengthen tendencies it was designed to oppose, especially "occupational individualism and defensive fraternal solidarity" (Bittner, 1970: 67). Moreover, it creates expectations that are impossible to achieve, so that everyone appreciates the hypocrisy of constant deviance among those who are supposed to be the models of conformity and who are charged with the task of keeping the lid on other people's deviance. The police officer learns that all he must keep up to is the appearance of conformity, and a significant part of his occupational socialization is learning that skill.

The primary "all-purpose central device" the police officer is subject to is provincial law (the Police Act) and departmental rules relating to various aspects of discipline. For example, the Ontario Police Act, R.S.O. 1970, lists a long schedule of offences which reads like a set of rules comparable to those existing in prisons and other forms of "total institutions." Many of the offences have a very broad definition, allowing interpretive latitude to those who have the power to use these rules in their interests. Thus, a police officer is guilty of "discreditable conduct" if he "acts in a disorderly manner, or in a manner prejudicial to discipline or likely to bring discredit upon the reputation of the police force" or if he "uses profane, abusive or insulting language to any other member of a police force," among other things. Furthermore, he is guilty of "discreditable conduct" by virtue of being found guilty under any other offence of the Police Act. He is guilty of "insubordination" if he "is insubordinate by word, act or demeanor." He is guilty of "neglect of duty" if he "without lawful excuse, neglects or omits promptly and diligently to perform a duty as a member of the police force"; "idles or gossips while on duty"; "fails to work in accordance with orders, or leaves an area, detachment detail or other place of duty, without due permission or sufficient cause"; "fails to report a matter that it is his duty to report"; "fails to report anything that he knows concerning a criminal or other charge, or fails to disclose any evidence that he, or any person within his knowledge, can give for or against any prisoner or defendant"; "omits to make any necessary entry in any official document or book"; "feigns or exaggerates sickness or injury to evade duty"; "is improperly dressed, dirty or untidy in person, clothing or equipment while on duty," among others. He is guilty of "deceit" if he "without proper authority communicates to the public press or to any unauthorized person any matter connected with the police force," among others. He is guilty of "corrupt practice" if he "directly or indirectly solicits or receives a gratuity, present, pass, subscription or testimonial without the consent of the Chief of Police"; "improperly uses his character and position as a member of the police force for private advantage"; "in his capacity as a member of the police force writes, signs or gives, without the consent of the Chief of Police, a reference or recommendation to a member or former member of the police force, or any other police force," among others. He is guilty of "unlawful or unnecessary exercise of authority" if he "is uncivil to a member of the public," among others. He is guilty of "consuming intoxicating liquor in a manner prejudicial to duty" if he "(a) while on duty is unfit for duty through drinking intoxicating liquour; or (b) reports for duty and is unfit for duty through drinking intoxicating liquour; or (c) except with the consent of a superior officer or in the discharge of duty, drinks or receives from any other person intoxicating liquor on duty; or (d) demands, persuades or attempts to persuade another person to give or purchase or obtain for a member of the police force any intoxicating liquor, while on duty." No mention is made of other drugs.

In addition, departmental orders on a wide variety of matters may be backed up by the provisions of the Police Act. For example, a police department may have a requirement that its officers reside in a certain geographical boundary, and an officer who does not comply is guilty of "insubordination" ("without lawful excuse, disobeys, omits or neglects to carry out any lawful order") (*Re Coates and Ontario Police Commission* (1979), 23 O.R. (2d) 568, 96 D.L.R. (3d) 560 (Div. Ct.)).

A recent case illustrates the extremes to which police administrators can go in using the discipline code to reproduce the appearance of internal order. According to the *Toronto Globe and Mail* (December 4, 1980):

> For sporting an extra quarter-inch of facial hair last January, [Constable Murphy] is facing dismissal from the force on which he has served for 11 years.
>
> Staff Superintendent John Webster, who ordered Mr. Murphy taken "off the street" because he refused to shave his mustache, testified yesterday that the public and press may take the matter lightly, but it is of the utmost seriousness.
>
> . . . . .
>
> "The press and public may think this is chicken" Supt. Webster said. "But we're dealing with life-and-death situations and this is serious business."
>
> "Without order and regulations, you have a rabble. It is the principle behind this. If an officer cannot obey regulations, how can you expect him to act in a life-and-death situation?"
>
> Although Mr. Murphy's neatly trimmed mustache would have conformed with the new hair regulations that went into effect in October, it did not conform with the former regulations.
>
> . . . . .
>
> Shown a picture of the 1976 version of the "notorious mustache" as Mr. Murphy's facial hair is referred to by policemen, Supt. Webster quipped: "I'd have done everything but charge him under the Criminal Code for a mustache like that."
>
> After the charge, Mr. Murphy stapled papers and performed janitorial work at the police college while collecting his $23,000-a-year salary.
>
> He now works for the intelligence bureau. . . .

As human beings and as workers, there is no reason to believe that police officers act in ways different from the rest of us. Police officers are likely to "gossip" among each other about departmental and other affairs; "idle" on duty (what else can you do on a midnight shift in a suburban area?); tell their non-police friends and family about some details of their work; have a snooze or some booze on the job; telephone in sick in order to have a "mental health day" of rest away from work; curse at their fellow workers; adjust their appearance to suit themselves, and so forth. It is reasonable to guess that every police officer has violated these rules and the multitude of others like them, and that most do so daily. The question to ask is when do police administrators decide to charge for a violation and what functions does it serve?

In the case of Mr. Murphy cited above, he wore a visible symbol that served as a constant reminder of a violation. In order to assert the symbol of organizational discipline and authority, a senior officer decided to use him. This, of course, is no different from the way rules, including criminal law rules, have always been used for the purposes of order. In eighteenth-century England the hegemony of the rulers was maintained by using the law as an ideological display of majesty, justice and mercy (Hay et al., 1975). Some people were charged and some were not, some were hanged and some were pardoned, all to the end of reproducing the order of the status quo. In the current century a proliferation of measures has given the authorities much greater discretion in the uses of the criminal law, but to the same end, and it appears to matter little that none of these measures has had much impact upon levels of crime and deviance (Rothman, 1980). Similarly, in the organizational context there is massive violation of the rules of order, but only selective invocation. The very existence of the rules and their selective use create "dependent uncertainty" (Cain, 1973: 181) for police officers, which, of course, is a primary means by which all punitive rule systems serve to discipline the lower orders (Foucault, 1977). Their selective enforcement serves as a "status enforcing ritual" (Manning, 1977b: 58) for the administration, reminding lower-ranking officers of their place and confirming for everyone their sense of order.

Another consideration is the way in which rules of order and discipline can serve to give licence in other areas. That is, the more the administration gives emphasis to conformity regarding the appearances code, the more it will exchange that conformity for licence in areas of importance to police officers in their actual work. The literature is replete with examples of superordinate-subordinate exchanges of this type, particularly between sergeants and constables (e.g., Cain, 1971, 1973; Ramsay, 1972; Muir, 1977). Bittner (1970: 55) makes the point lucidly:

> Because the real work of the policeman is not set forth in the regulations, it does not furnish his superior a basis for judging him. At the same time, there are no strongly compelling reasons for the policemen to do well in ways that do not count in terms of official occupational criteria of value. The greater the weight placed on compliance with internal departmental regulation, the less free is the superior in censoring unregulated work practices he disapproves of, and in rewarding those he admires, for fear that he might jeopardize the loyalty of officers who do well on all scores that officially count—that is, those who present a neat appearance, who conform punctually to bureaucratic routine, who are visibly on the place of their assignment, and so on. In short, those who make life easier for the superior, who in turn is restricted to supervising just those things. In fact, the practical economy of supervisory control requires that the proliferation of intradepartmental restriction be accompanied by increases in license in areas of behavior in unregulated areas. Thus, one who is judged to be a good officer in terms of internal, military-bureaucratic codes will not even be questioned about his conduct outside of it.

Similar to other persons who constantly face the possibility of being ascribed a deviant role, the police officer learns to be discreet (cf. Cain, 1971: 90n). Since everyone can potentially be found out as a violator, the person who is selected out is in a sense punished for failing to maintain proper cover rather than for the specific violation (cf. Rubinstein, 1973: 119).

From the administrative viewpoint, the enabling rules of discipline may also come in handy if administrators need to discredit an officer for other purposes. An officer who is publicly caught out in something objectionable, even if he is conforming with the recipe rules of the police culture, may have to be made expendable in order to keep the organizational image polished and the working rules intact. Administrators can engage in "deniability" (cf. Mann and Lee, 1979: 26) of the events or practices by trafficking in the "rotten apple" theory of police deviance. This view is also one which is easily understood and accepted publicly, and is a favorite line in press coverage of police wrongdoings (ibid.; Chibnall, 1977, 1979).[16]

Of course, police administrators may also want to sustain particular figures of disciplinary control as they do figures of crime control (cf. Ditton, 1979).[17] Too few invocations might indicate that things are "too good" and suggest the possibility of supervisor-subordinate collusion, or lax discipline. Too many invocations might also invite inquiry from top echelons, including a questioning of the supervisors' ability to discipline their men (Cain, 1973: 148). The likely compromise is a standard in-between these extremes, making it appear that everything is in order.

In sum, rules are used for order within the police organization in ways similar to those used by police officers in going about their business of ordering people outside their organization. While police officers may be "cats" pursuing the offending "mouse" in the criminal game, they themselves must constantly be wary of being pounced upon. The rules they use, and that are used against them, undoubtedly serve the interests of discipline and the appearances of order. However, questions remain concerning the deviance these rules serve.

Deviant Rules?

The police are placed in this situation of having to use several rule systems for multiple purposes because of the impossible mandate they have acquired in contemporary times. The police have defined, and had defined for them, a mandate so broad that it includes responsibility for crime control, other deviance control, and ultimately social order. The police have taken on this responsibility for social processes that are beyond the possibility of any one group's control in that they are embedded in the social, cultural, political and economic structures of society (Manning, 1971, 1977a). Consequently, like all other priestly bodies who claim such grandiose mandates, they must resort to the "manipulation of appearances" (ibid.) to sustain their legitimacy and maintain their hegemony. The major tool they have for this purpose is the various rules at their disposal. On behalf of the powers that be, and also on their own behalf, the police can display majesty, justice and mercy even while massive amounts of ordinary crime and deviance are unjustly and mercilessly perpetuated both outside and inside their organization.

This situation obviously creates organizational hypocrisy on several levels. In community relations, administration–line officer relations, and relations among specialized subunits of the police force, the organization appears as "a puppet dancing to one tune and singing another" (Manning, 1977a: 362), or more accurately, singing several others.

The impact of these circumstances on line officers is predictable. It is likely to make them secretive, cautious, conservative, suspicious and untrusting. Perceiving that the administration's "Ways and Means Act" can be used against them in the same way that they use their own version of the "Ways and Means Act" against citizens, line officers may adopt the attitude that rules are for arbitrary, selective purposes, to be used only in accordance with the sense of justice of those who have them at their disposal.

There is no easy solution to this situation short of fundamentally altering our view of the police mandate and changing the rule systems by which they operate. Certainly, changing a few rules to give greater appearances of procedural regularity will do nothing to change the present order of things, and it may well strengthen the tendencies one was seeking to alter. A wealth of socio-legal research, as well as research in other governmental and industrial organizational settings (e.g., on the police see Medalie et al., 1968; Chambliss and Seidman, 1971; Greenawalt, 1974; Zander, 1978; James, 1979; Chatterton, 1979; on prison guards see Harvard Center for Criminal Justice, 1972; on school principals disciplining students see Gaylin et al., 1978: 136ff), instructs us that new reforms and the rules that are supposed to bolster them are typically incorporated into existing practices and frequently strengthen the practices.

Of course, we are not suggesting that we should give up and no longer question what might be deviant rules and what might be appropriate changes to them. In order to encourage this questioning we must first foster wider appreciation of the ways in which punitive rules—for example, the substantive criminal law, the Police Act, administrative orders and disciplinary codes—are used, especially how they symbolically reproduce particular conceptions of order. At the same time there is a need for further extensive inquiry into the recipe rules which guide police actions, and to understand how these link with administrative and legal rules in their uses as weapons of conflict and justifiers of action. Only when we have a fuller appreciation of these processes can we decide what particular rules and rule systems might be deviant in what circumstances, and therefore what changes might be called for in the fundamental project of reallocating discretion (power) within the criminal process and society at large.

NOTES

1. Cobb (1957: 56) reports that 2,238 of the first 2,800 men enlisted in London's New Police were dismissed, including 1,790 for drunkenness on duty. Reiss (1971: 156, 164) states that in his large observational study of patrol operations in three American cities, "excluding any participation in syndicated crime, roughly 1 in 5 officers was observed in criminal violation of the law . . . [and]

roughly 4 in every 10 officers were observed in one of the more serious violations of rules [e.g., drinking and sleeping while on duty; neglect of duty; falsification of information]." A variety of ethnographic studies also document rule violation, for example, Rubinstein (1973), Cain (1973), Ericson (1981a, 1981b).

2. The historical record informs us that attempts at further enforcement as a means of achieving compliance typically leads to an amplification of the phenomena that one is attempting to eradicate. One example is witchcraft control in Renaissance Europe (Currie, 1968). Another example is the first regime at Kingston Penitentiary, where under the "Auburn" rules inmates were publicly whipped for infractions such as talking out of turn or idling while at work (for similar rules, albeit with different punishments, see our discussion of the Ontario Police Act in the section headed "Police Uses of Internal Disciplinary Rules"). Infractions and punishment rituals multiplied from the hundreds to the thousands within a decade, until a commission of inquiry intervened and decided that for the sake of order other means of internal discipline had to be developed (Beattie, 1977).
3. Part of the code in most police forces includes a requirement of silence to outsiders about any police matter. For example, the Police Act of Ontario code of offences includes the offence of "V. Breach of Confidence, that is to say, if he . . . (c) without proper authority communicates to the public press or to any unauthorized person any matter connected with the police force." On the other hand, when it is an internal matter the requirement is usually that the officer must talk. Typically, officers do not have a right to silence regarding disciplinary hearings.
4. This authority is implied in the oath of office for constables in Ontario, an oath that is almost identical to the one employed in England. The Ontario Police Act, R.S.O. 1970, c. 351, s. 64(1), includes the oath of office:

   > I, __________, do swear that I will well and truly serve Her Majesty the Queen in the office of constable (*or as the case may be*) for the __________ of __________ without favour or affection, malice or ill-will; and that, to the best of my power, I will cause the peace to be kept and preserved, and prevent all offences against the person and properties of Her Majesty's subjects; and that, while I continue to hold the said office, I will, to the best of my skill and knowledge, discharge all the duties thereof faithfully according to the law. So help me God.

5. Oliver (1975: 316) reports that one English constable, undaunted by his senior officer's desire not to prosecute, "applied to the court for a summons as a private person and . . . conducted a successful prosecution." Oliver questions, "Can the Chief Officer issue a lawful order instructing the constable not to proceed with his private prosecution, and if the constable persists in his intention, can he be disciplined for disclosing information which he gained as a police officer, to a third person?"
6. According to one RCMP witness to the McDonald Commission of Inquiry, RCMP officers are trained to believe that the RCMP Act overrides all other legislation (*The Canadian*, February 3, 1979, quoted by Mann and Lee, 1979: 55).
7. In an article by C. Blatchford in the *Toronto Star*, June 20, 1979, the president of the Metropolitan Toronto Police Association is quoted in response to public criticism after a policeman shot a black Jamaican immigrant in a "domestic"

situation. He offers the typical argument that policemen must make split-second decisions, and that it is necessary to have legal support in these situations.

> The force is deeply disturbed. People are saying we should back off in these potentially violent situations. Well, damn it, if we do that, we'll have one or two officers being killed, or citizens dying—innocent victims. And we'll be nailed for doing what we're *legally bound* to do.
>
> When we don't back off, we're called up on the carpet for doing our job, and accused of shooting by color—*my God, when you have to make a decision in a matter of three seconds, you don't have time to pick and choose who you're going to shoot.* [Emphasis added]

8. Ramsay (1972: 65) illustrates the point as follows:

> When the Saskatchewan liquor law was changed in 1968 to prohibit the prosecution of persons intoxicated in a public place, overzealous [RCMP] members thwarted its intent and kept their statistics up by charging Indians under the Criminal Code for causing a disturbance.

9. One exception to this is Criminal Code section 450(1)(c), which allows a police officer to arrest someone on suspicion that a warrant for the person's arrest is in force in the jurisdiction.
10. Ericson (1981a: chap. 6) reports in a study of detective operations within a Canadian municipal police force that of 41 requests for search warrants all resulted in the justice granting a warrant, all but two without question. In a sample of cases followed from beginning to end, there were 27 searches of a "building, receptacle or place," including 17 in which a warrant was obtained (although not always shown to the suspect) and 10 by consent without a warrant or incident to arrest.
11. See Skolnick (1966: 224) for an enumeration of reasons why the exclusionary rule in the United States is likely to have little impact upon the routine actions of detectives and other police officers.
12. McBarnet (1979: 31) reports that in Scotland, the Thompson Committee on criminal procedure "found it 'satisfactory' for judges to 'rubber stamp' rather than investigate requests for warrants."
13. McBarnet (1979: 29–30) observes in the English context:

> It is also an arrestable offence according to the 1964 Police Act to obstruct the police in the execution of their duty. Since this has been interpreted (Parker L.J.) as "the doing of any act which makes it more difficult for the police to carry out their duty" and might include simply refusing to answer questions and any sarcasm in one's manner (*Rice v. Connelly*, 1966), it is difficult to see how someone can avoid being arrested if the police have a mind to it. Furthermore, refusing to cooperate is not a far cry from resistance, which is, of course, an arrestable offence, nor is resistance far from another offence, assault.
>
> Indeed, in court, resisting arrest tends to be presented by prosecutors as indicative of guilt and therefore a justification of the arrest on the first charge anyway.

Rubinstein (1973: 269) reports that in some American jurisdictions, "citizens are lawfully deprived of the right to resist even the unlawful actions of policemen."

In *Moore v. R.* (1979), 5 C.R. (3d) 289, the majority of the Supreme Court of Canada held that a suspect's failure to provide identification to a police officer attempting identification for the purpose of issuing a summons without arrest amounts to an obstruction of the police officer. There was no law requiring the accused to identify himself in the circumstances; however, the conviction for obstructing police was upheld because the accused had factually obstructed the officer in the execution of his duty by not identifying himself. In an annotation to this case, the Director of the Federal Department of Justice Criminal Law Amendments Branch comments, ". . . the *Moore* case seems a further step in the law enforcement approach the Supreme Court has adopted in cases involving police powers."

14. Carlen (1976: 114) comments:

> The policeman's notebook is not only a strategic prop in establishing the certain meaning of disputed past events; it implies that certain meaning is *external* to the people involved. As Gerald Abrahams (1964) has pointed out:
>
> > "Theoretically the policeman's notebook is one of those documents that can be referred to in order to refresh memory, not to act as a substitute for memory. In practice it becomes used as if it were the constable's memory. This, let it be added, is a tendency in law in respect of many documents made by experts of various types."

15. A sociologist offers his version of the same thing:

> In some cases the press of the immediate situation makes it imperative for the officer to act at once, in the absence of "reasonable cause" that would pass a commonsense test. If his actions result in evidence of criminality he can then "back up" and figure out the way to proceed which will make his evidence admissible. If no such way exists, he may retroject into the situation the necessary elements to support the common sense basis of his typification of criminality. Since the officer is linguistically objectifying his own subjective reality, there are many ways in which he can stretch it in the light of his present knowledge. He can find out what *would* have constituted reasonable cause had he thought of it at the time, and simply say he *did* think of it at the time. He can testify to things he did not see which were there. He can anticipate the court's review and put in his initial report items which would have given him reasonable cause had they happened. Finally, and without much danger, he can simply perjure himself. Very few of his fellow officers will testify against him, and no one else is likely to be able to. [Buckner, 1970: 99–100]

16. Chibnall conducted research on the reaction of London's "Fleet Street" newspapers to massive corruption in the Metropolitan London CID (Scotland Yard) (on this situation, see Cox et al., 1977). Chibnall (1977: 165–71; 1979: 144) found that reporters were concerned with detectives' morale and willingly wrote stories claiming that the wrongdoings were limited to a small rotten core. "The impact of the revelations on the force as a whole was minimized by interpreting police deviance as a minority activity which leaves the vast majority of policemen untouched and untainted. The explanation of the occasional 'bent copper' was to be found in individual pathology rather than in the endemic features of police work and organization" (1979: 144).

17. Mann and Lee (1979: 141) suggest that in the RCMP,

> a standard number or quota of orderly room cases or disciplinary hearings is apparently considered by some officers as a mark of effective leadership. "With a subdivision this size we should be able to average four orderly room cases a month," an officer is reported as saying [Ramsay, 1972]. Cases are not difficult to generate since it is impossible to live by all the rules of the force.

REFERENCES

Abrahams, G.
1964. *Police Questioning and the Judges' Rules.* London: Oyez.

Arnold, T.
1962. *The Symbols of Government.* New York: Harcourt Brace and World.

Balbus, I.
1973. *The Dialectics of Legal Repression: Black Rebels Before the American Criminal Courts.* New York: Russell Sage Foundation.
Banton, M.
1964. *The Policeman in the Community.* London: Tavistock.
Beattie, J.
1977. *Documents Illustrating Attitudes Towards Crime and Punishment in Canada, 1830–1850.* Toronto: Centre of Criminology, University of Toronto.
Bittner, E.
1967a. "Police Discretion in Emergency Apprehension of Mentally Ill Persons." *Social Problems* 14: 278–92.
1967b. "The Police on Skid Row: A Study of Peace Keeping." *American Sociological Review* 32: 699–715.
1970. *The Functions of the Police in Modern Society.* Rockville, Md.: NIMH.
Black, D.
1968. *Police Encounters and Social Organization: An Observation Study.* Ph.D. dissertation, University of Michigan.
1972. "The Boundaries of Legal Sociology." *Yale Law Journal* 81: 1086–1100.
Blumberg, A.
1967. *Criminal Justice.* Chicago: Quadrangle.
Brock, E.
1968. *The Little White God.* London: Allen and Unwin.
Buckner, H.
1970. "Transformations of Reality in the Legal Process." *Social Research* 37: 88–101.
Cain, M.
1971. "On the Beat: Interactions and Relations in Rural and Urban Police Forces" in S. Cohen (ed.) *Images of Deviance.* Middlesex: Penguin.
1973. *Society and the Policeman's Role.* London: Routledge.
Carlen, P.
1976. *Magistrates' Justice.* London: Martin Robertson.
Chambliss, W., and R. Seidman
1971. *Law, Order and Power.* Reading, Mass: Addison-Wesley.
Chatterton, M.
1976. "Police in Social Control" in J. King (ed.) *Control Without Custody.* Cambridge: Cropwood Papers, Institute of Criminology.
1979. "The Supervision of Patrol Work Under the Fixed Points System" in S. Holdaway (ed.) *The British Police.* London: Edward Arnold.
Chibnall, S.
1977. *Law and Order News.* London: Tavistock.
1979. "The Metropolitan Police and the News Media" in S. Holdaway (ed.) *The British Police.* London: Edward Arnold.
Cloward, R., and L. Ohlin
1960. *Delinquency and Opportunity.* New York: Free Press.
Cobb, B.
1957. *The First Detectives.* London: Faber and Faber.
Cohen, A.
1955. *Delinquent Boys.* New York: Free Press.

Cox, S. et al.
1977. *The Fall of Scotland Yard.* London: Penguin.
Currie, E.
1968. "Crimes Without Criminals: Witchcraft and Its Control in Renaissance Europe." *Law and Society Review* 3: 7–32.
Davis, K. C.
1969. *Discretionary Justice.* Baton Rouge: Louisiana State University Press.
Ditton, J.
1979. *Controlology.* London: Macmillan.
Douglas, J.
1971. *American Social Order: Social Rules in a Pluralistic Society.* New York: Free Press.
Durkheim, E.
1964. *Rules of Sociological Method.* New York: Free Press.
Ericson, R.
1981a. *Making Crime: A Study of Detective Work.* Toronto: Butterworths.
1981b. *Reproducing Order: A Study of Police Patrol Work.* Toronto: University of Toronto Press.
Ericson, R., and P. Baranek
(Forthcoming.) *The Ordering of Justice.* Toronto: University of Toronto Press.
Feeley, M.
1973. "Two Models of the Criminal Justice System: An Organizational Perspective." *Law and Society Review* 7: 407–25.
Fine, B. et al.
1979. *Capitalism and the Rule of Law.* London: Hutchinson.
Foucault, M.
1977. *Discipline and Punish.* London: Allen Lane.
Freedman, D., and P. Stenning
1977. *Private Security, Police and the Law in Canda.* Toronto: Centre of Criminology, University of Toronto.
Gaylin, W. et al.
1978. *Doing Good: The Limits of Benevolence.* New York: Pantheon.
Giddens, A.
1976. *New Rules of Sociological Method.* London: Hutchinson.
Gillance, K., and A. Khan
1975. "The Constitutional Independence of a Police Constable in the Exercise of the Powers of His Office." *The Police Journal* 48, no. 1: 55–62.
Great Britain Royal Commission on Criminal Procedure
1980. *Police Interrogation.* 2 vols. London: HMSO.
Greenawalt, K.
1974. "Perspectives on the Right to Silence" in R. Hood (ed.) *Crime, Criminology and Public Policy.* London: Heinemann.
Habenstein, R.
1963. "Critique of 'Profession' as a Sociological Category." *Sociological Quarterly* 4: 291–300.
Harvard Center for Criminal Justice
1972. "Judicial Intervention in Prison Discipline." *Journal of Criminal Law and Criminology* 63: 200–228.

Hasson, R.
(Forthcoming.) "Tax Evasion and Social Security Abuse—Some Tentative Observations." *Canadian Taxation: A Journal of Tax Policy.*

Hay, D. et al.
1975. *Albion's Fatal Tree.* London: Penguin.

Ignatieff, M.
1979. "Police and People: The Birth of Mr. Peel's 'Blue Locusts.' " *New Society* 4, no. 882: 443–45.

James, D.
1979. "Police-Black Relations: The Professional Solution" in S. Holdaway (ed.) *The British Police.* London: Edward Arnold.

Kadish, M., and S. Kadish
1973. *Discretion to Disobey: A Study of Lawful Departures from Legal Rules.* Stanford: Stanford University Press.

Kaufman, F.
1974. *The Admissibility of Confessions.* Toronto: Carswell.

Laurie, P.
1972. *Scotland Yard.* London: Penguin.

Lukacs, G.
1971. *History and Class Consciousness.* Cambridge, Mass.: MIT Press.

Lundman, R. J.
1980. *Police Behavior.* New York: Oxford University Press.

MacGuigan, M.
1977. *The Report of Sub-committee on the Penitentiary System in Canada.* Ottawa: Information Canada.

Mann, E., and Lee, J.
1979. *The R.C.M.P. vs. The People.* Toronto: General Publishing.

Manning, P.
1971. "The Police: Mandate, Strategy and Appearances" in J. Douglas (ed.) *Crime and Justice in American Society.* Indianapolis: Bobbs-Merrill.
1977a. *Police Work.* Cambridge Mass.: MIT Press.
1977b. "Rules in Organizational Context: Narcotics Law Enforcement in Two Settings." *The Sociological Quarterly* 18: 44–61.
1979. "The Social Control of Police Work" in S. Holdaway (ed.) *The British Police.* London: Edward Arnold.
1980. *The Narcs Game.* Cambridge Mass.: MIT Press.

McBarnet, D.
1976. "Pre-trial Procedures and the Construction of Conviction" in P. Carlen (ed.) *The Sociology of Law.* Keele: Department of Sociology, University of Keele.
1979. "Arrest: The Legal Context of Policing" in S. Holdaway (ed.) *The British Police.* London: Edward Arnold.
1981. *Conviction: Law, the State and the Construction of Justice.* London: Macmillan.

McMullan, J.
1980. "Maudits Voleurs: Racketeering and the Collection of Private Debts in Montreal." *Canadian Journal of Sociology* 5: 121–43.

Medalie, R. et al.
1968. "Custodial Police Interrogation in Our Nation's Capital: The Attempt to Implement Miranda." *Michigan Law Review* 66: 1347–422.
Morand, Mr. Justice
1976. *Report of the Royal Commission into Metropolitan Toronto Police Practices.* Toronto: Government of Ontario.
Morris, P.
1978. "Police Interrogation in England and Wales." Paper for the British Royal Commission on Criminal Procedure.
Muir, W.
1977. *The Police: Streetcorner Politicians.* Chicago: University of Chicago Press.
Oliver, I.
1975. "The Office of Constable—1975." *Criminal Law Review* (June): 313–22.
Packer, H.
1968. *The Limits of the Criminal Sanction.* Stanford: Stanford University Press.
Ramsay, J.
1972. "My Case Against the RCMP" *Maclean's* (July): 19.
Rawls, J.
1955. "Two Concepts of Rules." *Philosophical Review* 64: 3–32.
Reiss, A.
1971. *The Police and the Public.* New Haven: Yale University Press.
Rothman, D.
1980. *Conscience and Convenience: The Asylum and Its Alternatives in Progressive America.* Boston: Little Brown.
Rubinstein, J.
1973. *City Police.* New York: Farrar, Strauss and Giroux.
Sanders, W.
1977. *Detective Work.* New York: Free Press.
Schur, E.
1980. *The Politics of Deviance.* Englewood Cliffs, N.J.: Prentice-Hall.
Scott, R.
1972. "A Proposed Framework for Analyzing Deviance as a Property of Social Order" in R. Scott and J. Douglas (eds.) *Theoretical Perspectives on Deviance.* New York: Basic Books.
Sherman, L. W.
1974. *Police Corruption: A Sociological Perspective.* New York: Doubleday.
Skolnick, J.
1966. *Justice Without Trial.* New York: Wiley.
Softley, P.
1980. *Police Interrogation: An Observational Study in Four Police Stations.* London: HMSO.
Strauss, A.
1978. *Negotiations.* San Francisco: Jossey-Bass.
Thomas, D. A.
1974. "The Control of Discretion in the Administration of Criminal Justice" in R. Hood (ed.) *Crime, Criminology and Public Policy.* London: Heinemann.

Toronto Globe and Mail
1980. "Splitting Hairs on Police Discipline," Dec. 4.
1980. "Police Quotas: Not Enough Tags a Ticket to Boss's Office," Dec. 13.

Turk, A.
1976. "Law as a Weapon in Social Conflict." *Social Problems* 23: 276-92.

Williams, D.
1974. "Prosecution, Discretion and the Accountability of the Police" in R. Hood (ed.) *Crime, Criminology and Public Policy*. London: Heinemann.

Wilson, J.
1968. *Varieties of Police Behavior*. Cambridge: Harvard University Press.

Zander, M.
1978. "The Right of Silence in the Police Station and the Caution" in P. Glazebrook (ed.) *Reshaping the Criminal Law*. London: Stevens.

Chapter 5

Organizational Deviance and Political Policing*

Austin T. Turk

Proposals to create or strengthen police forces have always aroused fears of police deviance. The adequacy of provisions for supervision and redress has been frequently questioned, and there has been a perpetual tension between demands for more effective policing and for insurance against police excesses. Over the past several years, the policing of political activities has become a focus of international and national concern, as accounts of illegal, politically troublesome, or ethically disturbing practices have been widely publicized. These accounts have generally provoked outrage and condemnation, and calls for tighter restraints to be imposed upon political policing. However, virtually all reform proposals insufficiently recognize the complex realities involved and are likely to result in, at most, a temporary lessening of the target agencies' effectiveness without necessarily curtailing the disapproved practices. The objectives in this article are (1) to clarify the meaning of deviance by and within organizations engaged in political policing, (2) to point out the structural sources of such deviance, and (3) to assess the potential impact of various proposals for preventing or stopping such deviance.

Deviance in Political Policing

There are two senses in which one may reasonably speak of deviance in political policing: demonstrable violations of legal rules and blameworthy failures to accomplish organizational objectives. Public attention has been directed almost entirely to the first; little has been said about the second.

Disclosures of questionable acts have neglected the problems of specifying and applying the relevant legal standards and have failed to disentangle legal from political or ethical criteria for identifying offenses. Nor

---

*Reprinted from *Criminology*, vol. 19(2), pp. 231–50, © American Society of Criminology with the permission of the publisher, Sage Publications, Beverly Hills.

This is a revision of a paper presented at the meeting of the American Society of Criminology, November 7–10, 1979, Philadelphia, Pennsylvania.

has individual deviance been clearly distinguished from organizational deviance, or external from internal deviance. These conceptual shortcomings are attributable to two sources: the ideological predilections of analysts—which tend to blur analytical distinctions and to override methodological questions—and (more important, in my view) the exceptional politicality (partisan bias), vagueness, and permissiveness of the legal rules for defining and dealing with political criminality.

Although it is difficult to extract clear legal criteria from such laws, it is nonetheless clear that whatever boundaries may exist have often been overstepped by security agents. Violations of legal restrictions upon such practices as electronic surveillance, intercepting mail, and accessing confidential medical and tax records have been accorded much attention in more democratic states, while gross violations of habeas corpus and other basic procedural rules have been emphasized in reports from more totalitarian countries. Stories of such violations are found in sources ranging from smuggled accounts by victims to official reports by commissions of inquiry. An occasional court case provides formal legal authentication. Written and verbal accounts by alienated former agents lend further credence to the view that illegal practices are common.

But assertions, however plausible, are not equivalent to legal tests; and legal tests are not necessarily equivalent to empirical tests. Because any statement or communication may be intended or doctored to further political interests, even sworn testimony in an open court is not to be trusted readily. "Official secrets" laws tend to inhibit even voluntary admissions or reports; and as long as it is possible successfully to invoke such sweeping justifications as "national security" or "reasons of state," even admitted "excesses" may turn out to be legally acceptable. A further complication is introduced by the possibility that issues of legality may be shelved until long after questioned operations have achieved their aims and been discontinued. (The Smith Act, for instance, was not found unconstitutional by the Supreme Court of the United States until 20 years after it was enacted, and it was used effectively to suppress the American Communist Party.)

Resistance to demands for information about policing operations is, of course, to be expected.[1] Secrecy is normative in security organizations, and scrutiny by any outsider is automatically considered threatening. When it is not possible to refuse or avoid giving information to external parties, it may be provided in a variety of misleading ways. Lying is a routine tactic whose use evidently is limited only by considerations of expediency: Is it necessary, and do the potential costs of being caught at it outweigh the present costs of revealing the truth? If lying is ruled out, there are alternatives such as providing only information very specifically requested (which presupposes a prior intimate knowledge of what is available); destroying or "misfiling" incriminating items before they have to be produced (ideally before their existence is known); fragmenting information into bits so that sequential and other connective patterns are hidden; and depicting offensive acts as merely the deviations of a few wrong-headed or overly zealous individuals (preferably no longer active, and ideally dead or otherwise incapacitated). Any imputation of illegal or improper behavior to the organization rather than deviant individuals is strongly contested. If all else fails and the evidence of illegal policies and programs is overwhelming, organizational deviance may be admitted—but blamed upon former leaders (such as Hoover of the FBI), whose pernicious influence has, needless to say, been eradicated by the present law-abiding leadership. Past organizational deviance is extremely unlikely to be admitted to be evidence of current, systemic organizational deviance.

Tactics of secrecy and scapegoating to protect the organization from external view are supplemented and facilitated by the information control principles of need to know and plausible deniability. Persons not directly involved in a program or situation ordinarily know little or nothing about it. Ignorance is beneficial to the organization because it reduces the chance and potential scope of intentional or accidental disclosure and facilitates both the detection of unwanted leaks and the dissemination of valid or false information through ostensible leaks. For individuals as well as organizations, ignorance may be beneficial because to know is to be more vulnerable to pressures to reveal what is known and to bear responsibility for the knowledge (obtaining, transmitting, retaining, applying, destroying). Administrative measures to apply the need-to-know principle thus serve to make the detection and confirmation of organizational deviance difficult even if secrecy fails: An individual can reveal only what she or he knows and may be used either as a conduit for misleading communications to outsiders or as a scapegoat for deviance which cannot be denied.

Useful as it is, the need-to-know principle does create as well as lessen risks. Individuals or units ignorant of one another's activities may find themselves blundering into one another's paths, with effects such as blowing cover, alerting targets, diverting resources, and undermining credibility. Knowledge, then, is essential even though the responsibility of knowing will sometimes be too politically costly to be accepted. The problem is to find the optimal mix of ignorance and knowledge in a milieu where either can be dangerous. The ideal solution is indicated by the principle of plausible deniability, in which persons or agencies construct procedural mazes sustaining the appearance of ignorance but the reality of knowledge. These mazes feature such devices as separating output from input channels and internal from external channels of communication. For instance, the internal command network may be separated to a considerable extent from the internal network through which original and feedback information is channeled to an agency's directorate, while both are largely insulated from the networks—themselves not identical—through which advisories to higher level political entities (e.g., a president or an appropriations committee) and other external parties are produced, and through which directives from such outsiders are interpreted and in some fashion implemented. The principle of plausible deniability extends, of course, beyond agency boundaries in any modern state ("one of the advantages a secret agency like the CIA provides to a President is the unique pretext of being able to disclaim responsibility for its actions"—Marchetti and Marks, 1974: 72). When deviance can be plausibly denied by insiders, and even more when denial is politically useful to powerful outsiders, substantiation of reported deviance becomes virtually impossible.

The foregoing considerations indicate that legal deviance in political policing cannot be defined in a priori terms independent of a specified political context. Nor is confirmation empirically possible apart from the observed political as well as legal consequences of disclosures. Aside from the rare instances where an agent or, even rarer, an agency is found by a court to be guilty of unlawful conduct, the most defensible sources of empirically usable criteria for defining illegalities are the published findings of official legislative committees and judicial commissions able to compel the submission of evidence (such as the Senate's Church Committee, 1976, and Canada's McDonald Commission, 1978 and continuing). In their absence, definitely second-best sources are the reports of fact-finding organizations such as Amnesty International and the International Commission of Jurists, which have at least internationally recognized and sometimes semilegal standing. To the extent that courts (including administrative tribunals) or investigative bodies provide details of specific instances, their accounts also serve to confirm the occurrence of illegalities. Beyond such sources, assertions of illegality are unsupportable—not only because the ostensibly applicable legal rules are designed to extend rather than limit the discretionary powers of political police but also because the kinds of practices condemned as illegal are in fact mandated by the nature of political policing.

Any conception of legal deviance in political policing inevitably clashes with the fact that such organizations are invented to prevent radical political changes. Though it can be argued that a legal system as a totality functions to maintain the given order, political policing agencies are assigned the specific task of detecting and neutralizing any present or potential deviations from the ground rules of conventional politics. The rationale for political policing is always stated as some version of the nebulous doctrine of "national security," and the generous formal authorizations are supplemented by secret directives that spell out what may be only implicit in the authorizations: Political and military considerations override any legal or ethical ones.[2]

Insofar as legal authorizations do not recognize the predominance of nonlegal considerations, it is quite possible for the same practice to be sometimes legal and sometimes illegal—depending upon what is required and the political consequences of disclosure. Legal deviance will be "real," that is, behavioral deviance only if the behavior in question results in a blameworthy failure. Success of individuals and units within an organization, as well as of the organization itself, defines conformity; failure defines deviance. But even that Machiavellian formula is too simplistic. In the politically volatile arenas of political policing, the differences between conformity and deviance may well depend more upon an individual's or agency's success in denying or transferring responsibility for failure (when it cannot be hidden) than upon demonstrated success in accomplishing control objectives.

While deniability may work in many instances, the negative consequences of major or repeated failures will be inescapable; and responsibility for such deviance will accrue to either organization or individual. If failure to achieve control objectives is the criterion of behavioral deviance in political policing, it is necessary to know these objectives. The problem of defining any organization's goals is not easily solved because original goals may be changed or displaced, formal and informal objectives may not be fully compatible, goals are formulated at different levels with varying specificity and varying compatibility with one another, goals undergo modifications in the course of implementing efforts, and the relationship between organizational and individual aims is problematic (cf. Silverman, 1971: 9–11).

The goal definition problem is especially difficult in the case of political policing agencies because (1) specific goals cannot be inferred from their legal authorizations; (2) secret directives and memoranda are unlikely to be accessible even to many people in an agency; (3) agency personnel are resistant to interviews or observation, and in interviews prefer to discuss generalities or safe topics and avoid relevant specifics; and (4) even high-level officials may not fully understand the complex structure of overt, covert, externally mandated, internally generated, agency and subunit objectives—as well as the relation between organizational and individual purposes (including their own). A working solution for now is to infer organizational goals from what is known or reported about the activities of such organizations. On that basis, the following are defined as the goals of political police organizations:

(1) maintenance and enhancement of the organization, especially by increasing control over environmental contingencies (cf. James Thompson, 1967: passim)
(2) gathering adequate (full) intelligence about political activities and potentials
(3) controlling politically significant (as assessed) communications by negative (censorship) and positive (propaganda) means
(4) neutralization (suppression) by violent and/or nonviolent means of disapproved political activities

(5) deterrence of the general population from any involvement in or consideration of disapproved political activities.

I hope we are now in a better position to suggest what may be empirically viewed as legal deviance (at least in regard to North American and, to a somewhat lesser extent, West European agencies) and as behavioral deviance in political policing (presumably more generally applicable). It will be recalled that legal deviance is defined by the published reports of official investigative bodies; behavioral deviance is defined as blameworthy (i.e., undeniable) failure to achieve organizational goals. In neither kind of deviance can the label be assumed; rather, *that a particular practice is deviant is considered nothing more than an estimate of the probability of its being so labelled if disclosed.*

What is probably legal deviance if deniability is not sustained vis-à-vis external scrutiny? There may be a scale of decreasing probability in the following order (If so, it seems likely that the deviance probability of moves against domestic targets will in each case be lower than for moves against foreign targets.):

(1) assassination or maiming (especially of prominent, influential, and/or ideologically significant figures such as Steve Biko of South Africa)
(2) "Geneva offenses" (using such outlawed and widely repugnant devices as germs, poisoned umbrellas, letter bombs, and cattle prods)
(3) torture resulting in less than grossly evident physical or psychological harms (e.g., the beatings, threats, sensory deprivation, and general terrorization routinely inflicted upon detainees in many countries, according to Amnesty International)
(4) character assassination (as in the Jean Seberg case)
(5) intervention in conventional politics (e.g., the FBI campaign against Martin Luther King, Jr., and—as some perceive it—the Watergate episode)
(6) violations of civil or human rights (ranging from the violations of records and communications laws revealed by the Church Committee—e.g., via electronic surveillance and interference in tax investigation, licensing, publishing, and so on—to the incarceration of political dissidents in Soviet mental institutions)
(7) economic or political harassment of individuals (e.g., black militants asserting conventional political rights)
(8) use of informants and spies (as in the infiltration and manipulation of academic and other cultural institutions)
(9) subversion of economic or other institutions (including the large-scale undermining of national—e.g., Chile—and international structures, as well as the pressuring of single enterprises—e.g., extortion of campaign funds from corporations by planting incriminating material in computer files).

What is probably behavioral deviance if deniability is not sustained vis-à-vis internal review? For example,

(1) mission failures (e.g., intelligence failures as in Iran, Nicaragua, and the Bay of Pigs; information control failures as in the KGB defection of Gouzenko and the infiltration of British intelligence by Kim Philby; neutralization failures as in the electoral victory of the Parti Quebecois; and general deterrence failures as in France, Russia, and Cuba)
(2) disclosure to external parties (e.g., Ellsberg's *Pentagon Papers* and Agee's memoir of his CIA experiences in Latin America)
(3) fraud (in either mission reports—as in FBI reports on the civil rights movement—or the use of funds—e.g., the embezzlement of secret propaganda funds by the South African Eschel Rhoodie).

If either legal or behavioral deviance in political policing is to be the object of empirical study, available evidence and the discussion to this point indicate the following to be reasonable working rules or hypotheses:

(1) Whatever is done in foreign countries is less likely to be defined as deviant, or as serious, than if done at home.
(2) Domestic operations against foreign nationals, foreign-born, and other minorities are less likely to be defined as deviant, or as serious, than operations against other (especially high-status) persons.
(3) Operations against organizations are less likely to be defined as deviant, or as serious, than operations against individuals. (This may be attributable to the values of individualism and/or the tactics of emphasizing isolated cases of deviance rather than programs of systemic deviance.)
(4) Legal deviance is much more likely to be attributed to individuals than organizations. (It is easier to punish individuals, and scapegoating will as far as possible be used to block the imputation of legal deviance to the organization.)
(5) Behavioral deviance will virtually always be attributed to individuals rather than to the normative demands, programs, procedures, or structural characteristics of the organizations in which they work.
(6) Legal deviance is more accessible to research than is behavioral deviance: (a) Individual legal deviance is more accessible than organizational legal deviance. (b) Organizational legal deviance is more accessible than individual behavioral deviance. (c) Individual behavioral deviance, if at all accessible, will be more so than organizational behavioral deviance.

Structural Sources

Organizational deviance, legal and behavioral, in political policing is a function of attempts to satisfy both overt and covert external demands without risking undeniable failure. For domestic or international political reasons, it is externally demanded that inconsistencies between legal authorizations and secret directives be deniable. To protect the organization (or individuals within it), the deniability of inconsistencies between secret directives and working goals will be internally demanded—and probably given even higher priority (e.g., Allen Dulles's revision of a report to the White House so as to mask the disagreement between CIA covert operations aims and intelligence analyses of preinvasion Cuba—Marchetti and Marks, 1974: 288–90).

The mandate to prevent radical changes in the distribution of power and privilege is incompatible with the idea of a legally or ethically limited effort to do so. If the price of organizational behavioral deviance (mission failure) is ultimately the collapse of the political system, it necessarily exceeds that of legal deviance. The internal structure of relative costs mirrors the external structure: behavioral deviance is "real," while legal deviance is at most a political overhead cost of doing business.

Ambiguity in laws defining political offensiveness, and permissiveness in the legal authorizations of political policing, cannot be reduced without making the political bias built into such laws more evident. In more democratic nations the legal systems are characterized by an explicit commitment to limit the state's right to impinge upon individual freedoms. In principle, the limits of state authority and the rights of private parties are to be clearly specified and effectively guaranteed. Private privileges, rights, liabilities, and immunities are proclaimed to be secured against despotism. The concept of political crime and the institution of political policing contradict the imagery of limited state power and inviolable individual freedom. It follows that the reality of political policing must be deniable: Secrecy is thus an essential feature of political policing agencies.

Paradoxically, the greater potential ideological costs of disclosing legal deviance in more democratic nations implies that deniability is even more important than in more totalitarian countries. It seems plausible that secrecy in more totalitarian contexts tends to be more an amplifying element in governmental terrorism than an operating principle for maximizing the deniability of legal deviance. (Political police organizations everywhere will of course try to insure the deniability of behavioral deviance, particularly by the organization.)

Individual deviance is inevitable if internal demads for results explicitly or implicitly preclude alternatives (e.g., the FBI's "suicide tap"—Watters and Gillers, 1973: 277, 306). For individuals as for the organization, the costs of mission failure are far higher than those of legal (externally disclosed) deviance. Internal considerations of legality will be limited to weighing the potential costs of external disclosure; therefore, little or no internal reinforcement of external demands for legal conformity is to be expected. This will be even more true when such external demands are seen as either the inauthentic ploys of conventional politics or the outcries of politically naive or suspect sources.

Individuals will, of course, make every effort to avoid responsibility for mission failures. Excepting those who try to find safety in the classic bureaupathic dodge of ritualism (Victor Thompson, 1964: 152–77; and Merton, 1968: 249–60, on "the bureaucratic personality" as well as his famous analysis of ritualism as a type of deviance, 203–7, 238–41), they will simultaneously try to be in position to receive credit for mission successes. Knowing they risk being left "out in the cold" as scapegoats if missions undeniably fail, or if legal deviance cannot be denied, agents are under pressure to cover themselves by furnishing fraudulently positive mission reports and hiding evidence of failure. The internal demand for success irrespective of the means by which it is achieved, coupled with the priority of organizational over individual deniability, leaves the individual with no recourse other than behavioral deviance if things go wrong. (Suicide and mental breakdown are apolitical possibilities.)

If individuals find the chance and probable cost of being caught in undeniable mission failure and/or mission report fraud unacceptable, defection may be perceived as the only option. Defection may be a matter of physically absconding or of violating the secrecy rules. Disclosures to external parties may be made in return for present or future support and refuge. Funds may be embezzled or otherwise misused to facilitate disclosures or merely escape from the organization.

The misuse of funds for other than defection may not even be considered blameworthy. If it facilitates mission success or organizational deniability of mission failure, it is far more likely to be approved than disapproved. If the misappropriation is not excessive and does not interfere with efforts to accomplish organizational goals, it may be accepted. (One reason for accepting minor fraud, as well as other potentially discreditable behavior, is that it makes the individual more vulnerable to pressures to satisfy organizational demands—including those for legal deviance.)

In a hierarchical organization designed in accord with the principles of need to know and plausible deniability, opportunities as well as incentives to deviance are present, one expects, to a greater extent than in more egalitarian and open organizations. The exceptionally clear and strong demand for results regardless of methods, along with the exceptionally weak legal restrictions upon both the definition of objectives and the methods for achieving them, makes legal deviance inevitable and behavioral deviance very probable in political policing. Under extreme pressures both to produce results and to sustain deniability of failures to do so, agencies as well as agents will have little reason to be concerned about legal deviance and every reason to engage in lesser behavioral deviance to avoid the costs of the maximally serious, "real" behavioral deviance of undeniable mission failure.

The internal structural sources of deviance by and within political police agencies derive from the external structural sources of conflict in politically organized societies. To the extent that human needs go unmet because of systemic factors causing variations in life chances, political legitimation cannot be assumed. As an overly general rule, the greater the degree of exploitation, the more necessary is domination. More concretely, the less secure or hopeful about their life chances people become, the less effective are educative and hortatory appeals for political loyalty likely to be. Where the consensual foundations of political identity weaken, the coercive methods for maintaining political dominance become increasingly the only inhibitor of radical political changes. Political distrust is amplified in a reciprocal process. That political policing intended to create, sustain, or restore legitimation tends also to erode legitimation is the ultimate irony of the enterprise. In reference to the goal of maximizing political stability, that is, accomplishing legitimacy for the system, political policing is itself behavioral deviance, in that it constitutes domination instead of a means for promoting actual, consensual legitimation. Proposition: The fundamental structural source of deviance *in* political policing is the deviance *of* political policing.

Proposed Remedies

A far from exhaustive review of the literature has turned up dozens of general and detailed proposals for curtailing deviance in political and/or regular policing. Many refer to all policing, several to political policing. Some specify particular agencies; others are addressed to particular practices. They may call only for changes in laws protecting human or civil rights, for reforms of the laws defining political crimes, or for more delimited legal authorizations of policing practices. Changes in organization and/or administrative procedures may be emphasized rather than changes in laws. External monitoring of police activities may be the focus; or internal reforms may be stressed—perhaps merely the disciplining of individuals. In many instances the public, the government, or anyone is enjoined to "do something"; or else the possibility of reform may be denied, with the proposed remedy being political revolution. Finally, the great majority of proposals are aimed at controlling legal deviance, relatively few at behavioral deviance (mission failure)—though a thorough review of the police administration and organization efficiency/productivity literatures would undoubtedly find more.

A tentative classification summarizes the kinds of proposals found so far: political, legal, and organizational.

Political

Conventional politics. The most extreme proposals call for the asserting of community control: direct accessibility and accountability to "the people'' (local residents or the general population), requiring decentralization and deprofessionalization of police (e.g., Hain et al. 1979: 20–23). Less extreme proposals call for ombudsmen or civilian review boards (e.g., Stark, 1972: 237–39).

Revolutionary politics. The conclusion that radical political change is the only possible remedy may be stated boldly (e.g., Hall et al., 1978: 396–97) or implicitly (e.g., Bunyan, 1978: 301–9).

Legal

Asserting immunities, that is, human and civil rights. For instance, the call may be to strengthen legal protection of the right of privacy with respect to immunities from illegal access to the person and personal space (e.g., tax, medical, and other confidential records—on which see Goldstein, in Wheeler 1969: 415–43).

Forcing disclosures. Proposals for such measures as freedom-of-information laws aim at eliminating or significantly reducing the legal basis for keeping organizational decisions and practices secret (e.g., Mann and Lee, 1979: 164–239).

Narrowing definitional and procedural discretion in political policing (e.g., Matthews, 1972: 164–239).

Organizational

Redefining goals. Most proposals of this kind are aimed at eliminating or reducing interventionism, which usually means retaining the intelligence-gathering function (though contracting its scope) but prohibiting ''dirty tricks'' and ''covert operations'' (e.g., Marchetti and Marks, 1974: 352–54).

Closer formal monitoring. This almost standard recommendation typically means establishing, revitalizing, or increasing the responsibilities and powers of ''watchdog'' committees such as the ''40 Committee'' to oversee CIA operations and budget control agencies such as congressional appropriations committees and the General Accounting Office (e.g., Marchetti and Marks, 1974: 350–52). The principle is that frequent detailed reviews of budgets, policy decisions, administrative structure and procedures, and effectiveness would be insured.

Separating functions. Either specialization among agencies or internal separation of responsibilities and powers is envisioned. The most extreme version appears to be for each function to be assigned to an independently staffed and separately reporting agency (Watters and Gillers, 1973: 403–9).

Improving personnel management. Apart from standard proposals for upgrading recruitment and training, ad hoc disciplining of individuals is the focus. Such proposals tend to stress either the purging of lower level "rotten apples" or the replacement of top leadership such as commissioners and directors (e.g., the myriad calls throughout the 1960s for ending Hoover's tenure as FBI "czar"). Kennedy's firing of Dulles, Bissell, and Cabell for misleading policy recommendations regarding the Bay of Pigs invasion (Marchetti and Marks, 1974: 52–53, 56) exemplifies the personnel management approach (as well as conventional politics).

Propositions advanced earlier about the nature and sources of deviance imply several criteria by which to assess the proposals just summarized. In brief question form,

(a) Are legal and behavioral deviance distinguished, and their relation adequately considered?
(b) Is the relation between organizational and individual deviance adequately considered?
(c) Are the difficulties of defining and confirming deviance adequately considered?
(d) Are the goals of political policing adequately considered?
(e) Are the internal and external structural sources of deviance, and their relationship, adequately considered?

Using these criteria leads to the following general conclusions:

1. Political proposals for open public control of a decentralized and deprofessionalized police are unviable, and imply avoiding instead of dealing with the relationship between organizational and individual deviance, simply by dissolving police organization and placing individual agents in full public view. There may be some potential for instituting (discreet) appeals through some form of ombudsman to inhibit some forms of legal deviance—especially if involving demonstrable harassment and violation of civil or human rights.

2. Public proposals for revolutionary political change become targets of political policing, so tend to be self-defeating.

3. Legal reforms alone are very unlikely to inhibit political policing to any significant degree. Freedom-of-information laws have had some limited value for investigative reporting, but the files and discretionary powers of the political police have never been significantly affected. Indeed, they are always explicitly or implicitly exempted in the formulation of such laws.

4. Organizational changes have the greatest chance to bring about some decrease in legal deviance, especially of individuals, but probably at the cost of some increase in organizational behavioral and legal deviance.

5. Goal redefinition and personnel management (disciplining) are unlikely to reduce organizational deviance, because goal redefinition is likely to result in goal distribution. "Cleaning up" one agency is not tantamount to a revision of the institutional goals of political policing. Personnel

management tactics may result in some reduction in individual behavioral deviance, but are unlikely to reduce individual legal deviance.

6. Closer monitoring is likely to produce some reduction in organizational legal deviance, and perhaps a slight reduction in individual legal deviance; a reduction in behavioral deviance is more probable. The monitors are, if not overawed as novices, more likely to be co-opted than to be really effective overseers.

7. Separating functions is likely to reduce organizational behavioral deviance—especially in reference to intelligence gathering and analysis—but the pressures to coordinate operations appear to preclude independence. To the extent that genuine separation is achieved, it is likely to be counterproductive in terms of the deviance generated by interagency rivalry and mission failures.

Conclusion

The Church Committee declared:

> The American people need to be assured that never again will an agency of the government be permitted to conduct a secret war against those citizens it considers threats to the established order [U.S. Senate, 1976, Book III: 77].

In light of its own findings, as well as those of others, such an assurance by the committee is hardly to be taken as other than the expression of a noble sentiment. No clear path to controlling the controllers is yet to be seen. Perhaps respect for the ideals of real democracy and social justice, elusive as they are, can somehow be made a serious concern of those who monitor, operate, and employ political police. Those holding such hope are true idealists, for to rely upon the honor of those who purport to defend a society means—to paraphrase Bordua and Reiss (1966: 76)—to trust in the capacity of the defenders to transcend instead of merely reflect its inadequacies. Whatever is proposed or tried, "in the long as well as in the short run, a civil police depends upon a civil citizenry" (Reiss, 1971: 220)—and their mutual civility depends upon eliminating the structural sources of incivility.

NOTES

1. While all organizations resist disclosure and monitoring, secrecy appears to be a special preoccupation in political policing. This is to be expected in organizations characterized by (1) an essentially open-ended mandate to prevent radical political shifts, (2) extraordinary discretionary power, and (3) concomitant vulnerability to blame and scapegoating if anything goes wrong. Such organizations are especially sensitive to the threat of penetration by external or internal opponents because organizational failure implies the collapse of the polity itself.
2. Whatever quantitative differences in political policing may be found, attempts to find qualitative differences between more democratic and more totalitarian

regimes seem doomed to failure. The evidence is by now overwhelming that the core attribute of political policing everywhere is the use of organizational and other resources "in a manner unrestrained by the constitutional order of the arena within which the contest takes place" (Selznick, 1960: 2; and cf. 267–68).

REFERENCES

Bordua, D. J., and A. J. Reiss, Jr.
1966. "Command, Control, and Charisma: Reflections on Police Bureaucracy." *American Journal of Sociology* 72 (July): 68–76.

Bunyan, T.
1978. *The History and Practice of the Political Police in Britain.* New York: Quartet Books.

Goldstein, A. S.
1969. "Legal Control of the Dossier," pp. 415–43 in S. Wheeler (ed.) *On Record: Files and Dossiers in American Life.* New York: Russell Sage.

Hain, P.; D. Humphrey; and B. Rose-Smith
1979. *Policing the Police.* Vol. 1: *The Complaints System: Police Powers and Terrorism Legislation.* London: John Calder.

Hall, S.; C. Critcher; T. Jefferson; J. Clarke; and B. Roberts
1978. *Policing the Crisis: Mugging, the State, and Law and Order.* London: Macmillan.

Mann, E., and J. A. Lee
1979. *RCMP vs. the People: Inside Canada's Security Service.* Don Mills, Ontario: General Publishing Co.

Marchetti, V., and J. D. Marks
1974. *The CIA and the Cult of Intelligence.* New York: Dell.

Matthews, A. S.
1972. *Law, Order and Liberty in South Africa.* Berkeley: University of California Press.

McDonald Commission of Inquiry into Certain RCMP Activities.
1978. "Freedom and Security: An Analysis of Policy Issues." Ottawa.

Merton, R. K.
1968. *Social Theory and Social Structure.* New York: The Free Press.

Reiss, A. J., Jr.
1971. *The Police and the Public.* New Haven, Conn.: Yale University Press.

Selznick, P.
1960. *The Organizational Weapon: A Study of Bolshevik Strategy and Tactics.* New York: Free Press.

Silverman, D.
1971. *The Theory of Organizations: A Sociological Framework.* New York: Basic Books.

Stark, R.
1972. *Police Riots: Collective Violence and Law Enforcement.* Belmont, Cal.: Wadsworth.

Thompson, J. D.
1967. *Organizations in Action.* New York: McGraw-Hill.

Thompson, V.
1964. *Modern Organizations.* New York: Knopf.

U.S. Senate
1976. *Intelligence Activities and the Rights of Americans. Final Report of the Select Church Committee to Study Governmental Operations with respect to Intelligence Activities.* Washington, D.C.: Government Printing Office.
Watters, P., and S. Gillers (eds.)
1973. *Investigating the FBI.* New York: Ballantine Books.

Chapter 6

Legitimizing Police Deviance*

Jean-Paul Brodeur

Introduction

As I came to be concerned with most of the issues raised in this paper as much through a personal experience as through academic research, I shall begin by saying something about this experience. I was involved for over two years as a consultant with a Quebec provincial commission of inquiry on police operations. This commission of inquiry, known as "Commission d'enquête sur des opérations policières en territoire québécois" was headed by attorney Jean F. Keable, and its report was released on March 6, 1981.[1]

The police operations investigated by this commission were similar in nature to those reported on by the American Church Committee,[2] namely, counterterrorism and what is more vaguely referred to as "antisubversion." These operations were conducted by Security Service squads in Quebec between 1970 and 1973. The Royal Canadian Mounted Police (RCMP), the Sûreté du Québec (SQ, Quebec's provincial police) and the Montreal municipal police each had such squads operating mainly in Montreal and its vicinity.

Even though I feel I have learned a good deal about the police through my participation in the Keable Commission's inquiries, I must admit that what I have learned has perplexed me instead of reinforcing whatever certainties I may have entertained on the nature of police deviance and on the ways to exercise control over it.

It is quite natural to assume that "police deviance" refers to the behaviour of a distinct professional group, namely, policemen. This obvious assumption further implies that if one wants to control police behaviour, one will have to develop rules which apply to the activities of this group of persons. Both this assumption and its implications seem to me to oversimplify matters. The police operations investigated by the Keable Commission, and quite a few other police operations, are dependent upon

---

*I wish to thank Professor Clifford Shearing and Mr. Philip Stenning for their extensive comments on an earlier draft of this essay. I would also like to thank Anne Butler of Butterworths for helping me bring the article closer to the standards of written English. Any remaining mistakes are, of course, my sole responsibility.

informers who, with the acquiescence of their police controllers, are deeply involved in illegal activities, and are paid on a regular basis.[3] Given this feature of police activity, any policy established to regulate police behaviour which was not also designed to control the infiltration of police agents would inevitably avoid the problem. The point made in the preceding remarks can be stated quite simply: When we talk about police control, it should not be taken for granted that we know precisely what the word "police" refers to. As a police force is an organization that thrives on its ever-expanding fringe (telephone company employees, post office officials, persons with access to confidential records, etc.), the control of police deviance cannot be effective unless this wider context is recognized.

I shall now briefly comment upon possible applications of the notion of deviance to police behaviour. It seems to me useful in this regard to distinguish between three sorts of police deviance. The first sort refers to delinquent behaviour that may be statistically related to persons who happen to belong to police organizations. It might be discovered, for instance, that a significant number of policemen cheat on their income tax (this is a purely fictitious example). Even though meaningful relationships could conceivably be drawn between the hypothetical "police personality" and cheating on income tax, this would not imply that this kind of behaviour could be theoretically identified as "police deviance." Those relationships would merely call attention to a possible explanation for the delinquent behaviour of citizens who happen to earn their living by working as policemen. This being said, there remain two sorts of police behaviour that do pertain to the issue of police deviance. A policeman may abuse the powers granted to him by his office either for personal gratification or to achieve, in some alternate fashion, what he perceives to be the institutional goals of the organization to which he belongs. The classic illustration of the first kind of abuse is police corruption; an example of the second sort, albeit not unproblematic, would be illegal arrest. Like most distinctions, it must be stressed that the one just drawn allows for some overlapping. Police brutality, for instance, depending on its context, may fall on either side of the distinction. Likewise, overzealousness in the pursuit of institutional goals could, in certain cases, be explained by an individual's ambition to be quickly promoted.

All of the police operations investigated by the commission of inquiry for which I was a consultant exemplify abuses of power in the pursuit of police institutional goals. A significant number of these operations were part of an RCMP program called "Disruptive Tactics." Its aim was to destabilize leftist movements and more generally to disorganize political dissidents in Quebec. In this paper, I shall raise questions pertaining to the legality of these and analogous operations. Questions of legal evaluation may seem straightforward enough: one describes an operation undertaken by the police and, on the basis of the facts, one tries afterwards to see whether the operation and the behaviour of those involved in its undertaking fall within the confines of the law, as it stands. The apparent simplicity of this procedure can be deceiving in the case of police operations. Before presenting more explicitly what I intend to do in this paper, I would like to say something about the difficulties involved in weighing police behaviour on the scales of the written law, in its present form.

Basically, the issues that I wish to raise are germane to the questions discussed by D. J. McBarnet in "Arrest: the Legal Context of Policing," an article published in 1979.[4] McBarnet answers in the negative a question that she expresses thus: "Is the law formulated to control the police?" (p. 28). Although I thoroughly agree with her answer, I would like to point out that this question can be interpreted in two ways. It might be interpreted to mean: "Are the legal checks upon police activities strong enough to efficiently protect civil liberties?" This is McBarnet's interpretation of her own question. One can also ask: "Can the police be successfully prosecuted if they breach whatever legal constraints bear upon their activities?" Although they are intimately connected, these two reformulations do not seem to me to be equivalent. The first one pertains to the legal protection of civil liberties and the second one to the control of police deviance as such. In this paper, I will be more concerned with the second reformulation of the question of legality.

There are, however, serious difficulties involved in an attempt to answer this question as I have reformulated it. Let me first illustrate one sort of difficulty. Not infrequently (at least in Quebec) the police will preempt charges of brutality by having their victim accused of resisting arrest and even of assault against the arresting officer(s). Hence, when the case goes to court, it is the guilt of the victim and not the abuse by the police that is at issue. If the citizen can prove himself innocent of the charges laid against him, he will be acquitted. However, this does not in any way mean that the policemen who have assaulted him will be prosecuted. In reviewing recent jurisprudence involving problematic police behaviour toward citizens, one is struck by the fact that in most cases it is the citizen that stands accused, the policemen acting as witnesses for the prosecution.[5] Being party to law enforcement, the police can successfully deflect the reach of the law when it could be directed against them.

Closely related to this first difficulty is a second one. As I have just said, police behaviour is often not the immediate object of jurisprudence; it is alluded to or explicitly discussed in cases where citizens are defendants. In some other areas, such as Security Service operations, there is very little jurisprudence. This situation raises a methodological issue. When we resort to legal analysis of broad notions such as *mens rea*, for instance, we have to rely on court rulings that were not made in relation to police behaviour at all. If we wish to use this jurisprudence in discussing police operations, we have to assume that it would apply as much to police behaviour as it does to the behaviour of any citizen. In other words, we have to assume that the law, as it would, in this case, be interpreted by the courts, is the same for all. With regard to components of the criminal justice system other than the courts—the police themselves, the Crown, the relevant political authorities—this assumption does not seem to me to be fully warranted, the scales often being tipped in favour of the police. It would be, I believe, rather incautious to postulate that this situation would be drastically reversed in the courts and that what applied in cases involving citizen behaviour would unequivocally apply in cases involving police behaviour.

Finally, a third problem arises when police behaviour is confronted with the law. I will try to express this problem in general terms, giving concrete evidence for it further on in this paper. This difficulty is similar to one that has been widely discussed in ethical theory.[6] It has been argued that any attempt to draw an equivalence between moral goodness and a given natural fact is doomed to failure because it transforms into mere tautologies questions that are perceived as meaningful by human beings. If we define, for instance, moral goodness as pleasure, a meaningful question such as "Is an excess of pleasure morally good?" should be reformulated thus: "Is an excess of moral goodness morally good?" Whatever answer is given to the reformulation, it seems that it would miss the issue raised by the original question.

This attempt to reduce ethics to worldly facts has been branded the "naturalistic fallacy" by ethical theorists. One could similarly coin the expression "legalistic fallacy" in reference to an attempt to reduce legality to existing laws. Even if one sets aside the substantial issue of deciding whether or not legality (in a given place and at a given time) should be made to coincide with existing laws, this notion retains a certain heuristic value as it reminds one not to assume that existing laws exhaust the field of what is legal at a given time, and thus transforming into tautologies or contradictions questions that are meaningfully raised.[7] I shall, for instance, provide explicit evidence that the RCMP asked questions such as "Is breaching this law illegal?" By regarding such a question as a contradiction, one not only ignores the fact that it is meaningfully raised inside police forces and that law enforcement policy is sometimes based upon a negative answer to it, but one also neglects to consider the important fact that raising such questions in the course of decision making is an expression of privilege and of power.

All the preceding remarks on the difficulties involved in confronting police behaviour with the law as it stands could indeed be summarized by saying that the police are institutionally endowed with a privileged status that bears upon their general observance of the law. This essay is intended to describe aspects of this privileged status. More specifically, after having given some background to the issues to be raised, I intend to discuss the following paradox. Control of police deviance that is not firmly grounded in law is bound to be ineffective, for reasons that I will present. I will, however, argue that far from providing a ground for control, the law provides legitimacy to police behaviour that is either deviant or conducive to deviance. I will suggest that this is no accident, as one of the basic functions of the criminal law is to legitimize for law enforcers activities that are legally prohibited to the citizens. I will furthermore argue that the police mandate, as it is presently formulated by the law, is in itself a source of police deviance. Finally, in my concluding remarks, I will briefly draw some of the consequences of the preceding analyses for articulating strategies to contain police deviance.

Background

My first task in developing my argument is to provide an illustrative background to the issues I propose to raise. During the night of October 7, 1972, members of the three main police forces operating in Quebec—the Montreal municipal police, the SQ and the RCMP—broke into the offices of a left-wing press agency and removed all of its files for disruptive purposes. Police involvement in this illegal operation, whose code name was BRICOLE, was revealed only in 1976 through the testimony of a former RCMP agent who had played a part in it.[8] On the day following the 1972 break-in, the press agency, suspecting that it had been the victim of a police operation, sent telegrams to the respective heads of the police forces concerned and registered letters to the Solicitor General of Canada, the Quebec Minister of Justice and the Quebec Ombudsman. All of these addressees were asked whether the police were responsible for the break-in. The press agency also filed a complaint at a Montreal police station. In all of its endeavours to find out whether the police were involved in the break-in, the press agency met with either denials or no answer at all.

After the disclosure of the operation in 1976, the RCMP Security Service headquarters asked the officer who had authorized the RCMP to break-in to prepare a report on it. This report was to be sent to the Solicitor General of Canada. In its original version, an excerpt of the report read:

> WHY ILLEGAL ENTRY:
>
> The primary objective of this Operation was to disrupt the MDPPQ and the APLQ and the second objective was information gathering. The *theft* was preferred over the *lawful search* by the persons involved as more disruptive: No need to return documents/No legal battle against *oppressive authority* and it would create more uncertainty in the milieu. Although a Warrant could probably have been obtained, it appear [*sic*] the MCP could not make a direct link between the MDPPQ/APLQ and a crime. Finally there was hope that the *crime* could be blamed on Andre MAHEU of the MILICE REPUBLICAINE who had asked the MDPPQ for a list of its supporters and, when refused, had become quite hostile.[9]

The above-quoted document was submitted on March 15, 1976. On the first of April of the same year, the head of the RCMP Security Service wrote a letter to the officer responsible for the March 15 report,[10] asking him to redraft it:

> In the event that the Honourable Fernand LALONDE, Solicitor General for the Province of Quebec, requests further information, would you and your staff review your BRICOLE report of March 15, 1976, plus attachments. *It is realized that it was originally written for internal consumption.* No doubt it could be redrafted with the same *factual* accuracy, perhaps a bit shorter, *with a language that would be more easily understood outside this Force.*[11]

The officer complied, and the previously quoted excerpt from his report, after redrafting, read:

> WHY ENTRY WITHOUT WARRANT:
>
> The primary objective of this Operation was to disrupt the MDPPQ and the APLQ and the second objective was information gathering. The *entry without warrant* was preferred over the *search with warrant* by the persons involved as more disruptive: no need to return documents/no legal battle against *"oppressive authority"* and it would create more uncertainty in the milieu. Although a warrant could probably have been obtained, it appeared the SPCUM could not make a direct link between the MDPPQ/APLQ and a crime. Finally there was a hope that the *removal of the documents* could be blamed on Andre MAHEU of the MILICE REPUBLICAINE, who had asked the MDPPQ for a list of its supporters and when refused, had become quite hostile.[12]

If one compares the two versions of the report on operation BRICOLE, it becomes quite clear that its redrafting purported to suppress all expressions in the original text that either implied or explicitly stated that the police had behaved illegally.

The three police officers who had authorized the participation of members of their respective forces in operation BRICOLE were, in the end, prosecuted. However, they were not charged under section 306 of the Canadian Criminal Code (breaking and entering) but under section 115. Section 306 carries severe penalties, ranging from imprisonment for 14 years to imprisonment for life, depending on whether or not the offence is committed in relation to a dwelling house. Section 115 is seldom invoked in criminal procedure: it states that anyone who, without lawful excuse, contravenes an Act of the Parliament of Canada is guilty of an indictable offence and is liable to imprisonment for two years (a much lighter penalty than those provided under section 306). It was alleged that these three police officers should have complied with section 443 of the Canadian Criminal Code and accordingly should have obtained a warrant for search and seizure; they were charged with having failed to do so. They pleaded guilty and were given an unconditional discharge[13] at the end of a rather unusual procedure, a *pré-enquête* ("pre-inquest") before a magistrate, that was held for the most part *in camera*. It was argued before the court that they had acted in the best interest of national security.

It must be stressed that their misconduct was legally defined in a way that strictly parallels the redrafting of the RCMP report on BRICOLE, "entry without warrant" being substituted for "theft." It is also significant that the RCMP officer who pleaded guilty to the charge laid under section 115 of the Criminal Code is the officer who redrafted the March 15 report on BRICOLE. For all practical purposes, this officer was in a position to dictate the terms of his own indictment and those of his co-defendants from the SQ and the Montreal municipal police.[14]

This play upon definitions of illegal behaviour is not unusual. Anyone familiar with the way in which police record their operations could indeed quote scores of examples. I will refer to one more case. During the night of April 27, 1972, two RCMP officers broke into the shed of a construction company by smashing the padlock with a metal instrument, and removed at least one case of dynamite and some electric detonators. This incident was described in a brief issued by the Solicitor General of Canada as an "unauthorized seizure of dynamite in a building-yard."[15]

Reflecting upon these and similar cases, I find myself in a quandary. Deviance as an object of scientific inquiry is not given as a natural fact but is established through definition. This point has been repeatedly made in criminology. It seems that what appears at first glance to be a form of police deviance is not only often, but quite systematically, defined out of the field of illegal behaviour. Policemen are rarely brought to trial for abusing their powers, and even when charges are laid, they seldom result in convictions.[16]

We seem, then, to be faced with a dilemma. If we comply with the canons of legal positivism, we may be compelled to acknowledge that police deviance is a pseudo-topic, as the criteria used for its definition are not strictly legal and thus appear arbitrary. We may, of course, disagree with legal positivism and maintain that in numerous instances police behaviour can reasonably be called deviant, even though such behaviour does not breach the law as it is formulated or even though it can be made to come within the law in official statements submitted to persons legally responsible for controlling the police (cabinet ministers, Crown attorneys, the courts, and so forth). The latter course is surely more promising for building theories; it may, however, prove to be frustrating if one attempts to do more than just theorize about police deviance, that is, if one strives to find and implement ways to control it.

This is a crucial point. Control can be either externally enforced or voluntarily complied with. Even though both of these processes (enforcement and compliance) are usually seen to be intricately bound together when inquiries into the dynamics of control are made, I shall briefly discuss them separately. The successful *enforcement* of control is dependent upon two sets of conditions, the first positive and the second negative. First, one must have a reliable apparatus to enforce the controls. Secondly, one must not meet with too much resistance on the part of the target of control. For if one meets with firm and persistent resistance, one is likely to exacerbate rather than control the situation, for example, by precipitating open confrontation and conflict. A consequence of these assumptions is that the less powerful a group to be controlled is, the more one can resort to enforcing control upon it; hence, for instance, the aggressive style of law enforcement against minorities. Conversely, the more powerful a group is, the more one has to rely upon *compliance* with the controls.

Now, not only is the police organization a powerful agency, but it is also the apparatus that is institutionally provided for the enforcement of control, albeit not upon itself. If one wishes to *enforce* controls upon the police, one flouts to some degree both previous conditions: the resistance is always quite firm and there is not even a reliable enforcing apparatus to quell it; hence, for instance, the *extreme* reluctance of the political class to confront the police. One is therefore forced to resort to forms of control which are grounded in compliance, and consequently encounters the difficulty of encouraging such compliance on the part of the police. The only way to generate such compliance is to provide strong legal grounds for it, thereby relying upon the powerful symbolism the law holds for an institution that is, at least in theory, devoted to upholding it.

In what follows I shall attempt to argue that because the conditions of its enforcement by the police are not explicit, the criminal law, as it now stands, does not provide this ground for compliance. In developing this argument I will focus initially on the criminal law in general and thereafter turn my attention more specifically to the police mandate as defined in the Police Acts and other legislation.

The Criminal Law

I will begin by stating a few general propositions regarding aspects of the criminal law. In spite of their generality, these propositions have an immediate bearing upon the subject of police deviance, as I shall suggest in the next section of this paper.

(1) Criminal law gives authority to the state—in effect to the criminal justice system—to punish certain kinds of behaviour. Punishment or retribution is effected by treating a culprit legally in more or less the same way as he has illegally treated his victim.[17] Since the institution of imprisonment is a general means of retribution, the punishment does not really mirror the nature of the crime. But the parallel between crime and punishment still holds, at least in that if any private citizen did to a fellow citizen what the criminal justice system does to someone convicted of a crime, he would be prosecuted for illegal behaviour. In short, the ways of doing justice are disquietingly similar to those of doing injustice.[18] In respect to punishment, the criminal law might then be characterized as a process of *legalized reciprocation*.

(2) Criminal law also defines certain kinds of behaviour as both illegal and punishable. It must, however, be borne in mind that most definitions of "crime" conjoin objective and subjective aspects of behaviour and are consequently far from being explicit. Section 283 of the Canadian Criminal Code thus defines "theft" as behaviour with a fraudulent intent; "fraud" is itself defined by section 338 as defrauding through the use of fraudulent means. This circularity occurs frequently, thus giving expression to a fundamental difficulty: the relative undefinability of ethical terms with which the criminal law is saturated (the semantic field of "malice").[19]

(3) A third proposition about the criminal law, and any law for that matter, is that it cannot be reduced to a sequence of sections and articles printed together under a legal heading. In order to be applied, any law has to be supplemented by custom (legal, social and linguistic), jurisprudence and legal doctrine. It must also be supplemented by other laws.[20] These supplements are often as important as the written criminal law itself. One consequence of this is that there can be no clear dichotomy between the law and its so-called application. If this is granted, it follows that there is little sense in alleging that the criminal law is clear about police deviance but is seldom applied. (One could cite in this connection section 26 [excessive force] and section 117 [misconduct of an officer in the execution of a process] of the Canadian Criminal Code.) The very fact that certain sections of the criminal law are seldom, if ever, applied says something about the law itself, which should be conceived *à la* Donald Black as a living process with definite patterns of behaviour.[21]

Although much has been written on this subject, there are two important points relating to it that I would like to discuss briefly. It is, I believe, a mistake to hold that it is for the most part informal practices that circumvent the law. These practices are to a significant extent *grounded* in law. I shall provide an extreme example of this. Covering up police deviance may be alleged to be one of the main reasons why there are few prosecutions. This is true enough; it is, however, no less true that covering up is *legally* authorized by section 41(2) of the Canadian Federal Court Act.[22] This section gives the Solicitor General of Canada legal authority to refuse, for purposes of national security, communication of documents that may be claimed by the courts or quasi-judicial bodies such as commissions of inquiry. It was systematically invoked by the Solicitor General to prevent the Keable Commission from gaining access to documents pertaining to the RCMP program called "Disruptive Tactics." The few operations carried out under this program that were finally made public proved to be examples of serious police wrongdoings (a break-in, the burning of a barn, a theft of dynamite and the issuing of a fraudulent terrorist communiqué). The extent of this wrongdoing has not yet been publicly revealed.

In her previously quoted article, McBarnet makes the same point about not divorcing the law from its enforcement (p. 27). However, when she writes that "deviation from legality is institutionalized in the law itself" (p. 39), she appears to reinstate the dichotomy at a superior level, namely, between the law and legal ideology. One could object even to this form of dichotomy and apply to legal ideology and rhetoric what she says about due process: that it is *for* crime control (p. 39). I would be inclined to see in the ideology of legality a process of extracting from the law any elements that can justify a widening of its reach.

(4) The previous assertions about the importance of supplements to the written criminal law are particularly relevant when we take into account the legal question of evaluating intent or intention in criminal behaviour. A deeply entrenched principle of law and legal doctrine states that *"Actus non facit reum, nisi mens sit rea"* (or, in the words of Lord Kenyon, "the intent and the act must both concur to constitute the crime"[23]). This doctrine of *mens rea*, whose explicit formulation dates back at least to the seventeenth century,[24] is to a significant extent reflected in the wording of criminal statutes, some of which in defining offences refer in either a general[25] or a specific way[26] to the requisite criminal intent. In numerous definitions, however, the nature of the requisite intent is not specifically mentioned. The legal doctrine of *mens rea* stands in these cases as a rule of interpretation of the criminal statutes, leaving ample space for litigation.

(5) The scope of possible litigation can be seen to be even broader if we notice that the legal notion of *mens rea* stands in effect for a whole cluster of variously related concepts. Such concepts are, to name just a few, malice, actual malice, implied malice, constructive malice, awareness, ulterior intent, foresight, basic intent, general intention and specific intention. Some of these concepts are far from clear, even though they are widely used in jurisprudence. In *Leary v. R.* (1977), for instance, Mr. Justice Dickson wrote in his dissenting opinion that there seemed "little reason for retaining in the criminal law—which should be characterized by clarity, simplicity and certainty—a concept as difficult of comprehension and application as 'specific intention.' "[27]

In some cases, basic concepts both overlap and fall under different logical and legal categories. I believe in this regard that *mens rea* can be construed either as a mental counterpart of the *content* of the act or as an endorsement of its *purpose* (it can, of course, be construed as both). This interfacing of intent defined as an awareness of the content of the act and as an endorsement of its purpose is firmly grounded in the Canadian Criminal Code: when specific about *mens rea*, the Criminal Code defines it in terms of both intent and purpose.[28] It is also grounded in ordinary language, which, as was noted by Mr. Justice Dickson in *Lewis v. R.*, frequently uses intent and motive (one's ulterior intention as it relates to the end of an act)[29] interchangeably.[30] However, the Canadian and British courts have generally held that motive and intent are basically different legal notions, motive not being exculpatory,[31] whereas a lack of awareness of the very nature of the act (*mens rea* as a mental counterpart) can stand as a legal defence. A telling example of the distinction is given by terrorism: no political motivation could ever render legal political assassination ("political execution"), kidnapping ("revolutionary arraignment") or bank robbery ("expropriation").

In a few instances, however, the two above-quoted interpretations of the principle of *mens rea*—awareness of the act and endorsement of its purpose—have tended to merge. In *R. v. Handfield* and in some related jurisprudence[32] Canadian courts have ruled that motive can have exculpatory effect (the defendant successfully pleading that his purpose was to play a joke, not to steal anyone's property).

In *Lewis v. R.* (1979), the Supreme Court of Canada laid down six basic principles designed to clarify the notion of motive in law. The court re-established (in its second principle) that motive is not exculpatory, although "proved absence of motive is always an important fact in favor of the accused and ordinarily worthy of note in a charge to the jury."[33] The intricate character of the relationships between motive and intent was explicitly acknowledged by the court in the formulation of its sixth principle: "Each case will turn on its own unique set of circumstances. The issue of motive is always a matter of degree."[34]

The difficulties surrounding the doctrine of *mens rea*, and particularly the clarification of the relationship between intention and purpose, are, I believe, quite real. It first seems that the legal doctrine of *mens rea* is so technical that it is divorced from everyday thinking. This poses a problem because an important number of legal decisions affecting, for instance, the prosecution of policemen are taken on an informal basis, where reasoning is much closer to a layman's thinking than to Supreme Court distinctions. Secondly, it is not clear whether the notion of purpose as it appears in certain sections of the Canadian Criminal Code coincides with the concept of motive as defined by the courts. The courts, as we have seen, generally hold that motive and intent are different legal notions. If this is granted, it would seem that one of two things is true. We could say, on the one hand, that legal definitions of specific intentions are seriously misformulated whenever they rely on the notion of purpose, because the law then defines specific intention by something that the courts have generally ruled to be different from intent. On the other hand, we could say that the jurisprudential notion of motive is significantly different from the notion of purpose as it is used in the Canadian Criminal Code to define specific intention. Finally, I shall remark that even jurisprudence is not wholly unequivocal: although it is generally held that motive is not exculpatory, it has been recognized to be so in cases where taking someone's property was claimed to be part of an innocent practical joke.

The point of these remarks, to which I shall return later, could be expressed by saying that ambiguities in the law favour those who have the power to take advantage of them. Not only do I believe that the police have such power, but I would like to stress that they are in a position to use this power where legal uncertainty can be decisive, that is, *not* before the higher courts, whose very function is to resolve legal ambiguities, but in the earlier stages of procedure, when the decision whether to prosecute or not has not yet been taken, or before the lower courts.

The Enforcement of the Criminal Law

I have, in the previous section, made a number of general remarks on the criminal law. I will now consider the consequences of these remarks for the field of law enforcement.

(1) The first remark was essentially that the criminal law involves a process of legalized reciprocation. The point of this remark was to draw attention to the fact that punishment legally duplicates criminality: the criminal law harms persons who have themselves harmed other persons either in themselves or in their property. It seems to me that this general proposition finds specific application in matters of law enforcement. I shall say in first approximation that law enforcement *operationally* duplicates law violation. Examples of this duplication are numerous and I will begin by giving a very simple one: in order to arrest a fugitive or a speeding motorist, police officers themselves may have to drive above speed limits. Two points should be made about this example. The first one is that it seems to illustrate convincingly what appears to be an *operational necessity;* it would be deemed rather obtuse to issue a directive prohibiting police officers, regardless of circumstances, from driving above speed limits. The second point I wish to make is that operational necessity (or what is perceived as such) can beget what appears prima facie to be unrestricted disrespect for the rule of law. In other words, it leads to operational deviance. It should be recognized that it is one thing to allow police officers to drive above speed limits for the purpose of arresting a suspect and quite another one for them to generally act as if traffic regulations did not apply to them.

I have said previously that there are numerous examples of law enforcement duplication of law violation. Here is a tentative list, which takes into account the distinction made between operational necessity and operational deviance:

A. Violation of the Law	*B. Operational Necessity*	*C. Operational Deviance*
murder manslaughter	killing (necessary force)	police executions[35]
assault	doing bodily harm (necessary force)	police brutality

all violations of property	authorized search and seizure	violations of property in order to get evidence, information or to "destabilize"
drug trafficking	drug seizure (buy and bust operations)	drug trafficking (buying without busting)
extortion	public protection	"police protection"
threat and intimidation	interrogating and tailing	blackmail and harassment
speeding	chasing	general disrespect for traffic regulations

The main purpose of this tentative list is to exemplify *very roughly* the dimensions of police operational duplication of law violation. Needless to say, it could be expanded and refined, if, for instance, undercover operations were taken into account. Other examples of duplication could also be provided on a more general level than individual offences. It is interesting to note in this respect that the most enduring result of nationalist terrorism in Quebec between 1963 and 1973 has been to precipitate in the province the establishment of a fullfledged state security apparatus (the Security Service of the SQ and the late premier Bourassa's Centre d'analyse et de documentation (CAD), patterned after the French SDECE). In struggling against violent separatism, the Quebec provincial police force has progressively evolved into an organization much more befitting an independent state than a province.

The second purpose of my comparative list is to raise an important question: Are the items listed in column C species (tokens) of the corresponding items in column A? Are they, in other words, violations of the criminal law? One should not hasten to give an abstract answer to this question, as raising it is in effect tantamount to asking whether the criminal law affords us, in specific cases, the means to discriminate items listed under column C from items listed under column B. The answer to this question is at best controversial, and not only for reasons pertaining to the actual content of the criminal law. In reviewing items under columns B and C, linguistic reification should be avoided. The items listed respectively under the headings "Operational Necessity" and "Operational Deviance" differ less from each other as *things* than as *scores* on a legal scale. The criminal law may conceivably be instrumental in discriminating between extremes on the scale; it is not certain, however, that any law could afford us a means of drawing a clear line between items not so widely separated (for instance, numerous cases of alleged police brutality).

(2) As I said above, the legal definition of a criminal offence combines objective (behavioural) and subjective (mental) elements. I also indicated

that the law is often not explicit regarding these subjective or mental elements. There are good reasons for this: in most criminal cases, the objective and subjective aspects of the alleged offence are not dichotomized, perceptible behaviour bearing witness to intention. If someone is seen leaving a bank in a hurry, covering his face with a hood and carrying a machine gun, there is little doubt about whether he has committed a hold up. The reverse obtains with alleged police deviance: since the factual descriptions of police wrongdoings are usually made by law enforcement agencies extremely sensitive to the public image of their members, these descriptions are most often pseudo-objective reformulations of police behaviour into occupational jargon.[36] This jargon is not only disconnected in principle from any intimation of a criminal state of mind, it is also laden with exculpatory comments.

The brief issued by the Solicitor General of Canada on the theft of dynamite by RCMP members is an example of what I have called a pseudo-objective reformulation. We have already seen that this operation was described as an "unauthorized seizure of dynamite in a building yard." This makes it seem as if the Security Service agents involved had not substantially broken the law but had merely failed to get an authorization, thus implying that the police could legalize breaking into a private company's shed and taking explosives from it.

The following is an example of an exculpatory statement. On October 4, 1971, two RCMP officers intercepted the car of a citizen who was driving along Avenue du Parc in Montreal. This citizen was subsequently taken to a hotel room in the suburbs of Montreal and interrogated for 17 hours, being obliged throughout the night to stand upright in order to keep awake. One of the purposes of this interrogation was to recruit him as a future police informer. This incident is referred to in a brief submitted by the Solicitor General of Canada to the Keable Commission.[37] It is presented as an "interview." This brief also mentions that according to the RCMP members involved in the incident, no violence was used against the citizen, although he was ordered by them to stand up so that he would not fall asleep during an interrogation that lasted until the following morning.

What we are presented with, then, are statements concerning "unauthorized seizures," "interviews," and so forth, and we have to decide whether the activities described in these statements are illegal. In other words, what has to be evaluated is whether a "technical offence" is also a substantial one. It must be noted that even to discuss reprehensible behaviour in those terms is to confer a privilege upon an offender.

(3) Before considering how this question about the legal status of an "offence" can be answered, it is relevant to ask *where* decisions regarding it are made within the criminal justice apparatus. The decision whether or not to lay criminal charges appears for a variety of reasons to require much more deliberation in cases of police deviance than in other cases (save,

perhaps, the prosecution of politicians and other members of the "power elites"). This decision is taken in numerous instances by quasi-judicial institutions, namely, commissions of inquiry, police boards, citizens' complaint boards, internal discipline committees, and so forth.[38] In other cases, it is taken through an exceptional judiciary procedure, for example, what in Quebec is called a *pré-enquête* ("pre-inquest").[39]

The point I wish to make about these different bodies is not that they are partial to the police; it is rather that the issues admitted before them as relevant to the interpretation of police behaviour are somewhat broader and less legally constricted, less technical, than those considered by a judge in a court of law. These bodies sometimes experience what I would call a "second innocence" about the matters of justice when confronted with presumed police misconduct, and their decision making is less mechanical than in the lower courts.

Let me illustrate from experience what I mean by "second innocence." The criminal justice system's capacity to rehabilitate in any way persons who have been punished has been the object of such intense criticism that it takes a certain amount of callousness to process a case in such a way that the person(s) implicated will be severely punished. This appears to be particularly true of cases involving police officers, where all the human and moral concerns that are typically repressed when dealing with ordinary offenders suddenly resurface. All the imperfections of our criminal justice system unexpectedly appear to dawn upon the toughest of prosecutors, who mull anew on such legitimate issues as: "What's the use of punishing him? What good will it do?"; "Hasn't he been punished enough? His name is all over the papers and his career is in shambles"; "Was what he did *really* illegal?" For instance, in operation HAM,[40] RCMP agents took hold of computer tapes listing the names of all the members of a political party and had them copied. The whole operation was completed secretly within a few hours at night, and the tapes were returned to the place they had been taken from. Although section 283 of the Canadian Criminal Code explicitly states that theft is committed when there is intent to *temporarily* deprive someone of his property, it was repeatedly argued before the Keable Commission that the tapes had not *really* been stolen by the RCMP, because they were returned within hours. Such common-sense interpretations of technical definitions appearing in the Criminal Code seem to carry much more weight when presented before quasi-judicial bodies who have to decide whether the case would stand up in court. Any uncertainty in the criminal law, which is riddled with uncertainties, is then put to use to counter accusations against the police.

(4) Our problem, then, is to see whether a pseudo-factual description of an act ("unauthorized seizure of dynamite") falls within the scope of the definition of an offence in the Criminal Code. This matter can be decided in two steps. The first step is to free the description of its biases. This is not

easily done. But even if an unbiased description of behaviour is finally produced, the crucial problem of judging whether or not there is criminal intent or *mens rea* remains.

(5) Criminal law makes it, I believe, extremely difficult to give an uncontroversial solution to this problem for basically two reasons.

First, as I have stated before, the criminal law uses both the vocabulary of intention (the mental counterpart of one's action) and of purpose (goal) in defining intent: the more specific the description of intent, the more it tends to merge with a definition of purpose. It follows that *three* sets of criteria can be and are actually applied in evaluating alleged police misconduct: *actus reus*, *mens rea* and what I shall call *finis reus*[41] (requisite purpose or goal). If *finis* and *mens* conflict (wilfully breaking the law in order to apply it efficiently) *mens* is neutralized by *finis*. We are left with a weak "technical offence" which is seldom prosecuted or, if it is, is likely to result in an acquittal or an absolute discharge. The same point can be made metaphorically. We have seen that one of the few instances in which motive has been recognized as disculpatory by the courts is the so-called "trick" or "joke" defence (stealing as part of a game). In a similar way, but with much more weight, a police officer accused of misconduct in performing his duties can in theory always plead that he did not really break the law but was actually playing the law enforcement game (a very serious game).

Second, the weight of the criminal law is directed against offenders who, as the saying goes, stand as naked subjects before the law (*mens rea* can also be defined as immoral preference of one's *particular* interest over the common good). But what are we to think about those who, far from standing as naked subjects before the law, have misbehaved as members of a law enforcement agency and who can therefore allege that their *mens* coincided with the *collective aim* of the agency? That the criminal law affords us no precise guidelines in cases involving complex organizations can be easily shown by raising such questions as: Are all officers who have planned and *authorized* at their own level an illegal police operation to be prosecuted as party to a conspiracy? What about those whose knowledge of the operation was restricted to what they needed to know?[42]

I shall now provide some illustration for the points I have just considered. Following the information laid against the officers who had authorized the APLQ break-in, Judge Vincent, who was to rule on the case, held a pré-enquête. A pré-enquête being a rather exceptional procedure, there are no clear rules about how it should be handled by the judge who is holding it. The RCMP was particularly worried that Judge Vincent would ask members of the force summoned before him as witnesses if they knew of other illegal police operations. Upon briefing officers who were to testify before Judge Vincent, it was discovered that at least one of them (Inspector Claude Vermette, who had been involved in operation HAM and believed that it was illegal) would admit that he knew about other illegal police operations.

Having thus learned that an RCMP officer was prepared to testify before Judge Vincent that operation HAM had been illegal, members of the Security Service who were stationed in Montreal sent a telex to Ottawa in order to seek legal advice from their headquarters:

> It would, therefore, be appreciated, if this operation was legal, that we be informed on what grounds it was legal so that insp. Vermette could change his testimony.[43]

They received the following reply:

> 3. It is important to turn the question on "HAM" around. We should ask in what way was "HAM" illegal? It must be remembered that every PUMA and every VAMPIRE operation necessitating entry into the target without consent prior to June 30, 1974, was technically a situation of trespass, a criminal offence. It is still technically an offence in spite of bill C-176 until such time in the future as some appeal court jurisprudence is developed.
>
> 5. There are many other cases in which there is no specific provision in law for this undertaking. *Are we then to lable* [sic] *illegal or unlawful many of our operations simply on that basis* and then perhaps draw relationship between that and BRICOLE?
>
> 6. Assuming that defense counsel raises objections at every appropriate time when the questioning is going beyond the relevance of a case at hand, there would seem to be no alternative if the judge persists for that same defense counsel to ask for an adjournment to give us an opportunity to discuss with the Solicitor General whatever proper legal intervention might be introduced.[44]

Paragraphs 3 and 5 of the telex are clear enough: the basic aim of the law is to provide the police with authority for undertaking such operations as they deem necessary. So deeply entrenched is this assumption that the lack of specific legal provisions granting such authority is only seen as a contingency that provisionally allows for certain operations to be deemed "technical offences," until duly legitimized by the courts. What are those police "technical offences"? My position is that they are cases where the police knowingly (*mens*) breach the law (*actus*) for what they consider law enforcement purposes (*finis*). Such purpose quashes malice, thus yielding what I shall call disaccountable behaviour.

One could indeed retort that the courts might not see it this way. However, let me first point out that the *law* can be invoked to prevent the courts from ruling on these cases: this is precisely what was suggested by the RCMP in paragraph 6 of the above-quoted telex. According to testimonies made before the Keable Commission, several hundred PUMA and VAMPIRE operations were conducted during the 1960s. I personally do not know of one single instance where members of the RCMP Security Service were prosecuted for trespassing.

It does happen that such cases come before the courts. I shall briefly discuss *R. v. Gabourie (Nos. 1 and 2)* (1977) and *R. v. Dass* (1979); both of these cases involved police interception of private communications. According to section 178.16(1) of the Canadian Criminal Code, a private communication that has been intercepted by use of an electronic or other technical device is inadmissible as evidence unless the interception was lawfully made. Part IV.1 of the Criminal Code sets the conditions under which interception of private communications is legal.

In *R. v. Gabourie (No. 1)* (1977), it was argued by defence counsel that evidence obtained through interception of private communications was inadmissible because the listening device had been implanted before the police were given legal authority to do so. The court ruled that the evidence was admissible:

> From this, it appears to me that the installation of the hook-up is merely a preparation for the interception and not part of the interception. Accordingly, it cannot be said that the installation of the hook-up prior to the date of authorization renders the interception unlawful.[45]

In *R. v. Gabourie (No. 2)* (1977), it was also claimed in defence that intercepted private communications were inadmissible as evidence because the Solicitor General of Canada had failed to give the defendant the notice that is required by law (90 days after the interception). In response to that claim, the judge said:

> Now, I do not believe that if the Solicitor General of Canada had failed to give Fred Gabourie the notice required in this case by s. 178.23 of the Code, that the omission would render the interception inadmissible.[46]

Even more interesting is *R. v. Dass* (1979). Although the police had legal authorization for intercepting his private communications, Mr. Ashok Dass appealed his conviction on two counts of criminal conspiracy. He claimed that the installation of the listening device had implied trespassing, making the whole process of the interception unlawful and thereby rendering the intercepted communications inadmissible as evidence. The court explicitly rejected the Crown counsel's argument that the authority to install a bugging device carried with it by implication the authority to enter premises by force or by stealth in order to implant the device:

> The authority to intercept private communications is not an authority to break the laws. If in effecting an interception a law-enforcement officer commits a trespass . . . the authority to intercept gives the law-enforcement officer no protection.[47]

This clearly appears to contradict my previous argument.

In this regard, I would first like to stress that *R. v. Dass* is not a case in which the police were being prosecuted. What had to be decided by the Manitoba Court of Appeal concerned the admissibility of evidence whose obtainment had implied police trespassing. As in *R. v. Gabourie* the court came squarely on the side of the prosecution by ruling that the evidence was indeed admissible:

> The fact that there has been a trespass or some other civil or, indeed, criminal wrong in the planting of the device does not invalidate the authorization to intercept, and thus does not render the interception unlawful. The authorization granted by the court is an authorization to intercept private communications. How that authorization is carried out is not germane to the issue of the admissibility of the evidence flowing from the interception. If a trespass has been committed, then those who have committed the trespass will be answerable in some other criminal or civil forum.[48]

The crux of the matter is that the police officers involved in this alleged trespassing were, predictably, *never* made answerable "in some other criminal or civil forum." Not only were the police not prosecuted, but they even contributed financially to Mr. Dass's application for leave to appeal the Manitoba Court of Appeal judgment to the Supreme Court of Canada.[49] The Crown felt confident that the Supreme Court would uphold its claim that legal authority to install a listening device implies the authority to make surreptitious entries in order to implant the device. This confidence was, in my opinion, at least partly justified: once the interception of private communications is legalized, how can it not be legal to implant a listening device, even if it implies surreptitious entry (is there some other way to bug a dwelling place or a private office?)? The Supreme Court did not reach a decision on this matter as Mr. Dass was refused permission to appeal.

In making admissible evidence whose adducement implied either illegal entry or discretionary interpretation of the conditions set out in Part IV.1 of the Canadian Criminal Code, rulings such as those in *R. v. Gabourie* and *R. v. Dass* in fact provide legitimacy to police operations which overstretch the limits of legality.

The points made in (5), above, could perhaps be generalized and made to apply to any individual who assumes a public persona by acting as a member of an institution or an agency dedicated in theory to the common good (members of Parliament, functionaries, priests, doctors, lawyers, and so forth). The traditional answer to institutional or occupational deviance is to control it through internal discipline and regulations. This traditional answer raises two difficulties. If internal discipline is strictly enforced, those submitted to it can claim to be the victims of double accountability (both the law and internal regulations and *procedure*). If it is not, the citizen can complain that there is a double standard of accountability: an internal lenient standard for those belonging to a powerful organization and a harsher one for those who have no institutional status.[50]

The remarks made under (2) to (5), above, would tend to suggest that the criminal law does not afford us an unequivocal and efficient means for deciding whether items listed under column C of the tentative list in (1), above, fall within the scope of the offences listed under colum A. This suggestion must, of course, be qualified, the law being fairly clear in certain instances. The cases of unlawful search and police corruption come to mind in this regard. They are, however, quite different. Obtaining a search warrant is specific to police work, whereas the legal provisions concerning corruption are not restricted to police corruption. More importantly, perhaps, a police officer accused of corruption cannot invoke convincingly the collective aim of the organization to minimize his criminal responsibility, whereas a police officer who fails to get a search warrant can (the three police officers prosecuted for their part in operation BRICOLE actually did and got an absolute discharge).

The real issue raised by police deviance concerns what I have called operational (agency) reciprocation, for this is the area where police misconduct is grounded in its legal function. If it is granted that the criminal law does not impose sufficient constraints on police behaviour, should we not expand it and then declare somewhat redundantly that whatever the intent the police should not break the law while enforcing it? That would amount to declaring that the police, acting as such, are subject to strict liability.

Taking this course implies one basic assumption: that it is *possible* for the police to enforce the criminal law without breaking it.[51] Before making this assumption, we should examine the police mandate, remembering that law enforcement to a significant degree operationally mirrors lawbreaking.

The Police Mandate

Legally Defining the Police Mandate

The mandate of the police forces operating in Quebec is defined in sections 39 and 67 of the Quebec Police Act (*Loi de Police*). I shall not quote these sections of the Quebec Police Act, because definitions of the police mandate are fairly standard and usually comprehend, with varying degrees of emphasis, four basic functions: order maintenance, prevention and repression of crime, the enforcement of regional or jurisdictional by-laws and statutes, and the provision of certain services.

Legally defining the police mandate is actually more complex than merely quoting sections of different police Acts. To the extent that the police mandate concerns law enforcement, the scope of this mandate is a direct function of the laws to be enforced. For instance, any increase or decrease of legal criminalization has a corresponding effect upon the scope of the police mandate.

Other problems pertain to special mandates that are issued by political authorities and intended for policing agencies such as the RCMP Security Service. The legal status of these special mandates is both unclear and unclarified by the courts, owing to their confidential character.

Let me illustrate the dimensions of the problems involved. A 1975

Canadian Cabinet decision, "The Role, Tasks and Methods of the RCMP Security Service," was made public in 1978 by the McDonald inquiry into RCMP wrongdoings. It read thus:

> The Cabinet agreed that:
>
> (a) the RCMP Security Service be authorized to maintain internal security by discerning, monitoring, investigating, deterring, preventing and countering individuals and groups in Canada when there are reasonable and probable grounds to believe that they may be engaged in or may be planning to engage in:
>
> (i) espionage or sabotage;
> (ii) foreign intelligence activities directed toward gathering intelligence information relating to Canada;
> (iii) activities directed toward accomplishing governmental change within Canada or elsewhere by force or violence or any criminal means;
> (iv) activities by a foreign power directed toward actual or potential attack or other hostile acts against Canada;
> (v) activities of a foreign or domestic group directed toward the commission of terrorist acts in or against Canada; or
> (vi) the use or the encouragement of the use of force, violence or any criminal means, or the creation or exploitation of civil disorder, for the purpose of accomplishing any of the activities referred to above.

This directive is *partly* patterned after section 16 of the Canadian Official Secrets Act (OSA): that section of the OSA allows the Solicitor General of Canada to authorize on his own the interception of private verbal communications of individuals engaged in subversive activities (according to the Canadian Criminal Code, this authorization is normally issued by a magistrate). Section 16 of the OSA enumerates *five* kinds of subversive activities. This enumeration is retained in the Cabinet directive. There are, however, significant differences between the Security Service mandate, as formulated by the Cabinet, and section 16 of the OSA. Clause (v) of the Cabinet directive speaks of both *domestic* and foreign groups, whereas the OSA only mentions foreign groups. The Cabinet directive also adds a *sixth* category of subversive activities to those already included in section 16 of the OSA.

This raises a problem: Can the Solicitor General of Canada legally authorize on his own the electronic surveillance of the individuals and groups included in the *expanded* list of targets that is found in the Cabinet directive? There can be no question that these individuals and groups were to be effectively submitted to electronic surveillance: paragraph (a) of the Cabinet directive explicitly authorizes the "monitoring" of their activities. Another problem concerns the operational and legal meanings of such expressions as "discerning," "deterring" and "countering." If the operations investigated by both the McDonald and Keable commissions are any indication of the meaning of these words, it is unlikely that they only refer to lawful activities. "Discerning," "deterring" and "countering" can respectively be translated into infiltration, intimidation and destabilization.

All of the previous questions may be reduced to one basic issue: To what extent can a Cabinet directive overrule the law? If the answer given is that it cannot in any way, it becomes difficult to avoid the conclusion that special mandates such as the one quoted above are likely to produce police operational deviance, at least in the form of "technical offences." But again, should it be called "deviance"? If the testimonies made before the Keable Commission have any significance, they bear witness to the fact that these special mandates are considered by the police to be the *very expression of the law.*

Crime Control: Containment or Management?

Notwithstanding the percentage of police activity devoted to it, it is generally agreed that crime control is now the core of the police mandate.[52] A basic characteristic of the police mandate with regard to crime control is that it is *all-encompassing:* it is somehow taken for granted that controlling criminality as defined by the Criminal Code is a feasible task. With reference to the criteria used to evaluate police performance (clearance rates and the like) we may also say that it is assumed that crime control is, for all practical purposes, equivalent to crime repression. This last assumption, at least, seems to me completely unwarranted. In what follows I will provide evidence for this statement by examining the results of the investigations of several commissions of inquiry into alleged police deviance in Quebec.

Since 1894, there have been several commissions of inquiry on the police in Quebec. The main inquiries were those headed respectively by Alderman Rainville in 1894, by Judge L. J. Cannon in 1909–10, by Judge Louis Coderre in 1924–25, by Judge E. Fabre Surveyer in 1943, by Judge Lucien Cannon in 1944, by Judge François Caron from 1950 to 1954, by the lawyer Jean-François Duchaine from 1977 to 1980[53] and by the lawyer Jean F. Keable from 1977 to 1981. With the exception of the Surveyer inquiry, all these investigations have focused on police operations undertaken in the Montreal area, and fall into two categories. Duchaine and Keable investigated police operations directed against terrorism, while the others examined police response to prostitution and gambling and, to a lesser extent, violations of the regulations governing the sale of alcohol. Although these categories (terrorism and morality) are very different, these inquiries have common features which are worth reflecting upon.

Montreal's Red-Light District (1880–1944): A Law Enforcement Ghetto.

The Rainville, L. G. Cannon, Coderre, Lucien Cannon and Caron reports make very repetitious reading; indeed, they seem at times to be no more than different versions of the same report. In order to understand this, something should be said about the situation that prevailed in Montreal and which remained substantially unchanged between 1880 and 1944.[54] Although it was illegal and quite offensive to French-Canadian Catholic morality, prostitution was blatant in Montreal during this whole period. There are, in fact, old photographs which show people literally queuing at the entrances of the brothels, which were for the most part located in a downtown area known even to French-speaking Montrealers as the "Red Light." This situation was periodically denounced by various civic and religious pressure groups, resulting in public inquiries into police deviance (then euphemistically called "police tolerance"). Reports would then be issued and were soon forgotten after a brief, sensational exposure in the press. What put a damper on the fortunes of the Red-Light District was the Canadian Army, which, in 1944, wrote to the municipal council threatening to declare Montreal out of bounds for all soldiers if the Red-Light District was not closed down (the army was concerned about the number of soldiers who were contacting venereal disease). Prostitution was then progressively reorganized, and became less visible.

Witnesses interrogated in the course of these public inquiries were sometimes quite candid about the reasons why the Red-Light District was allowed to prosper. First of all, high-ranking police officers, municipal judges and aldermen all believed that prostitution could neither be eradicated nor significantly curbed and argued that the most that could be done was to keep it from spreading to all parts of the city. Secondly, they did not wish to make it legal, because that would have meant going against the grain of a public opinion strongly influenced by the Catholic Church. The solution hence appeared to be to control prostitution and related activities through *containment:* such illegal activities would be restricted to a fairly small area and would be highly visible. All persons involved in these illegal activities being well known to the police, the police were then in a position to regulate the situation by alternately pulling and loosening the leash. In so doing the police replaced crime repression with a certain form of crime management and profited from the fringe-benefits that it afforded them—money and information—thus becoming partly corrupted.

The Late Front de Libération du Québec (FLQ): A Security Service Colony

The Keable and Duchaine inquiries were concerned with police repression of terrorism in Quebec for a period that extended approximately from 1969 to 1973. Part of what the Keable Commission investigated has been well publicized, to some extent because the federal McDonald inquiry on RCMP wrongdoings has conducted a parallel investigation into the same police activities.[55] There is, however, an important part of the Keable inquiry that has not received as much attention, although it has already been made public both through the commission's hearings and its final report. This part of the investigation dealt with the infiltration of the FLQ by police agents, in November 1970 and during the following years.

For those not familiar with recent Canadian history, I shall very briefly recall events that took place in 1970. The FLQ was a terrorist organization responsible for much violence in Quebec from 1963 to 1972. In October of 1970, the FLQ abducted Mr. James Richard Cross, a British diplomat, and a few days later Mr. Pierre Laporte, a Quebec Cabinet Minister. Mr. Laporte was subsequently killed by his captors; members of the FLQ who had kidnapped Mr. Cross finally freed him in exchange for safe-conduct to Cuba, their hiding-place having been discovered by the police. These political kidnappings led to the proclamation of a state of apprehended insurrection in Quebec and to the intervention of the army, thus generating a major crisis in Canadian history.

To begin with, the police forces in Quebec completely failed to prevent the kidnappings. As the Duchaine report makes abundantly clear, the police forces were quickly overwhelmed by the task of finding where the first hostage was held; after the second abduction, they went into what was described by police officers as a "panic."[56] There was severe criticism of their impotence after the crisis, and they decided that they were not going to be caught unawares a second time.

Having succeeded by November of 1970 in infiltrating the FLQ cell that provided outside support to the group that had abducted the British diplomat, the combined anti-terrorist forces operating in Quebec devised a strategy for the aftermath of the crisis, which was still in progress. (Mr. Cross was to be liberated only on December 3, 1970). This strategy first called for the intimidation and destabilization of persons and groups suspected of leanings toward the FLQ, to prevent it from developing into a mass movement. However, persons who belonged to cells already infiltrated by the police were to be allowed to operate, within certain limits, under close police surveillance. Thus, as the Keable inquiry has shown, the late FLQ gradually became a Security Service colony.

One of the infiltrators was controlled by the anti-terrorist squad of the Montreal municipal police, and the information that she transmitted was distributed to other anti-terrorist sections (Sûreté du Québec and RCMP).[57] As a result of this, after November 14, 1970, the vast majority of FLQ communiqués were seen by the police before they were distributed. In other words, despite their violent content, their publication was "approved" by the police. Indeed, an RCMP officer testified that he had been told by colleagues in the Montreal police department that the special paper used by the FLQ to authenticate its communiqués was channelled to them by the anti-terrorist squad of their department. Furthermore, it has now been established that a Montreal police officer provided money that he knew was to be used by an FLQ cell to buy equipment for a projected kidnapping (including a polaroid camera to take photographs of the intended hostage).

In another instance, although they were forewarned of every detail (place, date and persons involved) of a planned theft of dynamite, and even though they followed an FLQ reconnaissance party to the scene of the future crime, the Montreal police did nothing to stop the theft when it took place. This list could be considerably extended. For example, the following acts of terrorism all took place under close police surveillance: Molotov cocktail throwing, placement of a bomb at the back of a postal station[58] and attempted extortion against an airline company. A police infiltrator also played a significant part in recruiting a team, most of whom were juveniles, for a robbery and in selecting the target of the robbery (a bingo hall). This time, however, the police were waiting and everyone was arrested.

At the end of 1971, the terrorist ideologue Pierre Vallières, who was then in hiding, had an article published in the Montreal daily *Le Devoir*. This article called for the FLQ to disband and work toward the goal of Quebec independence through democratic means by joining the Parti Québécois. A few days after the appeal by Vallières, an RCMP team issued a fraudulent terrorist communiqué denouncing him as a turncoat and urging the FLQ to resume the armed struggle. The police, it seemed, were worried about losing their colony.

However different from the repression of prostitution and related activities in Montreal during the first half of this century, this second brief case study does bear features in common with it. Both cases exemplify a strategy of *containment* that is generated by a tacit admission of failure to repress or prevent a certain form of criminality. The implementation of this strategy brings about a reorientation of the police mandate, crime control giving way to crime management. Crime management finally begets police deviance, in the form of either the discretionary granting of impunity to lawbreakers, or provocation, or corruption. Crime management also blurs the line between law enforcement and law violation, the police informer and the undercover agent being typical inhabitants of "a lawless land." I am inclined to believe that any law enforcement field where the police are very highly dependent on informers (such as in narcotics cases) involves a certain amount of crime management.[59]

A further inference could be drawn, at least tentatively, from the preceding remarks. It is widely recognized that deprived minorities are a favoured target of police action. To the variety of factors adduced to explain this situation, one could add police operational strategies: a group of people whose physical and social lives are confined within the boundaries of a ghetto becomes readily available for police encirclement and penetration.

Conclusion

Before concluding, I shall briefly summarize the points I have made. I began with the assumption that in order to be complied with, police control had to be grounded in law. I then proceeded to examine whether the criminal law, as it stood and was applied, did provide such ground. Not only did I try to show that prosecution of alleged police deviance was legally bound to be irredeemably controversial, but I argued that one of the basic functions of the criminal law was to legitimize for the police what was prohibited to the citizens. Recent Canadian legislation on the interception of private communications serves as both an illustration and a symbol of this point. In the Statutes of Canada, Bill C-176 is referred to as the Protection of Privacy Act. It has been made part of the Canadian Criminal Code under the heading "Invasion of Privacy"; this part of the Code sets out the conditions under which the police can legally proceed to intercept private communications. We have reviewed court decisions that tended to dilute the conditions bearing upon the admissibility of evidence obtained under Part IV.1 ("Invasion of Privacy") of the Criminal Code.

Postponing the inference that the law should be expanded to provide the controls that are now lacking, I decided to inspect the police mandate in order to find whether it could be fulfilled in *strict* accordance with the law. With regard to special mandates that are given to an apparatus such as the RCMP Security Service, I suggested that it was unlikely that they could be. On the basis of two case studies, I further tried to show that in order to fulfil duties which far exceeded their operational capabilities, the police were led to translate crime control into crime containment, with the latter giving way to crime management. This discussion could be summed up by saying that police impotence breeds police deviance.

It would then seem that we are faced with a contradiction: the proliferation of desirable legal checks upon the behaviour and operations of the police will only add to their impotence, thus generating more deviance. A frequently raised objection to the exclusionary rule, for instance, is that it increases police dependence upon confessions of guilt, thereby generating unlawful pressures on suspects in order to obtain their confession.

However, this contradiction may not be insurmountable. It could be seen as revealing the shortcomings of the orthodox strategy of solving problems of deviance. This strategy is to legislate and to criminalize whatever forms of deviance one wishes to deter. There are at least two objections to such a strategy.

The first objection is that such criminal legislation is bound to be so complex that it is doubtful that it could be enacted. I shall, in this regard, refer the reader to the second case study undertaken above. One of the points that can be inferred from this study is that it shows, at least in part, how simplistic it is to accept without question the symbolic dichotomy between law enforcers on the one hand and lawbreakers on the other hand. What, for instance, would be the legal predicament of a paid police informer acting under the ambiguous direction of his police controller?

A second objection to the orthodox strategy is that it is bound to produce legal formalism if it ignores the fact that police operational deviance is partly grounded in what is perceived, sometimes legitimately, as operational necessity or constraints. Instead of a definition, I shall give an example of what I mean by "legal formalism." I have already alluded to that example. Section 178.12 of the Canadian Criminal Code (Part IV.1, "Invasion of Privacy") requires the police to obtain legal authorization from a magistrate in order to intercept private verbal communications. This protection of privacy is, however, severely restricted, as we have seen, by section 16 of the OSA, which allows the Solicitor General of Canada to issue on his own an authorization for invading the privacy of persons suspected of subversive activities (domestic and foreign). "Subversive activities" is a blanket term that can be made to apply to almost every sort of political dissent. What is then conceded by a piece of legislation is taken back by another one, which bows to the operational pressures of police security work.

There are also numerous risks inherent in the orthodox strategy. The imperative of checking the exercise by the police of the powers they have at present may be so mesmerizing that resisting with due force their legal acquisition of new and more threatening powers is neglected. In a recent interview, the Commissioner of the RCMP proposed that his force be granted access to all computer data banks that the federal government possesses on the citizens (medical files, income tax files, unemployment insurance files, and so forth).[60] It may be much more important to counter such access than to build a legal machinery making, for example, the prosecution of police brutality easier (section 26 of the Canadian Criminal Code [use of excessive force] could, in this respect, be expanded).

A second risk is that legislative control can actually lead to a widening of the scope of legitimation afforded by the law to police operations. Eventually, for instance, a well-intentioned endeavour to control the interception of private communications will produce further legislation or jurisprudence legitimizing trespassing by police when they are implanting a listening device that they have legal authority to use.[61]

The contradiction referred to at the beginning of this section is in fact generated by the incorrect assumption that the only source of police impotence is and always will be a lack of or a decreasing of police powers through legal checks.[62] That need not be the only interpretation of my remark that police impotence breeds police deviance. It may be that the true source of police powerlessness to control crime is in the sweeping nature of their mandate, which includes tasks other than crime control and is not specific with respect to crime control. Unlawful political dissidence and labour unrest, victimless breaches of the law, petty robbery, rape, and white-collar fraud are *very* different things, although they can all qualify as "crimes." If there is, furthermore, any sort of failure—be it political, institutional or operational—to distinguish between crimes and regulatory offences which carry penalties, then crime control becomes an all-encompassing activity.[63]

Therein lies perhaps a second strategy of uprooting police operational deviance: a redefinition of the police mandate, which could lead to a refocusing of their presently dissipated activities. This redefinition of the police mandate would imply several things. It would imply, first of all, a specification of the police function and a referral to other agencies of peripheral duties that the police have come to assume, although they bear no relation to the core of their mandate (crime control).

It would also imply that the criminal law itself be re-evaluated and its scope restricted, thus allowing the police to concentrate efficiently on crimes that are harmful to society. It may be that decriminalization of citizens' behaviour would more effectively check police deviance than criminalization of delinquent police behaviour. It would finally entail a renegotiation of the police mandate between police organizations and the community they are supposed to protect.

I shall add one last remark. It is clear that the two strategies I have briefly discussed do not constitute rigid alternatives. Obviously, the law should embody necessary checks that are now wanting (against, for instance, police provocation and the abuses of long-term infiltration). But I do not believe that all efforts should be invested in this direction alone and that the crucial necessity of reconsidering what can be requested and reasonably expected from the police should be ignored.

NOTES

1. *Rapport de la Commission d'enquête sur des opérations policières en territoire québécois* (Quebec: Ministère de la Justice, 1981). All references to the commission and its report will be respectively made under "Keable Commission" and "Keable Report."
2. U.S. Senate, *Intelligence Activities and the Rights of Americans*, Final Report of the Select Church Committee to Study Governmental Operations with respect to Intelligence Activities (Washington, D.C.: Government Printing Office, 1976).
3. A detailed report on police infiltration has recently been published in the United States. See *Socialist Workers Party et al. v. The Attorney General of the United States et al.*, United States District Court, Southern District of New York. *Final Report of Special Master*, published by the Political Rights Defence Fund (New York, 1980). The Special Master was Mr. Justice Charles D. Breitel.
4. In Simon Holdaway (ed.) *The British Police* (London: Edward Arnold, 1979) at 24–40.
5. See, for example, *R. v. Biron* (1975), 23 C.C.C. (2d) 513; *R. v. Gabourie (No. 1)* (1977), 31 C.C.C. (2d) 471; *R. v. Dietrich* (1978), 39 C.C.C. (2d) 361; *R. v. Dass* (1979), 8 C.R. (3d) 224; *Morris v. Beardmore* (1980), 2 All E.R. 753; and recent judgments by the Supreme Court of Ontario in *R. v. Dedman* (1980) and by the Supreme Court of Canada in *Colet v. R.* (1981).
6. See R. M. Hare, *The Language of Morals* (Oxford: Clarendon Press, 1961) at 79–93.
7. Under the "legalistic fallacy," such sentences as "Deviation from legality is institutionalized in the law itself" become contradictory. This example is taken from McBarnet's previously quoted article (p. 39).

8. This agent was at the time being prosecuted for another offence: he had placed a bomb at the back of the house of a well-known Montreal businessman. While testifying in that case, the agent declared that he had done "much worse for the Force" than what he was presently being prosecuted for. Upon questioning he revealed his part in the police break-in that went under the code name BRICOLE. He was at the time of the break-in working for the RCMP.
9. Keable Commission, public exhibit P-95; the emphasis is mine. The acronyms "APLQ," "MDPPQ" and "MCP" stand respectively for "Agence de presse libre du Québec," "Mouvement pour la défense des prisonniers politiques québécois" and "Montreal Community Police" (Montreal's municipal police department). The APLQ and the MDPPQ were both targets of operation BRICOLE.
10. Several RCMP officers took part in the writing of this report and of its different attachments.
11. Keable Commission, public exhibit P-126; the emphasis is mine.
12. Keable Commission, public exhibit P-127; the emphasis is mine. The acronym "SPCUM" refers to the Montreal municipal police department.
13. Unconditional discharge is given according to section 662.1 of the Canadian Criminal Code. It is an exceptional outcome in a criminal procedure.
14. The influence of the police over prosecutors has been long recognized. See Brian A. Grosman, *The Prosecutor* (Toronto: University of Toronto Press, 1969) at 21. One can also cite the Law Reform Commission of Canada: "It is the crown prosecutor, then, not the police, who has legal responsibility for laying charges and conducting prosecutions. In practice the day by day business of deciding whom to prosecute and on what charges is left to the police." See *Diversion*, Law Reform Commission of Canada, Working Paper 7 (Ottawa: Information Canada, 1975) at 8.
15. Keable Commission, public exhibit P-108. The phrase in quotation marks is a translation from the French: "Prise non autorisée de dynamite sur un chantier de construction."
16. One of the investigations into police corruption that produced the most indictments and convictions of police officers was conducted in Chicago between 1970 and 1976. It had to invoke the Hobbs Act (a U.S. federal statute against extortion affecting interstate commerce) to prosecute police officers who were shaking down bars in downtown Chicago. See Herbert Beigel and Allan Beigel, *Beneath the Badge: A Story of Police Corruption* (New York: Harper and Row Publishers, 1977). Since 1978, the Montreal municipal police (SPCUM) has shown some readiness to prosecute its members. Approximately 14 officers were prosecuted between May and December 1978. The approximate figures for 1979 and 1980 are respectively 23 and 13 prosecutions. According to my sources, the charges most often laid were theft, assault and sexual offences. They seem to pertain more to self-interest deviance than to operational deviance. The interpretation of these figures is very difficult, because of the reluctance of the SPCUM to give information about internal discipline. I do not know, for instance, who the victims were in the cases involving theft. They may have been citizens, fellow officers or the police department itself.
17. Nobody went further than Jeremy Bentham in trying to devise a penology that would mirror criminality. See his *Principles of Penal Law*, p. II, bk. I, chap. 8

(p. 408 of vol. I of John Bowring's edition of *The Works of Jeremy Bentham* [Edinburgh, 1843]).

18. For an early and definitive statement of this paradox, see Plato, *The Laws*, bk. 9, 860b and c. For a contemporary statement, see Peter Macnaughton-Smith, *Permission to be Slightly Free* (Ottawa: Ministry of Supply and Services, 1976) at 32–33. This study was undertaken for the Law Reform Commission of Canada.
19. The controversy about the undefinability of ethical terms has been the topic of moral theory ever since the publication of G. E. Moore's *Principia Ethica* (Cambridge: Cambridge University Press, 1903).
20. For instance, the most explicit definitions of "unlawful political dissidence" are not to be found in the Canadian Criminal Code but in the Official Secrets Act, Revised Statutes of Canada (R.S.C.) 1970, c. 0-3, modified in 1974 by the Protection of Privacy Act, Statutes of Canada (S.C.) 1973–74, c. 50.
21. See Donald Black, *The Behavior of Law* (New York: Academic Press, 1976).
22. R.S.C. 1970, c. 10 (2nd Supp.).
23. In *Fowler v. Padget* (1798), 101 E.R. 1103, 7 T.R. 509.
24. It is to be found in Sir Edward Coke's *Institutes of the Laws of England*, pt. II, chap. 20: ". . . for the intent maketh felony and so are the books to be intended."

    Mens rea has been widely discussed in legal doctrine; it has also been the object of extensive jurisprudence. However, after the landmark case *R. v. Prince* (1875), it seems that some of the most significant developments were made with regard to the notion of strict liability as it bears upon offences which are not criminal but prohibited in the public interest. A recent judgment by the Supreme Court of Canada (*R. v. Sault Ste. Marie* (1978), 3 C.R. (3d) 30) is a case in point. In this ruling, which concerned the offence of pollution, the court articulated a judicial middle ground between offences in which *mens rea* must be proven by prosecution (criminal offences) and offences of absolute liability. The doctrine of *mens rea*, as it applies to criminal offences, is little affected by this judgment:

    > The doctrine of the guilty mind expressed in terms of intention or recklessness, but not negligence, is at the foundation of the law of crimes. In the case of true crimes there is a presumption that a person should not be held liable for the wrongfulness of his act if that act is without mens rea. . . . Blackstone made the point over 200 years ago in words still apt: "to constitute a crime against human law, there must be first a vicious will, and secondly, an unlawful act consequent upon such vicious will." . . . *I would emphasize at the outset that nothing in the discussion which follows is intended to dilute or erode that basic principle.* [*R. v. Sault Ste. Marie* (1978), at 34–35; the emphasis is mine]

25. For general intent, see, for example, sections 245 and 287 of the Canadian Criminal Code.
26. For specific intent, see, for example, sections 246, 283 and 302 of the Canadian Criminal Code.
27. *Leary v. R.* (1977), 37 C.R.N.S. 60 at 82–83.
28. For uses of "intent," see, for example, sections 283 and 306 of the Canadian Criminal Code; for "purpose," see sections 300, 301 and 302; see also section 4 of the Narcotic Control Act (R.S.C. 1970, c. N-1). In its draft legislation on sexual offences, the Law Reform Commission of Canada has proposed to define sexual interference—formerly rape, attempted rape and gross indecency—as

touching either directly or indirectly "for a sexual purpose . . . another person without the consent of that person." See *Report on Sexual Offences* (Ottawa: Law Reform Commission of Canada, 1978) at 49.

29. This definition is a paraphrase of G. Williams' *Criminal Law* as quoted in *Lewis v. R.* (1979), 10 C.R. (3d) 299 at 309.
30. *Lewis v. R.*, at 308.
31. Motive is generally incriminating and can be used as circumstantial evidence for *mens rea*. See *Cloutier v. R.* (1940), 73 C.C.C. 1; *R. v. Hicklin* (1868), L.R. 3 Q.B. 360; *R. v. Lewis* (1903), 7 C.C.C. 261. Section 423 (2)(b) of the Canadian Criminal Code states that conspiracy to effect a lawful purpose by unlawful means is an indictable offence.
32. See *R. v. Handfield* (1953), 17 C.R. 343 (Que. C.A.). See also *R. v. Kerr* (1965), 4 C.C.C. 37 (Man. C.A.); *R. v. Wilkins* (1965), 2 C.C.C. 189 (Ont. C.A.); *R. v. Chapman* (1969), 3 C.C.C. 358; *R. v. Clark* (1971), 17 C.R.N.S. 56; *R. v. Paris* (1972), 15 C.R.N.S. 111.
33. *Lewis v. R.*, at 312.
34. *Lewis v. R.*, at 314. Since the very controversial ruling by the House of Lords in *D.P.P. v. Smith* (1960), the relationships between motive and *mens rea* have been the object of intense debate in the United Kingdom. Anyone believing that all is clear in this field should read the very thorough discussion conducted in *Hyam v. D.P.P.* (1974), 2 All E.R. 41. The accused appealed a murder conviction before the House of Lords on the basis that her motive was not homicidal. The appeal was dismissed by a split decision (three to two). In his dissenting opinion, Lord Diplock said that he believed that all judges agreed that if the English law of homicide "were based on concepts that are satisfactory, both intellectually and morally," the appeal would be allowed.
35. On this, see John B. Wolf, "Enforcement Terrorism" in *Police Studies* 3, no. 4 (Winter 1981): 45–54. Wolf makes an interesting distinction between agitational terrorism (what we normally mean by "terrorism") and enforcement terrorism (police terrorism).
36. On this, see chap. 5, "Laundered Language," of W. Edward Mann and John Alan Lee, *The RCMP vs The People* (Don Mills, Ontario: General Publishing Co., 1979) at 67–86.
37. Keable Commission, public exhibit P-109b, quoted in the report at 340–41. The standard RCMP expression used to refer to such incidents was "confrontation interviews." Hundreds of those were conducted in Quebec between 1970 and 1973. See the Keable Report at 339.
38. Sections 7 and 10d of the Montreal municipal police department's code of professional ethics parallel sections 117 and 26 of the Criminal Code (see *Gazette officielle du Québec*, 14 juin 1978, 110e année, no. 29; *Règlement sur la déontologie et la discipline des policiers de la Communauté urbaine de Montréal*, A.C. 1711-78, 24 mai 1978). It can be foreseen that allegations concerning the making of a false return to a process and the use of excessive force will first have to be made before the complaint board for the Montreal municipal police department, where they are initially treated as disciplinary faults. If they are judged serious enough by that board, they may be channelled to a criminal court. Thus, less serious criminal offences can be treated as disciplinary faults.

39. Section 455.3(1)(a)(ii) of the Criminal Code states that in certain cases a justice of the peace may hear witnesses in order to determine whether an information is grounded in fact. This inquest is held before the preliminary inquiry; it is a rather exceptional procedure. Such an inquest was held when three police officers were indicted for their part in the BRICOLE police operation.
40. Operation HAM was conducted during the night of January 9, 1972. It was a very elaborate operation, directly supervised by the RCMP Security Service headquarters in Ottawa and authorized at the highest level of the service. Members of the RCMP broke into the offices of Messageries Dynamiques Inc., a private company that was doing business with the Parti Québécois. The Parti Québécois is a provincial political party devoted to the cause of Quebec's political independence; some of its members had been elected to the Quebec provincial Parliament in 1972. The RCMP took hold of computer tapes which listed the names of all members of the Parti Québécois and provided some information on them; it had the tapes copied during the same night by a friend of an ex-member of the RCMP who played an important part in the operation. This friend did not know that he was partaking in an RCMP operation. The original tapes were returned to the Messageries Dynamiques before the end of the night. The copies of the tapes were sent to Ottawa to be printed out; they were finally destroyed, with their print-outs, in 1975.
41. I intentionally use the Latin *finis reus* to stress that, like *mens rea*, this expression refers to a *field* of related concepts (motive, motivation, purpose, institutional goal, operational necessity) which interfaces with the conceptual field of *mens rea*.
42. It is standard procedure in Security Service operations to restrict information given to an operative to the minimum needed for him to perform his task in a particular context. Thus, if a team of agents is to act as look-outs during an operation involving surreptitious entry, they will not generally be told what the team performing the entry is going to do inside the place they are breaking into. Well over 50 persons were informed on a "need-to-know basis" in the RCMP operation HAM. The "need-to-know basis" is but another example of the symmetry between law enforcement and law violation: the fragmentation of groups into insulated cells is the corresponding practice in the field of terrorism.
43. Keable Commission, exhibit H-35, para. 4, quoted in the report at 411.
44. Keable Commission, exhibit H-36, quoted in the report at 374 and 412 (the emphasis is mine). A PUMA operation is a clandestine search which does not imply seizure. A VAMPIRE operation consists of implanting a listening device (referred to as a "technical source"). Bill C-176 is the Protection of Privacy Act.
45. *R.* v. *Gabourie (No. 1)* (1977), 31 C.C.C. (2d) 471 at 476.
46. *R.* v. *Gabourie (No. 2)* (1977), 31 C.C.C. (2d) 485 at 490.
47. *R.* v. *Dass* (1979), 8 C.R. (3d) 224 at 246.
48. *R.* v. *Dass* (1979), 8 C.R. (3d) 224 at 245–46.
49. This information was communicated to me personally by one of Mr. Dass's lawyers.
50. Such a situation, where neither the public nor the police are satisfied with the internal enforcement of discipline, was described by Mr. Justice René Marin in his report on RCMP internal discipline. See René Marin, *Le rapport de la commission d'enquête sur les plaintes du public, la discipline interne et le règlement des*

griefs au sein de la Gendarmerie Royale du Canada (Ottawa: Information Canada, 1976).

51. The 1968 report of the Royal Commission on Security (the Mackenzie Report) admits that violations of the spirit, if not of the letter, of the law are unavoidable in the field of Security Service operations. These operations have so far been the responsibility of the Canadian police and particularly of the RCMP. It is in no way certain that this conclusion of the Mackenzie Report does not also apply to regular police operations. See section 57 of the abridged version of the *Report of the Royal Commission of Inquiry on Security* (Ottawa: Queen's Printer, June 1969).
52. For a recent overview, see Peter K. Manning, *Police Work* (Cambridge, Mass.: MIT Press, 1977) at 90 et seq.
53. Lawyer Jean-François Duchaine did not actually head a commission of inquiry; he conducted an investigation into the October Crisis on behalf of the Quebec Ministry of Justice. He did not have the legal powers of a commissioner.
54. These dates are approximate; it is quite possible that the Montreal Red-Light District was in existence before 1880. On this, see Jean-Paul Brodeur, *L'ordre délinquant* (Montreal: Hurtubise [forthcoming]).
55. These activities included theft of dynamite, the burning of a barn, the APLQ break-in, the issuing of a fraudulent FLQ communiqué, the reproduction of the list of members of the Parti Québécois and the intimidation of citizens in order to recruit them as informers.
56. See Jean-François Duchaine, *Rapport sur les événements d'octobre 1970* (Gouvernement du Québec: Ministère de la justice, 1980) at 65–67 and 253–56.
57. As the Keable Report makes clear, the infiltrator whose activities I have referred to was not the only one who had penetrated the FLQ. If one adds to her activities those of a similar kind performed by other informers, one can perhaps surmise the degree of control that the police were in a position to exercise on FLQ terrorism. Indeed, one police officer went so far as to declare to a Quebec government investigator that "in 1972, we [the police] were the FLQ." See the Keable Report at 236.
58. Through their informer, the police had replaced the dynamite used in making the bomb with dummies. This fact was not revealed in court when the terrorist was later prosecuted, after having spontaneously confessed to his crime during a routine police check (he was in hospital, following a traffic accident).
59. On this, see Edward Jay Epstein, *Agency of Fear* (New York: G. P. Putnam's Sons, 1977) at 103–110.
60. See *Le Devoir*, February 10, 1981, p. 2.
61. Since this paper was written, the McDonald Report on the RCMP Security Service has been released. The report recommends that surreptitious entries made by the police in order to install a listening device should be legalized.
62. The Duchaine Report shows that granting the police unmeasured powers during the October Crisis of 1970 did nothing to solve the hostage problem. It probably precipitated the killing of Mr. Laporte by hardening the resolve of his abductors. It did not speed the liberation of Mr. Cross, who was freed more than six weeks after the recourse to the War Measures Act. It has left a deep scar on Quebec's public opinion and has damaged, perhaps irretrievably, the image of the police in the province.

63. The volume of Canadian criminal law is evaluated thus by the Law Reform Commission of Canada: "700 Criminal Code sections, 20,000 federal offences and 20,000 in provincial law not to mention the welter of municipal laws": *Our Criminal Law*, a report by the Law Reform Commission of Canada (Ottawa: Information Canada, 1976) at 12.

Chapter 7

The Role of Police Boards and Commissions as Institutions of Municipal Police Governance*

Philip C. Stenning

Introduction

Research and writing on control of the police has tended for the most part to concentrate on those aspects of the internal administration, management and reward structures within police forces which are thought to encourage (or at least not discourage) proper police practices. In this essay, some aspects of the structures of external control over police forces are examined within the Canadian context. Until very recently, extremely little research of significance has focused on the various structures which have been established to provide for the government of police forces, the relationships between the police themselves (especially the chief) and these governing authorities, and the influence of politics on their operations. By examining the historical and modern development of one type of police governing authority in Canada, this essay takes a first tentative step in filling this gap in existing knowledge about police accountability and control, and in identifying some important issues for further study.

Policing in Canada is undertaken by a variety of public, quasi-public and private bodies operating under widely divergent mandates.[1] Thus, existing public police forces here include a federal police force (the Royal Canadian Mounted Police) operating under a federal legislative mandate;[2]

---

*This essay is based on research commissioned by the Commission of Inquiry into Certain Activities of the Royal Canadian Mounted Police (the McDonald Inquiry), and completed in 1979. The author wishes to express his gratitude to the commission for its support of this research, as well as to the numerous persons and organizations across Canada who so willingly and extensively co-operated in this research. The views expressed in this essay are those of the author, and do not necessarily reflect those of the commission or of others who participated in the research on which it is based. This essay was presented as a paper at the 52nd Annual Meeting of the Canadian Political Science Association, Université du Québec à Montréal, June 4, 1980.

two provincial police forces (the Ontario Provincial Police force and the Quebec Police Force/Sûrete du Québec), each operating under provincial statutes;[3] a large number of municipal police forces, most of which operate under a combination of provincial statutes and municipal by-laws;[4] and a host of special-purpose police forces (e.g., harbour and railway police), each operating under specific federal or provincial statutory mandates.[5] To further complicate matters, the federal police force provides police services, under contract, to eight of the ten provinces, and to a large number of municipalities in those same eight provinces, and the Ontario Provincial Police force provides such services on a similar basis to a number of municipalities in that province.

The concerns of this essay are limited to the operation of *municipal police forces*—that is, those police forces established by municipalities under the authority of provincial legislation and/or municipal by-laws. More particularly, the essay focuses on the evolution, status and role of a particular kind of special-purpose body—known colloquially as a local police board or commission[6]—which has been adopted by a number of these municipal jurisdictions as the governing authority for their municipal police forces. The essay will also touch on the role of the provincial police commissions which have been established in seven of the ten provinces, but only to the extent that this role impinges on the government of municipal police forces. The essay will not concern itself, however, with the particular issues which arise over the government of municipal police services which are provided not through an autonomous municipal police force, but by an external police force (e.g., the RCMP or the OPP) under contract with a municipality.

Although the focus of the essay will be on police boards established to govern municipal police forces, it will be readily apparent that many of the issues and principles that arise out of a discussion of the status and role of such boards have implications of a much more general nature relating to the governance and control of policing in a democratic society. The purpose of this essay is to draw out these more general issues and principles and illustrate their application and significance in the context of the governance of municipal police forces in Canada.

The essay begins with a brief description of the historical origins of modern municipal police forces in Canada, emphasizing the traditional connection between the police and the lower judiciary. The essay then describes the development of modern municipal police boards, and discusses some possible explanations for the original adoption of this mode of police governance. This discussion focuses particularly on two dominant themes—the shift from judicial to non-judicial control of the police, and the struggle between provincial and municipal governments for domination over the structure of municipal police governance. There follows a description of the current variety of municipal police boards found in Canadian jurisdictions, and of their mandate and the functions they perform. Four significant influences on the role of municipal police boards in governing their forces—the notion of police independence, the concept of police professionalism, the rise of police unionism, and the modern resurgence of provincial influence over municipal institutions—are then described and discussed. The essay next considers the matter of the accountability of police boards themselves, and describes some recent controversies which this issue has generated in the Province of Ontario. This discussion, as well as the essay's conclusions, focuses particularly on the issue of the role of politics in the government of municipal police forces, and the different positions which have been propounded on this controversial issue. The extent to which this debate has been coloured by the historical association between the police and the judiciary is also considered.

The Origins of Municipal Police Forces in Canada

At the time of Confederation in 1867, policing systems were already well established in many parts of Canada. Kelly and Kelly (1976: 1) note that the first "policeman" in the colonies which later became Canada appeared on the streets of Quebec City in 1751. During these early days, in both Upper and Lower Canada, and later on the West coast and in the Maritimes, the power to appoint constables resided exclusively in judicial officers, usually called justices of the peace. These early constables, then, although they performed a variety of protective functions, such as watching for fires and patrolling the streets at night (the so-called "night watch"), were in essence officers of the law whose primary function was to perform the administrative tasks (such as the serving of writs and summonses, and the making of arrests) which were necessary to the effective performance of the judicial process. In fact, until quite late in the nineteenth century, their remuneration (for those who were remunerated) was usually determined in accordance with a well-established tariff associated with the performance of these administrative tasks. Thus, a constable would receive so much money for each summons served, each arrest effected, and so forth (McDougall, 1971b: 15–16).

With the great industrial development and urbanization of the late eighteenth and nineteenth centuries, the basic community structures within which the early constables were able to work to maintain order and preserve the peace began to break down. In particular, the increased mobility of the population (itself spurred by the rising demands for labour to service new industrial enterprise, and facilitated by the development of more sophisticated transportation technologies) meant that communities themselves, particularly urban ones, no longer had the capacity for self-policing on which the early system of constabulary had relied so heavily for support. Under these circumstances, it became increasingly evident, both in England and in Canada, that a new system of policing would be required to cope with the problem of maintaining order in these new urban environments. In Quebec, the authorities initially resorted to the militia for this purpose (Barot and Berard, 1972), a tactic which was perhaps understandable in light of the recent conquest of that territory by the British. Elsewhere in the country, however, and in Quebec as well once civilian government was re-established, the traditions of local responsibility for, and control over, policing were not to be so easily swept aside,[7] and the authorities sought to adapt the old system of constabulary to meet new demands. At first, therefore, the power of appointing the new urban constables, and of thereby creating the first modern municipal police forces in the larger urban centres, remained with judicial officers such as the justices of the peace and the newly established "police magistrates." In some instances, grand juries were given such powers of appointment.[8]

This assignment of responsibility for the municipal police to the lower judiciary was a clear reflection of the prevailing practice with respect to the government of the police in England at the time (Critchley, 1978), and is understandable not only by reference to the history of the police in the mother country, but also in the context of the absence, at the time, of any structure of locally elected municipal government. It is important to understand, furthermore, that while today we think of justices of the peace and magistrates as purely judicial officers, this was not the case in the eighteenth and early nineteenth centuries. Justices of the peace in particular, at that time, were charged with a whole range of functions and responsibilities, which included not only, or even primarily, judicial functions, but also administrative functions of local government (see Moir, 1969). The fact that the responsibility for the government of municipal police forces originated with the judiciary in Canada, however, is of cardinal importance in understanding subsequent developments with respect to the government of these forces.

The nineteenth century saw the emergence, both in England and in Canada, of local municipal government, and with it some highly significant transformations in the arrangements for the government of municipal police forces. After the failure of the reformers to achieve the election, rather than appointment by the central authorities, of justices of the peace in Upper Canada, one of the first steps toward responsible elected local government was the creation, during the 1830s, of five-member elected boards with local government powers in the province's towns (Aitchison, 1949). These boards were called boards of police[9]—a nomenclature that is indicative of the fact that the term "police" originally had a much broader meaning than is normally ascribed to it today. As the editor of *The New Municipal Manual for Upper Canada* noted in 1859, referring to the power of municipalities in Upper Canada at that time to "establish, regulate and maintain a police":

> The word "police" is generally applied to the internal regulations of cities and towns, whereby the individuals of any City or Town, like members of a well governed family, are bound to conform their general behaviour to the rules of propriety, good neighbourhood, and good manners, and to be decent, industrious and inoffensive in their respective situations . . .; but the word, as here used, has a still more restricted meaning, for it is intended to apply to those paid men who in every City and Town are appointed to execute police laws, and who in many respects correspond with Constables of Rural Municipalities. [Harrison, 1859: 158]

While the justices of the peace retained control of the police in the smaller towns and rural areas, the incorporation of the cities and larger towns of Upper Canada during the 1830s and 1840s saw this control pass to the newly established mayors and their elected local councils. These newly elected officials were granted authority and powers that would astonish their modern counterparts, including not only the administrative, but in some cases also the judicial powers that had formerly been exercised by the justices of the peace. The Act incorporating the City of Toronto in 1834,[10] for instance, gave to the city council the authority "to regulate the police of the said City," and imposed on it the duty to "from time to time, employ so many Constables for the said City as to them may seem necessary and proper, and pay them such sum per annum for their services as to the said Common Council shall appear just." Such constables were "bound to obey the orders of the Mayor and Alderman, or any or either of them, in enforcing the laws of this Province, and the ordinances of the said City." Another section of the Act provided that:

> The Mayor and Alderman, or any one or more of them shall have full power and authority to take up, arrest or order to be taken up or arrested, all or any rogues, vagabonds, drunkards and disorderly persons, and as the said Mayor or Alderman, or any two of them, shall see cause, to order all or any such rogues, vagabonds, drunkards and disorderly persons to be committed to any workhouse that may hereafter be erected, or else to any House of Correction, there to receive such punishment, not exceeding one month's imprisonment, or the common stocks, as the said Mayor and Alderman, or any two of them, shall think fit.

In addition to these substantial powers, the Act provided that the mayor, assisted by the alderman or any one of them, were constituted as a court of record called "the Mayor's Court of the City of Toronto," having "the like powers and . . . the same jurisdiction over crimes and misdemeanours arising within the City . . . which the courts of General Quarter Sessions of the Peace [i.e., the justices of the peace] within this Province now or hereafter shall have by law."[11]

From these provisions it will be apparent that as a result of the efforts of the nineteenth century municipal reformers in Upper Canada, not only the executive and administrative powers of the justices of the peace (including their control over municipal police forces), but also their judicial powers, were transferred without discrimination into the hands of the new local politicians. The fact that control over municipal police forces was transferred to elected municipal politicians not as a discrete policy decision, but as part of a wholesale transfer of local government power from justices of the peace to locally elected politicians, and that this local government power included virtually the whole administration of justice (including the lower courts), is critical to an understanding of subsequent developments with respect to the government of municipal police forces. For clearly, at a time when even judicial authority over the disposition of criminal cases was viewed as appropriately placed in the hands of elected local politicians, there could be no doubt that control of the police was just as properly placed in the hands of these same politicians. The seeds of doubt on this matter only began to arise with the emergence, later in the nineteenth century, of the notion that certain aspects of the administration of justice (and most particularly judicial functions) were not only not appropriate to be left in the hands of locally elected politicians, but were not even appropriately subject to the control of elected politicians at all, be they locally or centrally elected.

By 1849, with the passage of the Baldwin Act,[12] the power to establish, maintain and regulate a municipal police force had been granted by statute to the elected council of every city and town in Upper Canada, and during the succeeding 130 years this power was extended to include the councils of townships and villages as well as, more recently, regions in Ontario. Furthermore, provincial legislation gradually changed this from an option to a mandatory requirement for the cities and larger municipalities.[13]

While Upper Canada (later Ontario) has been chosen as an example to illustrate the origins of municipal police forces, a similar history can be traced in each of the other jurisdictions of Canada. The essential feature of this history is that of the gradual transfer of control over municipal police forces from judicial officers to locally elected municipal councils. The timing of this transfer of control varied enormously from one jurisdiction to another. Control of the City of Charlottetown Police force, for instance, did not finally pass from the city's magistrate to the police committee of the city council until 1941,[14] more than a hundred years after many city and town councils in Upper Canada first gained control of their municipal police forces. In every jurisdiction in Canada, however, this transfer of control over municipal police forces has occurred.

The transfer of control of municipal police forces from the hands of judicial officers to those of locally elected politicians involves two important dimensions. Since the judicial officers involved had always been persons appointed by the provincial, rather than the local, authorities, the transfer represents not only a shift in control from an appointed judicial officer to a body of elected politicians, but also a shift in control from a provincially appointed authority to a locally elected authority. It is these two aspects of the shift in control—the shift from judicial to non-judicial control, and the shift from central to local control—which have been at the heart of the long controversy over the control of municipal police forces.

The Origins of Local Municipal Police Boards

Within a very short time after the earliest manifestations of this radical shift in the control of municipal police forces in Upper Canada from the justices of the peace to the new municipal councils, a significant reaction to it occurred. Just nine years after the passage of the famous Baldwin Act of 1849, the legislature of Upper Canada enacted the Municipal Institutions of Upper Canada Act.[15] From the point of view of the control of municipal police forces, this statute initiated a radical reversal of the policies effected through the reform legislation of the preceding 30 years. For while the right of city and town councils to establish, regulate and maintain their own municipal police forces was preserved, it was, in the case of cities but not of other municipalities, made subject to the requirement for the creation of boards of commissioners of police. Section 374 of the Act provided for these police boards in the following terms:

> 374. In every City there is hereby constituted a Board of Commissioners of Police, and such Board shall consist of the Mayor, Recorder and Police Magistrate, or if there is no Recorder or Police Magistrate, or if the offices of Recorder and Police Magistrate are filled by the same person, the Council of the City shall appoint a person resident therein to be a member of the Board, or two persons so resident to be members thereof, as the case may require.

The earliest legislative provision for the creation of a local police board illustrates the kind of flexibility that has been built into so many of its successors in other jurisdictions in order to strike some kind of compromise between municipal and provincial interests in the governance of municipal police forces. Both the recorder and the police magistrate were judicial officers who were appointed by, and held office during the pleasure of, the Crown (i.e., the province). They were both *ex officio* justices of the peace. The recorder's salary was fixed by the provincial government, and was paid out of the same fund as that of county judges. The police magistrate's salary, however, was fixed and paid by the municipal council. The recorder had to be a barrister of not less than five years' standing.

The flexibility in the composition of the boards established by the Act, however, derived from section 352 of the Act, which provided that:

> 352. A Recorder or a Police Magistrate shall not in the first instance be appointed for any Municipality, until the Council thereof communicates to the Governor its opinion that such an officer is required.

In theory, therefore, if a city council decided that it did not need a recorder or a police magistrate, it could have a police board consisting of the mayor and two residents of the city appointed by the council. Thus, at the city council's option, the composition of the police board could vary from, on the one hand, the mayor and two judicial officers appointed by the province, to, on the other hand, the mayor and two other persons appointed by council. Alternatively, it could be composed of the mayor, one judicial appointee of the province, and one person appointed by the council. There seems to have been no requirement that appointees of council should not also be members of council, so in theory a board could consist of the mayor and two other members of council.

It is not clear whether these theoretical options envisaged by the Act were reflected in practice, but it seems likely that most, if not all, of the five cities in Upper Canada at that time would have had both a recorder[16] and a police magistrate, and therefore a police board composed of the mayor and two provincial judicial appointees.

The significance of the concept of this police board, however, lay as much in the nature of its status and authority, as in its composition. The members of the police force were appointed by the board and held office at the pleasure of the board. Although the size of the police force remained within the discretion of the city council, it nevertheless had to be "not less in number than the Board reports to be absolutely required." The board, as well as thus determining the minimum size of the force, was required to, "from time to time, as they may deem expedient, make such regulations for the government of the force, and for preventing neglect or abuse, and for rendering the Force efficient in the discharge of all its duties." Most importantly, the constables appointed to the force were required by the Act to "obey all the lawful directions, and be subject to the government of the Board." The salaries of members of the force were to be fixed and paid by the council, but the council was required to pay for "all such offices, watch-houses, watch-boxes, arms, accoutrements, clothing and other necessities as the Board may from time to time deem requisite and require for the accommodation and use of the force."

The scheme of this legislation makes it quite clear that it was intended that the board should have a considerable degree of autonomy and independence from the dictates of the municipal council, no matter what its composition may be. The powers and functions of the board were not powers and functions delegated by the council, but statutory powers and functions conferred directly on the board itself. From this it is clear that even if the board were composed of three members of the council (i.e., the mayor and two aldermen appointed to it by council), it could not in any sense be considered a committee of council. Indeed, it is precisely this notional independence from the local council which constitutes one of the major characteristics of many of the modern, as well as of the original, police boards in Canada. While this notional independence existed irrespective of the actual composition of the board, it will be readily apparent that the extent to which such notional independence was translated into real independence in practice almost certainly hinged very much on the actual composition of the board.

Two important aspects of the compromise which this early conception of a police board represents should be emphasized here. In the first place, it represents a compromise between provincial and municipal control of municipal policing and police policy, since a majority of the members of the board could be, and in most cases probably were, provincially appointed. In this context, it is important to bear in mind that since Confederation, municipalities have never had any constitutionally defined sphere of jurisdiction. For, while the legislative jurisdiction of the federal and provincial legislatures is defined constitutionally by the British North America Act[17] (principally by sections 91 and 92 of the Act), all municipal authority is delegated constitutionally by the provincial legislatures. The significance of this constitutional arrangement, of course, lies in the fact that the municipalities have no constitutional claim to any jurisdiction over any municipal service, including policing. This means that the extent of municipal control over municipal policing is legally and constitutionally, if not politically, entirely at the discretion of the provincial legislature. Indeed, even the definition of policing as a municipal service is constitutionally within the exclusive jurisdiction of the provincial legislatures.

The second important aspect of the police boards envisaged by Ontario's early legislation is the compromise it represents between judicial and elected political control over municipal policing and police policy. The significance of this compromise in the context of Upper Canada in 1858 is by no means clear, and, more particularly, must be recognized as potentially quite different from the significance of the inclusion of members of the judiciary on municipal police boards in the present era. This is because, in the intervening years, the status and role of the lower judiciary have undergone major changes. As has been noted earlier, the notion of the political independence of the judiciary (especially the lower judiciary) which is so familiar to us today, but which, in the case of the lower judiciary, has doubtfully been totally realized even today in all jurisdictions in Canada (see, e.g., Alberta, Board of Review, 1975: 7–8), was apparently unknown in the Upper Canada of the mid-nineteenth century.

Similarly, the notion that the functions of the lower judiciary should be confined principally or exclusively to judicial duties was virtually unheard of at this time. Under these circumstances, the transfer of control over municipal police forces in the cities from the municipal council to a board composed of a majority of lower judicial officers should probably most accurately be interpreted as little more than a transfer of control from local back to provincial authorities. With the changing status of the lower judiciary during the ensuing 120 years, however, the significance of this compromise has come increasingly to be interpreted in terms of a transfer of control from political to non-political authorities (see, e.g., Edwards, 1980: 72). Clearly such an interpretation suggests quite different issues about the nature of municipal policing and of the municipal police function than are raised by the interpretation which emphasizes the municipal-provincial dimensions of the compromise. For it suggests that at the heart of the compromise lies a conception of the municipal police function as being not simply another municipal service over which municipal and provincial governments may struggle for control, but as a judicial or quasi-judicial function over which the influence of elected politicians of any kind should be reduced or eliminated altogether. This ambiguity over the role of the judiciary as members of police boards lies at the heart of the controversies which have surrounded such boards ever since their inception as institutions of municipal police governance in Canada over 120 years ago.

The Original Justifications for Police Boards

Adequate research has not yet been completed to explain the radical reversal of policy which the inclusion of the requirement for police boards in the 1858 Act seems to reflect. Some speculation on this question can be made, however. In the first place, it is clear that the idea for the creation of such boards derived not from England (still the colonial power), but from the United States. In England, with the exception of the Metropolitan London force, which was under the control of the Home Secretary, control over municipal police forces had been given to local municipal councils without reservation by the Municipal Corporations Act of 1835. The "watch committees" which this statute required municipalities to set up to govern their municipal police forces were composed entirely of members of the elected municipal councils. The composition of these watch committees remained unchanged until 1964, when the new English Police Act of that year required their membership to consist of two-thirds municipal councillors and one-third local magistrates (Critchley, 1978).

According to Fosdick (1969: 77), the idea of a "board of police" as an institution of municipal police governance first emerged in an ordinance proposed (but never passed) in New York in 1844. The board proposed by this ordinance was to be composed of seven senior officers, including the superintendent, of the New York City police department, and was to be charged with "general administrative functions." This idea was taken up and put into effect for the City of Philadelphia in 1850, but later in the same year the composition of this board was changed so that it consisted of the marshal of police and the presidents of the respective town boards of the communities within the police district. Three years later, a "board of police commissioners" was established to govern the New York City police force, which was clearly the model on which the police boards required under the 1858 Upper Canada statute were based. The New York board consisted of the mayor, the recorder and the city judge. According to Fosdick:

> Apart from the fact that the chief of police was selected by the mayor with the board's approval, the board had full powers of appointment and dismissal of all members of the force and was charged with general administrative duties. [1969: 78]

Noting that "the origin of this novel experiment, particularly in its relation to police organization, cannot be exactly determined," Fosdick explains the change (which, he says, "came into instant and widespread favor") in the following terms:

> The office of mayor had not yet been associated with broad executive powers, and appointments, as well as administrative responsibilities, were lodged in the common council. The decade just referred to [i.e., 1845–55], however, witnessed the waning influence of the council as an administrative body. This change was undoubtedly due in part to the rising democratic sentiment which brought with it a pronounced distrust of the legislative departments of the government, both state and local. It was due, too, to the growing complexity of municipal functions and the increasing difficulties of supervision through committees of council. [1969: 76–77]

Fosdick also noted that, in creating the police board in 1853, "the legislature had hoped to eliminate the political favoritism and ward control which prior to that time had dominated the [police] department." This hope, he added, was justified only in part, mainly because "the recorder and the city judge, serving *ex officio*, took little interest in the affairs of the force, and control was gradually assumed by the mayor" (1969: 80–81).

To what extent similar considerations led to the adoption of the provisions of 1858 in Upper Canada can only be guessed at, at the present time. McDougall (1971a) has asserted that the 1858 provisions were enacted with the intention of "removing the police from politics." Referring to the period immediately prior to the introduction of these measures, he wrote that,

> by the 1830's cities and towns were authorized to appoint full-time police forces if they wished. Members of these forces were still appointed annually and their selection was based on patronage. The political character of appointees proved nothing short of disastrous when riots and religious rivalry shattered the peace of the community, since the faction in control of the municipal government was not above using the police as a partisan force. [1971a: 11–12].

Although McDougall cites no specific source for this last allegation, there seems little reason to believe that it is not accurate (cf. Quebec, 1855: 15). The notion that this early police board could "remove the police from politics," however, is not without problems. In the first place, within the context of Upper Canada in 1858, there seems little enough reason to believe that the recorder and police magistrate who were to form the majority of the membership of such boards were in fact, or even in theory, any less "political" than the members of the municipal councils which they replaced, although undoubtedly they reflected different political interests (i.e., central rather than local interests). In the second place, it seems strange that a measure the intention of which was to "remove the police from politics" would nevertheless provide that the mayor should have, *ex officio*, a seat on the police governing authority, and that the council should have power to fix the size (subject to a minimum) and salaries of the force. Nor would the flexibility built into the provision governing the composition of the governing authority, whereby it could consist of three members of the council, seem to be compatible with an unequivocal intention to "remove the police from politics."

Finally, the fact that the requirement for a police board was not extended to towns which maintained their own police forces gives pause again to question the true motivations behind the creation of this institution. One would have thought that if the sole motivation had been to "remove the police from politics," there would have been little justification for not insisting that any municipality which maintained a municipal police force should have a police board. Yet to this day there are only two jurisdictions in the country which have legislated such a requirement.[18] Part of the reason for this may have been the small size of many municipal forces (sometimes no more than one constable). In such circumstances it might be thought somewhat ridiculous to insist that one policeman should be governed by a board consisting of three persons. Nevertheless, this does not in itself seem to be an adequate explanation of the distinction which such legislation has consistently made between large and smaller municipalities.

A much more plausible explanation for the creation of police boards would seem to be the desire of the central (provincial) authorities to remove the municipal police forces out of the control of local political interests and back into the sphere of their own political influence. In this context, the creation of police boards as institutions of government of municipal police forces may be seen not so much as a measure to "remove the police from politics," as an attempt to move the control over municipal police forces from one sphere of political interests toward another. Clearly, it would always be very much in the interests of the proponents of such a change to create the impression that the new governing authority is in some way demonstrably less "political" than its predecessor. In this context, the preference of the advocates of police boards for having the majority of their membership comprised of members of the judiciary seems readily explicable, and the provision whereby such boards could still, in certain circumstances, be composed entirely of locally elected politicians becomes understandable as a necessary concession to the contemporary realities of the struggle for power over municipal institutions between municipal and provincial authorities (Aitchison, 1949).

The notion that characterizations of municipal police forces and their governing authorities as autonomous "non-political" institutions may be little more than a strategy invoked to justify their removal from one sphere of political interests to another is not a new one. In his penetrating study of municipal police forces in the United States, Fogelson (1977) has amassed a great deal of evidence in support of his claim that the move toward municipal police autonomy from local government, and consequent changes in the structure of municipal police government, in that country were no more nor less than a means whereby control over these forces could be shifted from lower- and lower-middle-class immigrants to upper- and upper-middle-class native-born Americans. Similarly, Critchley (1978), in his classic study of the British police, has demonstrated quite clearly how the struggle for power over local forces between the justices of the peace and the locally elected municipal councils in the nineteenth century can most convincingly be understood in terms of a struggle between two quite clearly identifiable political factions (representing the landed aristocracy and the new middle-class bourgeoisie respectively) for control over these forces.

Whether the apparently sudden political *volte face* of the 1858 Act in Upper Canada can be understood in terms of an analysis such as this remains to be demonstrated. As an analytical framework, however, it would seem far from implausible, and should not too readily be discarded in favour of the more commonly heard explanation of the measure as representing an attempt to "remove the police from politics." The notion of the "independence" of municipal police forces and of their governing authorities, however, is one which requires further elaboration and which will be considered in more detail later in this essay. For the moment, the 122-year history of municipal police boards in Canada, and their current status, must be briefly described.

The History of Police Boards in Canada

Police boards are not unique in Ontario, although historically that has been, and remains today, the province in which they are most commonly found. The model for a police board which the Act of 1858 established in Upper Canada has, with a few important exceptions, remained substantially unchanged in Ontario. With the advent of Confederation in 1867, the place of recorders on such boards was taken by the new, federally appointed, county court judges.[19] Despite their federal appointment as judges, however, the power to appoint them as members of police boards remained with the provincial authorities. In 1936, the power of municipal councils to fill vacancies in the membership of police boards resulting from vacancies in either or both of the judicial offices concerned (i.e., county court judge and magistrate) was removed,[20] thus guaranteeing without exception both the judicial character, and the provincial control over the appointment, of the majority of the members of police boards. For a short period (1946–58)

Crown attorneys (also provincial appointees) could be appointed as members of police boards instead of magistrates,[21] but in 1958 this requirement that the third member of such a board was to be either a magistrate or a Crown attorney was abolished, and instead the third member was now to be "such person as the Lieutenant-Governor in Council may designate."[22] From this time on it became the practice to appoint lawyers or businessmen, so that the tradition of the majority of board members being judicial officers ended. In 1979, the Ontario government finally succumbed to long-standing pressures from a variety of sources (including the judiciary themselves)[23] and removed the requirement that at least one member of a police board had to be a county or district court judge,[24] thus signalling the end of the legal requirement for judicial representation on most police boards in Ontario. Despite this legislative change, however, the present provincial solicitor general has publicly stated his intention to continue to appoint members of the lower judiciary to membership of police boards whenever this is possible.[25]

With the regionalization of police forces in the province, beginning with the creation of the Metropolitan Toronto Police Force in 1956, provision was made for five-member regional police boards.[26] Like the municipal police boards, the regional boards consist of a majority of members appointed by the provincial authorities. One of these, however, must still be a county or district court judge, and in Metropolitan Toronto another must also be a provincial judge.[27] These regional police boards in Ontario, and the Charlottetown board in P.E.I., are now the only police boards in Canada whose membership is required by law to include at least one (and in the case of Toronto, two) members of the judiciary.

In the other provinces the institution of police boards has historically been received with considerably less enthusiasm than in Ontario. Although it is not intended to review in detail here the experience which each of these jurisdictions has had with police boards, a very brief summary will give some idea of the rate at which this institution spread in Canada after its initial introduction in Upper Canada in 1858.

The first province to adopt the concept of a police board after Ontario was Manitoba. The charters of the cities of Brandon and Winnipeg, both enacted in 1882, permitted, but did not require, the establishment of police boards as the governing authority for their respective police forces.[28] The establishment of such a board was made mandatory for the city of Winnipeg four years later,[29] but such a requirement was not imposed on the city of Brandon until 1949.[30] Police boards have not been created for any other municipalities in this province.

The charters of the cities of Vancouver and New Westminster, enacted in 1886 and 1888 respectively, each required the establishment of a municipal police board.[31] In 1893 this requirement was extended to every city and town in the province,[32] but three years later the requirement was lifted in the case of towns.[33] Police boards of one form or another have existed in British Columbia ever since, and it is now the only jurisdiction which legally requires every municipality which maintains its own municipal police force to have a police board.[34]

In 1907 and 1908 respectively, police boards were established for the cities of Moncton[35] and Fredericton,[36] and in 1961 legislation was enacted permitting the council of the city of St. John to establish a police board for the government of its police force.[37] These are the only municipal police forces in New Brunswick that have ever been subject to the governance of police boards.[38] In 1908 police boards were made optional for cities in Saskatchewan,[39] but in 1915 this provision was amended to require all cities in the province to establish police boards.[40] Legislation establishing a police board for the City of Charlottetown was enacted in 1938, and this remains the only police board in Prince Edward Island.[41]

The concept of a police board was not introduced generally into Alberta until 1951, when such boards were made optional for the province's city police forces.[42] In 1968, this option was extended to include any municipality having its own police force,[43] and in 1971 police boards were made mandatory for the governance of police forces in the larger municipalities.[44] At the present time all 11 municipal police forces in the province are governed by police boards.

With the exception of the Public Security Council of the Montreal Urban Community, which was established in 1969 to oversee the creation of (and subsequently to govern) the city's new unified police department,[45] police boards have been unknown in the Province of Quebec, which has the largest number of municipal police forces of any province (196 at the last count). With the exception of the Montreal force, each of these forces is governed directly by the local council.

Police boards were unknown in Nova Scotia until 1974 when the province's new Police Act, enacted in the face of considerable opposition, required the establishment of police boards for the government of police forces in the larger municipalities, and made them optional for the smaller ones.[46] Currently all 25 municipal police forces in the province are governed by police boards. There has never been any police board in the Province of Newfoundland.

It will be apparent from this brief historial summary that any realistic assessment of police boards in Canada must bear in mind that some provinces have had long experience with this institution, while for others it represents a new and unfamiliar form of police government. Historically, the majority of the experience with municipal police boards in Canada has occurred in Ontario and the western provinces. In Quebec and the eastern provinces, with some exceptions, this institution has been virtually unknown until very recently. There appears to be no obvious explanation for this fact.

The Current Variety of Police Boards in Canada

The composition of police boards in Ontario has been described in some detail not only because they were first introduced there, but also because at present the majority of police boards in Canada are to be found in Ontario, and because that province's police boards have been the subject of the most persistent controversy in recent years. It should not be imagined, however, that the police boards in Ontario are, or ever have been, in any sense typical of all police boards in Canada. In fact, nothing could be further from the truth, and the most striking finding which emerges from a review of the history of police boards in Canada is the amazing variety of forms in which this institution has manifested itself. Indeed, almost the only things these various police boards have in common are the fact that they have all played some role in the government of municipal police forces, and that they all have had at least a notionally separate identity from that of their local municipal councils.

In terms of their composition alone, it is possible to identify no fewer than 38 different models of police boards during the institution's 122-year history in Canada, ranging from boards whose members were all appointed by the provincial authorities,[47] through boards whose members were all chosen by and/or from among the members of the local council,[48] to boards whose members were chosen through direct public election to office.[49] Composition, however, has been by no means the only source of variety among Canadian police boards. Other important dimensions of variety have included their size, status, degree of autonomy, authority, powers and functions.

Obviously this great variety poses some problems for theoretical analysis, since it is arguable that police boards do not represent a sufficiently homogeneous category for such analysis. In this essay it is clearly not possible to describe the whole range of variety which this institution has manifested over the years.[50] Some, but by no means all, of this variety may be illustrated, however, through an examination of those police boards which exist at the present time in Canada. But before entering upon such a review, some contextual statistics are required.

There are currently approximately 450 municipal police forces in existence in Canada, almost three-quarters of which are to be found in the provinces of Ontario (128) and Quebec (196). These forces range from forces of one or two members in some rural municipalities, to forces of over 5,000 members in the metropolitan areas. The fact that there is thus no such thing as a "typical" municipal police force in Canada goes a long way toward explaining why there is also no such thing as a "typical" police board.

The majority of municipal police forces in Canada are not now, nor have they ever been, governed by police boards. Rather, they are subject to the direct control of their local municipal councils, or committees thereof.

The majority of municipal policemen, however, do now belong to police forces that are governed by police boards. This is explained by the fact that a few large metropolitan police forces, which are subject to the governance of police boards, account for the great majority of municipal policemen in the country (Canada, Statistics Canada, 1978).

At the present time there are approximately 130 police boards in existence in Canada, more than half of which are in the Province of Ontario (71). The police forces governed by these boards thus represent less than one-third of all the municipal police forces in the country. It has already been noted that the establishment of a police board for the governance of a municipal police force in any given jurisdiction may be either a local option or a mandatory statutory requirement. While the exact number of the existing police boards which are optional rather than mandatory was not ascertained during the research undertaken for this essay it must be noted that this number is not insignificant. In Ontario, for instance, 34 of the 71 police boards currently in existence are optional boards.[51]

The significance of whether a board is optional or mandatory lies, of course, in the implications this has for the status of the board. If a board is a mandatory board it will by definition have some guaranteed legal autonomy vis-à-vis the local municipal council, whatever its composition. An optional board, however, may or may not have such autonomy depending on the nature of the option. While in some jurisdictions the dissolution of optional boards, once established, is subject to the consent of the responsible provincial minister (usually the attorney general),[52] in others it is not.[53] Obviously, where a police board's very continued existence is within the discretion of some external authority such as a municipal council or a provincial government minister, however, any autonomy which might be claimed for it may be regarded as fundamentally undermined.

The significance of a police board is related, of course, not only to the size of the police force that it governs, but to the size of the budget that it administers. While by no means all police boards in Canada have complete control over their forces' budgets, once approved by the local council, in most cases they do, and such budgets are often of very sizeable proportions indeed. The budget for the Metropolitan Toronto Police Force, for instance, which, once approved by the Metropolitan Toronto Council, is administered exclusively by the Metropolitan Toronto police board, stood in 1980 at an unprecedented $202 million, and represented the largest single item (almost 13 per cent) of Metropolitan Toronto's operating budget. Over 80 per cent of this police budget is paid out of funds raised through local taxation, the remainder being supplied through a provincial grant. When it is appreciated that the Metropolitan Toronto police board is comprised of five persons, a majority of whom are appointed by the provincial authorities and are not locally elected office-holders, and that the board enjoys complete autonomy vis-à-vis the Metropolitan Toronto Council, the potential for controversy over this institution can be readily understood. Indeed, a review of the history of police boards in Canada leaves little doubt that the issue of control over the municipal police budget has been the greatest source of controversy over this institution.

With this contextual information in mind, some of the essential features of the variety among existing police boards in Canada can be described.[54]

Size of Boards

Most existing police boards consist of three or five members. The great majority of the boards in Ontario (61 out of 71), all boards in Saskatchewan, and the boards in Fredericton and Charlottetown are three-member boards. In addition, in Alberta, where municipalities have the option of establishing boards of three or five members, many have opted for three-member boards. The option for three-member or larger boards also exists in Nova Scotia, but research for this essay did not reveal whether any municipalities there have chosen the smaller boards. All 12 boards in British Columbia are five-member boards, as are the two boards in Manitoba, and the ten regional boards (including Metropolitan Toronto) in Ontario. Some of the Alberta boards are also five-member boards (e.g., Calgary and Edmonton), although again research did not reveal how many. Larger boards exist in Montreal (with a seven-member board) and in Nova Scotia (where legislation permits municipalities to create boards of any size, provided they consist of a minimum of three members). In Halifax, for instance, the board currently consists of 12 members (the entire city council plus one nominee of the provincial attorney general).

Composition of Boards

The composition of existing police boards varies greatly. Members of all boards acquire their positions either *ex officio* or through appointment by either provincial authorities or municipal councils. The variations in the composition of police boards may thus be considered in terms of the two dimensions of (1) how membership is acquired and (2) who acquires membership. The mayor or other head of the municipal council is an *ex officio* member of the board in all jurisdictions in British Columbia and Saskatchewan, as well as in Fredericton, Charlottetown, Brandon (Manitoba), and in all jurisdictions in Ontario (including Metropolitan Toronto) except the nine regional jurisdictions. Provincial authorities in British Columbia and Ontario have the power of appointment of the majority of members of all police boards in those jurisdictions, but in all other cases control over the selection of the majority of the members of boards is in the hands of municipal authorities. The only police boards with respect to whose membership provincial authorities have no control at all are those in Alberta, Saskatchewan and Winnipeg.

In Ontario, British Columbia, Alberta and Fredericton the law provides that the majority of members of a police board must be persons who are not members of the municipal council. In all the other jurisdictions members of council form the majority on police boards. As was noted earlier, the only existing police boards which include members of the judiciary in their membership are those in Ontario and Charlottetown.

From the foregoing, it will be apparent that the categories of persons who are eligible for appointment to police boards are: (1) members of the municipal council, (2) members of the lower judiciary, and (3) other unspecified persons. In some cases, these other unspecified persons are required to be residents (e.g., in Brandon, Manitoba), ratepayers (e.g., in Fredericton), or electors (e.g., in Winnipeg) of the municipality concerned.

As to the actual membership of existing police boards, preliminary research suggests that the majority of members of police boards are drawn from the ranks of civic politicians, lawyers, businessmen, school principals and teachers. Other "professional" people (e.g., doctors, psychiatrists, chartered accountants) are also found on some boards, as are social and community workers in small numbers, and on two of the ten urban boards studied, former military officers, and "housewives" were also members. The labour movement, women and persons under 35 years of age seem to be particularly underrepresented, as are ethnic minorities. As previously noted, at least one member of every board in Ontario is a member of the judiciary, but elsewhere this is rare or non-existent. It is very uncommon for members of boards to be ex-policemen. There are instances in which persons sit as members of more than one police board; this, however, is rare. More comprehensive research is required to substantiate these preliminary findings.

The Political Character of Boards

Most of those persons interviewed on the subject of the composition of boards during the research in preparation of this essay seemed to be agreed that appointments to police boards tend to be "political" in the sense that those who exercise the power of appointment are free to exercise their political judgment in the choice of appointees, subject, of course, to the statutory requirements with respect to qualification for appointment (e.g., that the appointee is or is not a member of the municipal council, or is a judge, or is a resident of the municipality, etc.). This is not to say that all such appointments are made strictly on the basis of partisan political loyalties. It is recognized, however, that sound political judgment may often commend appointment of actual or potential opponents, or persons with no declared political affiliations. The commonly heard characterization of police boards as "non-political"—a characterization often employed by those who wish to contrast police boards with other "political" police governing authorities (e.g., municipal councils)—seems to be derived not so much from the nature of individual appointments to boards, as from the fact that in some jurisdictions (e.g., Ontario, British Columbia, Nova Scotia and New Brunswick) police boards are required to be composed of members appointed by more than one appointing authority, and in some jurisdictions (British Columbia, Alberta, Ontario and New Brunswick) a certain number of appointees must be persons who do not hold municipal political office. This characterization, however, if it is intended to refer to anything other than the fact that some boards have as a majority of their members persons who are not at the time elected politicians, is one which, to the author's knowledge, has never been either clearly enunciated or empirically substantiated.

Tenure of Office of Board Members

The term of office of members of police boards varies greatly, and to some extent depends on the source of appointment. Persons who are appointed in their capacity as civic politicians, of course, may serve only as long as they retain their seats on council, although in many instances such appointments are made on an annual basis. Re-appointments for successive terms are not uncommon, however. Other appointees are frequently appointed for longer terms, usually of two or three years, and re-appointments of such persons are not uncommon either. In some jurisdictions, appointment to, and retention of, membership of boards is dependent on residence within the community concerned. The British Columbia Police Act is unique in providing for a maximum period (six years) of membership of a police board. The legislation governing police boards reveals no other provisions guaranteeing the tenure of members of boards, and it would appear that members of police boards all serve "at pleasure."

Part-time, Short-term Nature of Board Membership—Implications

With the exception of the chairman of the Metropolitan Toronto Board, all chairmen and members of police boards serve on a part-time basis. In many jurisdictions, members of police boards serve without remuneration. This is the case even with respect to members of some of the boards serving major cities in Canada.

The part-time nature of almost all, and the short-term nature of a great many, appointments to municipal police boards probably represent their two most important characteristics, with respect to the implications they have for the role and status of police boards. They exert a strong inhibiting influence not only on the ability of board members to develop expertise with respect to their functions as board members, but on the ability of police boards to engage in long-term policy planning and development for the forces under their jurisdiction. They also contribute in large measure to a heavy dependence of police boards on chiefs of police for information, expertise and the development of long-term planning. Indeed, next to the "political/non-political" argument, these implications seem to be those which are most often cited in favour of police boards whose membership is not dependent on the members holding elected political office.

The problems generated by part-time and short-term membership of police boards, however, are not limited to those members who hold elected office, although, as noted above, appointed members seem generally to serve for longer terms. Most members of police boards have quite substantial commitments and responsibilities beyond those they owe to their function as board members. Opinions vary substantially on the extent to which this may impair their contribution to the work of police boards. Those who hold the view that it does, however, frequently cite it as a reason why heads of municipal councils should not be chairmen of police boards. Those who support the idea of mayors being chairmen of boards, on the other hand, will often, while conceding that mayors sometimes are unable to devote adequate attention to police board business, argue that the mayor is the most appropriate person to represent the interests of the municipality that should be prominently reflected in the governance of the police force.

The part-time nature of boards inevitably means that they do not shoulder the main burden of the administration of the police forces under their jurisdiction, but function more in a supervisory capacity. As a result, the day-to-day administration of the police force, as well as the initiation of policy development and planning, resides in many cases solely with the chief of police and his staff. The fact that most police boards do not have any separate staff, apart perhaps from the services of an administrative secretary and a stenographer, further contributes to this division of responsibilities.[55]

Most police boards meet formally on an average of once a month, although some of the boards in larger urban areas meet more frequently.[56] A board which actively engages in contract negotiations with its police personnel, as some boards do, will often have to meet more frequently for the purpose of such negotiations. Regular meetings of police boards, however, generally last from two to four hours. Most police board members, therefore, are not expected to devote more than a day a month to this responsibility. Despite this, a number of board members interviewed in different cities during the study referred to problems of absenteeism of members at meetings. These problems were most frequently associated with board members who were also members of municipal councils and had to attend to competing civic responsibilities. One chief of police interviewed during the study, however, explained some of this absenteeism in another way. Politician members of police boards, he suggested, tend to handle "crunch issues" by absenting themselves.[57]

Chairmanship of Boards

Another very important implication of the part-time, short-term nature of police board membership is the manner in which it contributes to the significance of the role of the chairman of the board. Often, as a result, the chairman becomes, by default, by far the most active and influential member of the board.

The chairmen of most municipal police boards tend to be either mayors or other heads of municipal councils, or lawyers. Judges are chairmen of a minority of police boards in Ontario (14 out of 71). Except in British Columbia (where the mayor is *ex officio* chairman of the board) and Montreal (where the chairman of the MUC Public Security Council is appointed as such by the lieutenant governor in council) chairmen of boards are normally elected as such by the board members annually.[58]

The Mandates of Modern Police Boards

The statutory mandates of police boards in Canada vary considerably. They do, however, share the common feature of being vaguely defined by legislation. In this connection, an interesting comparison may be made with the quite specific legislative definitions, which are to be found, of the mandates of the more recently established provincial police commissions, of which more will be said below. The provisions of the Ontario Police Act may be considered as a case in point, the only sense in which the Ontario legislation is atypical in this regard being that the definition of the mandate of police boards in Ontario is somewhat *less* vague than in other provincial Police Acts.

Section 41 of the Ontario Police Act defines the mandate of the Ontario Police Commission (the provincial body) in terms of 14 specific functions which are enumerated in the section. By comparison, the mandate of a municipal police board is defined in sections 14 to 17. Section 14 gives a board the power to determine the size of the force, and the accommodation, equipment, and so forth, which it requires. Section 15 gives a board the authority to appoint the members of the force, and section 16 allows it to make by-laws, not inconsistent with provincial regulations enacted under the Act, "for the government of the police force, for preventing neglect or abuse, and for rendering it efficient in the discharge of its duties." Finally, section 17 provides that a board "is responsible for the policing and maintenance of law and order in the municipality," and that "the members of the police force are subject to the government of the board and shall obey its lawful directions." The Ontario Police Act gives no indication of what may or may not be a "lawful direction" for the purposes of this section, and a review of pertinent judicial decisions yields no guidance on this matter beyond the bald assertion that "neither the board nor a municipality not having a board can lawfully give directions to any member of a police force prescribing the duties of his office."[59] Since duties of police constables in Ontario are more or less specifically enumerated in section 55 of the Act, this judicial interpretation of section 17 is of little value in discerning the mandate which is contemplated for police boards under that section. It will be apparent that the language in which this mandate is expressed is almost identical to that of the original Upper Canada statute of 1858 (see above, at 168).

In many jurisdictions, the role of the police board which is provided for in the relevant provincial statutes is much less specific than this. The statutes governing police boards in Nova Scotia and Winnipeg, for instance, give to the relevant municipal councils almost complete freedom to define, by by-law, the role of these boards.[60] As a result, the mandate of the police board in Winnipeg has undergone radical changes at the hands of the city's municipal council in recent years.[61]

The result of such provisions is that the degree to which responsibility for, and control over, municipal police forces is shared between police boards and their municipal councils varies greatly from one jurisdiction to another. In terms of extremes, one could say that boards in Ontario have more than the lion's share at present (municipal councils there do not even have ultimate control over the size of the police budget),[62] while those of Winnipeg and Fredericton are effectively limited to that of holding hearings into public complaints against members of their police forces, and (in the case of the Winnipeg board) hearing appeals from disciplinary decisions of the police chief and "advising" him on community relations and crime prevention policies.[63]

Adequate empirical research into the role of police boards in the governance of Canada's municipal police forces has not yet been undertaken. A preliminary review of the operations of police boards in ten of Canada's major cities, however, reveals the following range of functions.

Preparation and Control of the Police Force Budget

Although control of the budget of a police force would seem to be a vital function for anybody charged with the government of a police force, by no means all police boards in Canada have this responsibility. In those cases (the majority) where police boards are involved in the preparation of the budget, the final approval of the budget generally lies with the municipal council, and the board must accept any limitations which may be placed upon it by council. In Ontario and British Columbia, however, the provincial police commissions are given final authority to resolve disputes between a municipality and its police board over the budget.[64] Control of the budget, of course, carries with it a great deal of power, including the authority for determining the size of the force and the provision of equipment, accommodation and facilities.

Collective Bargaining

In a great many jurisdictions, the board plays no role in collective bargaining other than that of providing those responsible (usually civic officials, such as city managers, personnel directors, finance commissioners, etc.) with information they may require for this task. It will be readily apparent that the role of those boards which have no control over the police budget or over the collective bargaining process is already substantially circumscribed by comparison with those boards which have control in both of these areas.

Promulgation of Rules and Regulations

The rules and regulations promulgated by boards, along with the collective agreements and the chief's standing and daily or weekly orders, constitute the principal administrative documents governing the operations of municipal police forces. Such rules and regulations, which almost all boards have authority to promulgate, cover such matters as the duties of various ranks in the administration of the force; police procedures such as the handling of lost and found items; the treatment of persons in custody; the care of equipment and its use; reporting procedures; the maintenance of police records and access to them; relations of members of the force with the media and other persons seeking information about police matters; the offering of rewards; the treatment of informants; the conditions under which officers may perform special pay duties, and so forth.[65] They may also deal with other personnel under the board's jurisdiction, for example, auxiliary policemen, parking control officers, by-law enforcement officers, school crossing guards.

Supervision Over Recruitment, Hiring, Promotions, Suspensions and Dismissals

In most, but by no means all, jurisdictions the police board has final authority over these matters. In some jurisdictions, however, the appointment of the chief of police must be either made by (e.g., in Nova Scotia), or ratified by (e.g., in Alberta), the municipal council.

General Policy Direction or Approval

A few boards—but definitely a minority—are highly active in the initiation and direction of police policy, some even striking committees (sometimes including appointed community representatives) or hiring consultants to develop policy and make recommendations in particular areas. The majority of police boards, however, seem to rely almost exclusively on the chief of police to generate policy issues and proposals for the board's approval. Interviews with board members and chiefs of police in ten major Canadian cities generated the following list of examples of topics with respect to which boards played some role in policy formulation:

- meeting the policing needs of particular areas of a city
- recovery of stolen articles from pawn and second-hand dealers

- preventing suicides in police cells
- security measures for apartment and other buildings
- assistance to other police departments
- recruitment from other police departments
- treatment of ethnic minority groups
- installation and use of communication systems
- dissemination of accident reports
- support of force members taking educational courses in community colleges, universities, and so forth
- setting of departmental goals and objectives
- whether routine police presence should be maintained at a hospital
- the placing of shotguns in police vehicles
- the hiring of experts to perform psychological testing of recruits
- the establishment of a tactical unit
- the establishment of a domestic crisis intervention unit
- hot pursuit by police vehicles
- dealing with the problems of prostitution
- treatment of juveniles

Public and Community Relations

This is seen by many police boards as one of their major functions. It is accomplished in a variety of ways, including attendance at public meetings; speeches to community groups, schools, and so forth; attendance at municipal council and committee meetings; promotion of "police week"; the award of citations to members of the public who have assisted the police; and receiving and responding to deputations and representations from citizen groups on matters of concern to the police.

Internal Disciplinary Matters and Public Complaints

Almost all police boards have supervisory and appellate jurisdiction with respect to the disposition by the police chief of internal disciplinary matters and public complaints against the police. In many cases, boards also have original powers of investigation and inquiry with respect to such matters. Frequently, however, such powers are subject to provincial regulations governing procedures in such matters. The great potential for conflict between these responsibilities and the other functions of boards has led to much serious questioning of the appropriateness of the exercise of such powers by them.[66] Concern is particularly expressed about the difficulty of creating the appearance of impartiality in the exercise of such powers, when boards may be so involved in the supervision of the administration of their forces through their other responsibilities. The fact that such concerns are frequently expressed by members of boards themselves[67] contributes to the probability that reforms in this area may be not far off.

Miscellaneous Functions

Police boards also perform a variety of other miscellaneous functions. These include such matters as the review of reports by the chief of police on matters connected with the administration of the police force, and on crime within the force's jurisdiction; consideration of requests for information on policing matters from municipal councils and other civic authorities (e.g., a transit commission), providing such information, and sometimes consulting with such bodies; hearing grievances of force members pursuant to the terms of a collective agreement; review of reports on the use of firearms by police force members involving death or injury to a third party, and making reports thereon to the provincial police commission; the award of merit marks and commendations to police force members for outstanding service.

In addition to these functions, police boards in some of the larger cities of Canada have quite extensive responsibilities with respect to the licensing of persons carrying on various businesses within the jurisdiction of the board. Such businesses include taxicab, newspaper vending, second-hand goods dealing, fruit and vegetable vending businesses, door-to-door salesmen and a host of other concerns.[68]

While the list of functions just described may seem to constitute an impressive mandate for police boards, it must be stressed that many police boards do not enjoy all of these powers and responsibilities, and a good many enjoy only a few of them. Furthermore, the mere fact that a police board enjoys a particular mandate is no indication of the extent to which a board will exercise that mandate in practice. Again, adequate empirical research into the actual work of police boards is sadly lacking, but preliminary studies in this area suggest that in practice most police boards (and there are notable exceptions) play a very passive and minimal role in the governance of their police forces, even when they enjoy a theoretically expansive mandate in this regard. Some of the factors which may account for this have already been identified in this paper. They include the short-term, part-time nature of most police board membership, the perceived lack of the requisite expertise on the part of police board members, the absence of clear definitions of police board mandates, and the lack of adequate staff and support services to allow police boards to take a vigorous, independent approach to their mandate. All of these factors encourage a situation in which police boards develop a heavy reliance on their chiefs of police and the forces themselves for the information and the support services necessary for the exercise of their responsibilities. The result in many cases seems to be that police boards come to be little more than rubber-stamp agencies of approval and public relations for the policies and procedures adopted by their chiefs of police.

Four other important factors, however, have to be considered in any attempt to account for such emasculation of the role of police boards in governing their police forces. These are the notion of police independence, the notion of police professionalism, the rise of police unionism, and the growing influence of provincial agencies—especially provincial police commissions—in the control of municipal police services.

The Notion of Police Independence

After reviewing the historical common law status of the constable in England, Marshall (1965: 33) commented:

> In the twentieth century there has been contrived out of the common law position a novel and surprising thesis, which is sometimes now to be heard intoned as if it were a thing of antiquity with its roots alongside Magna Carta.

Marshall was referring to the thesis of police independence. A leading English constitutional lawyer, in a brief to the Royal Commission on the Police, described the notion of police independence as "obscure," and concluded that "there can . . . be little ground in law for the assumption that the discretion exercised by a chief constable is peculiar to himself" (Great Britain, Royal Commission on the Police, 1962b: App. 2, at 33). Nevertheless, the notion of the independence of the police has attracted a substantial degree of support from the courts in England[69] and Canada,[70] as well as from a variety of commentators, including the English Royal Commission on the Police[71] and, most recently, the English Royal Commission on Criminal Procedure.[72]

Space does not permit a detailed account here of the content and origins of this notion of police independence. Statements of the concept of police independence vary greatly,[73] but one of the more extreme (and most often quoted) versions of the concept is that offered by Lord Denning in the English case of *R. v. Metropolitan Police Commissioner ex parte Blackburn*. Referring to the constitutional status of the Commissioner of the Metropolitan London Police, he said:

> I have no hesitation, however, in holding that, like every constable in the land, he should be, and is, independent of the executive. He is not subject to the orders of the Secretary of State, save that under the Police Act 1964 the Secretary of State can call on him to give a report, or to retire in the interests of efficiency. I hold it to be the duty of the Commissioner of Police, as it is of every chief constable, to enforce the law of the land. He must take steps so to post his men that crimes may be detected; and that honest citizens may go about their affairs in peace. He must decide whether or not suspected persons are to be prosecuted; and, if need be, bring the prosecution or see that it is brought; but in all these things he is not the servant of anyone, save of the law itself. No Minister of the Crown can tell him that he must, or must not, keep observation on this place or that; or that he must, or must not, prosecute this man or that one. Nor can any police authority tell him so. The responsibility for law enforcement lies on him. He is answerable to the law and to the law alone. . . .

> Although the chief officers of police are answerable to the law, there are many fields in which they have a discretion with which the law will not interfere. For instance, it is for the Commissioner of Police, or the chief constable, as the case may be, to decide in any particular case whether enquiries should be pursued, or whether an arrest should be made, or a prosecution brought. It must be for him to decide on the disposition of his force and the concentration of his resources on any particular crime or area. No court can or should give him direction on such matters. He can also make policy decisions and give effect to them, as, for instance, was often done when prosecutions were not brought for attempted suicide; but there are some policy decisions with which, I think, the courts in a case can, if necessary, interfere. Suppose a chief constable were to issue a directive to his men that no person should be prosecuted for stealing any goods less than £100 in value. I should have thought that the court could countermand it. He would be failing in his duty to enforce the law.[74]

Until very recently, the applicability of the notion of police independence to police forces in Canada has received little attention, either by the courts or by commentators. Rather, on the basis of a few decisions of the Canadian courts in which the concept has been given more or less passing recognition,[75] its applicability in Canada seems to have been assumed. Court decisions governing the civil liability of municipalities and provincial governments for the actions of municipal police officers have been cited to justify an immunity for the police from the normal processes of democratic accountability and control.[76] Marshall (1965: 45), however, has concluded that "no such immunity and no general constitutional autonomy can be inferred from the much-handled civil liability cases."

Given the terms of modern police legislation in Canada, along with the fact that most of the Canadian cases which are relied upon in support of the notion of police independence were decided prior to the enactment of these legislative provisions, the applicability of this concept in Canada today remains highly questionable, and a thorough analysis of this question is long overdue. The likelihood of judicial review of this matter, however, has recently been greatly enhanced by the Quebec Court of Appeal's decision in the case of *Bisaillon v. Keable and the A.-G. of Quebec*.[77] In that case, Mr. Justice Turgeon, with whose opinions on this matter the other two members of the court concurred, thoroughly reviewed the legislation governing the police in Quebec, and concluded that the notion of police independence, as it has been expounded by the English courts, is not applicable in the Province of Quebec. This is the first reported case in which any superior court in Canada has so explicitly rejected the application of the English jurispurdence on this matter. The fact that Mr. Justice Turgeon chose not to refer to any of the extant Canadian case law on the subject, however, as well as the fact that the judgment is being appealed to the Supreme Court of Canada, ensures that judicial consideration of this matter in Canada is by no means at an end yet.

Even assuming the validity (not to mention the desirability) of the concept of police independence and its applicability in Canada, however, two things are quite clear. First, the concept itself has exerted a considerable influence on the relationship of police boards to the forces that they govern, encouraging a posture of substantial restraint, and a tendency to favour a limited interpretation of their mandate, by the former,[78] and a good measure of hostility toward attempts to impose democratic control on the police, by the latter.[79] Secondly, the precise implications of the notion of police independence for the relationship of a police board to its police force are the subject of substantial disagreement among police chiefs and police board members alike across Canada. This disagreement ranges from those who believe that the chief of police of a municipal police force is, in consequence of his independent status, not subject to any directions from his police board with respect to law enforcement policy or operations, and that a board has no right of access to police-held information pertaining to such matters, to those who believe that a board is entitled to issue instructions to its chief of police on any matter pertaining to the operations of the police force, and that, as one police board chairman put it, "there is nothing in that department which I am not entitled to be privy to."[80]

The Notion of Police Professionalism

McDougall (1971a) has described in fascinating detail, for Ontario, the historical emergence of the notion of police professionalism and its relationship to the notion of police independence and to the ongoing struggle between provincial and municipal authorities for control over municipal policing. His analysis leaves little doubt that the development of the notion of police professionalism tends to favour central rather than local interests in this struggle. Fogelson (1977) has illustrated a similiar tendency with respect to city police forces in the United States, as has Critchley (1978) in relation to the development of municipal policing in England. The implications of the development of the notion of police professionalism for the role of police boards in Canada, however, has not been systematically studied. Nevertheless, there can be little doubt that, along with the notion of police independence, the notion of police professionalism has had its influence in encouraging restraint and passivity on the part of police boards in their governance of municipal police forces. No better illustration of this influence could be found than the following description, published recently by the Ontario Police Commission, of the proper relationship between a police board and its chief of police:

> The primary rule is that the Chief of Police is charged with the responsibility for the control of the conduct of his men, particularly as it relates to the wide discretionary power which they exercise. Boards of Commissioners of Police represent civilian control of the force much the same as national governments represent civilian control of the Military Forces of the nation. National governments rarely have the technical knowledge to command armies, and

> must rely heavily on the expertise provided by the "general staff". Likewise, Boards of Commissioners of Police, by the very nature of their composition, must rely heavily upon their Chief of Police for the expertise required to operate the police force. They must spell out general policy through regulation and direction, but in the administration of the Force, they must rely upon the Chief of Police, otherwise the Board is assuming the prerogative of the Chief, and is, in effect, becoming the Office of the Chief, for which the Board has neither the time nor the expertise. [Ontario Police Commission, 1978: 116]

During interviews conducted while the research for this essay was being prepared, the influence of police professionalism on the police board/police chief relationship was constantly reiterated. One police chief commented, for instance, that the investigative techniques used by the members of his force are the chief's responsibility and that he does not normally inform his police board about them. These are, he urged, "professional matters with respect to which members of the police commission are amateurs." For the police board to attempt to give instructions with respect to what investigative techniques should be used would, in his view, be inappropriate, and would be comparable to "a hospital board telling a doctor how to operate."[81]

The Rise of Police Unionism

Closely associated with the trend toward police professionalism, although doubtfully consistent with such a concept, has been the significant development of structures of collective bargaining for the police. Although full-fledged police unionism is in many jurisdictions both prohibited by law and considered undesirable by the police themselves (cf. Reiner, 1978), this is by no means the case in all jurisdictions, and police unions now flourish in a number of Canada's major cities. The principal significance of these developments for the role of police boards is the extent to which matters of a non-economic nature that were once thought to be within the exclusive prerogative of the police chief and his governing authority have now been recognized as falling within the scope of collective bargaining and related arbitration processes. For many police boards, and especially those which do not have responsibility for collective bargaining, this trend has effectively resulted in significant loss of jurisdiction. Decisions that have major implications for the allocation of resources (e.g., the organization of the shift system, the issue of whether patrols should be manned by one or two officers, etc.) are increasingly being made not by chiefs in consultation with their police boards, as was previously the case, but by municipal labour negotiators, arbitrators and the courts (see, e.g., Arthurs, 1971; Swan, 1980). Furthermore, the fact that police associations and unions are organized on a provincial as well as a municipal basis has encouraged a tendency toward centralization in the definition and resolution of specific issues which further erodes the practical autonomy of individual police boards in their relations with their police forces. This, in turn, has been a major factor in the resurgence of provincial influence over the governance of municipal police forces, to which we turn next.

The Resurgence of Provincial Influence

During the last 35 years, post-war Canada has witnessed major overhauls of provincial legislation governing municipal policing, beginning with the enactment of the Ontario Police Act in 1946.[82] Invariably, such overhauls have involved a significant increase in the influence and control of provincial authorities with respect to municipal police forces. Standardization in the form of provincial regulations, uniform discipline codes and procedures for handling public complaints against the police, and the provision of systems of inspection and monitoring of municipal policing services by provincial agencies have characterized this period. The only provinces which have not yet completely revamped their policing legislation in this way are Manitoba and Newfoundland.

The principal vehicles of this growing provincial influence over municipal policing in recent years have been the new provincial police commissions. First introduced in Ontario in 1962, such commissions now exist in seven provinces,[83] and somewhat similar mechanisms of provincial authority are to be found in an eighth (Alberta).[84] Prince Edward Island and Newfoundland do not at present have such commissions, although the former province has enacted legislation, which is not yet in force, to establish one.[85]

Consisting usually of three or five members, often serving on a part-time basis, provincial police commissions play a role which, for the most part, consists in the provision of advisory services and technical and support services (e.g., co-ordinated criminal intelligence services to combat organized crime) to local authorities and municipal police forces. In some cases they run provincial police training facilities to which municipal police forces have access. While in no case does any provincial police commission have direct responsibility for the government of municipal police forces, in many cases such commissions are endowed with substantial powers to inspect local forces, to monitor the adequacy of municipal policing services, and to hold public inquiries into various aspects of municipal police services. Most provincial police commissions also have appellate jurisdiction with respect to the disposition, by municipal police chiefs and/or police boards, of internal disciplinary charges and public complaints against municipal policemen.

While most provincial police commissions are currently quite small organizations, some (notably those in Ontario, Quebec and British Columbia) are not. The Ontario Police Commission, for instance, currently has a staff of approximately 50 persons (not including the staff of 70 at the Ontario Police College, for which the commission is responsible), and in

1979–80 had an operating budget in excess of $7 million, of which just under half related to the commission's head office, the remainder being for the operation of the Ontario Police College.[86]

The precise impact of the growing influence of provincial authorities on the role of municipal police boards is difficult to gauge accurately. There is no doubt, however, that it has been substantial. The way it is perceived by some municipal police board members is amply illustrated by the following comments contained in a letter to the author from the chairman of the police board of a medium-sized Canadian city:

> While a degree of autonomy still remains in the hands of local Boards, this has been substantially eroded over the past few years, on the one hand through the development of the [provincial] Police Commission through mandatory and uniform practices regulations, and on the other hand by the steadily encroaching influence of police unions on administrative matters. Since the principal authority of the Boards is now to develop and control budgets on behalf of the individual municipalities, there may not be the same current need for the Board to be independent of the Municipal Councils. The need for Provincially-appointed Board Members is no longer as significant or important as the [provincial] Police Commission assumes an ever-enlarging role in the development of policy and standards for police departments throughout the Province. The principal concern in this regard, however, is that the [provincial] Police Commission is totally lacking in municipal representation on the one hand while heavily influenced and advised by the police unions on the other hand.

Another medium through which provincial authorities are able to exert a growing influence over municipal police policies is that of their ultimate control over prosecutions. To a limited extent, this relationship is entrenched in legislation. Section 59 of the Ontario Police Act, for instance, provides that a local Crown attorney (who is responsible to the provincial attorney general, and not to local authorities) may call in the provincial police force to handle problems arising even in an area which is under the jurisdiction of a municipal police force and its police board, and charge the cost of such services to the municipality. Furthermore, section 12 of the Ontario Crown Attorneys Act[87] empowers Crown attorneys to cause charges "to be further investigated, and additional evidence to be collected"—a provision which seems to envisage some degree of control by Crown attorneys over investigations by municipal police forces.[88] In New Brunswick, the provincial Ministry of Justice has adopted formal policies whereby the laying of criminal charges, applications for search warrants and applications for wiretapping orders by the police are subject to strict supervision and control by provincial Crown prosecutors (Gregory, 1979: 14–15). As was noted earlier, however, police boards are at present virtually unknown in this province, and New Brunswick appears to be unique in its adoption of such comprehensive policies of supervision of the actions of municipal police forces. Nevertheless, the New Brunswick experience serves to illustrate what a powerful source of control the provincial control over prosecutions can be.

Public Accountability of Police Boards

Since police boards are mostly statutory bodies which are notionally independent vis-à-vis both municipal and provincial authorities, the question of their public accountability is inherently problematic. With few exceptions, police boards are not required to report to any representative body.[89] Nor, in strict legal terms, are most of them subject to direction from anyone. Furthermore, the majority of the meetings of most police boards are held in private, as sanctioned by law,[90] and in most cases the rules and regulations promulgated by such boards, despite the fact that they have the force of laws, are not public documents. In at least one court decision, these and other documents relating to the operations of a police board have been held to be legally immune from public scrutiny.[91]

Under these circumstances, public accountability of such boards, such as it is, tends to be accomplished through indirect rather than direct means. Such indirect means include the lack of guaranteed tenure of board members, the ultimate control over the police budget by municipal councils or provincial police commissions, and the powers of supervision, monitoring, and inquiry vested in provincial police commissions and provincial prosecutorial authorities already described.[92]

It will be apparent that many, and in some cases most, of these indirect means of achieving public accountability of police boards are at the disposal of provincial rather than municipal authorities. It is the combination of this absence of direct local accountability of police boards with the fact that the substantial funds which they administer are either mostly or entirely raised through local taxation, which has given rise to most of the recent controversy over the legitimacy of such boards as institutions of municipal police governance.

Recent Developments—An Institution Under Attack

The history of police boards in Canada is marked by persistent controversy, and in recent years this controversy has shown no signs of abating. In Ontario during the 1970s three separate local government review commissions, appointed by the provincial government, independently recommended the abolition of police boards as they currently exist in the province, and advocated the return of control over municipal police services to elected municipal councils.[93] A fourth recommended no substantial change in existing arrangements.[94] Of these four commissions, the Robarts Commission on Metropolitan Toronto and the Waterloo Region Review Commission were the most thorough in examining the question of the governance of municipal police forces.

The Robarts Commission stressed "the importance of policing to the local community both as a service on its own and in its interrelationships with other local services," as well as "the principle of fiscal accountability, which holds that the spender of public funds should be responsible for raising them." The commission argued that the present arrangements for governance of the police force "have made it virtually impossible for either the public or its local elected representatives to make an informed assessment of the policies of the police commission and to evaluate the management and operation of the police force" (Ontario, Royal Commission on Metropolitan Toronto, 1977: vol. 2, at 276). Commenting on the commonly heard view that some municipal services need to be "protected from politics," the commission suggested that "this attitude ultimately reduces to a view of politics as a sinister process and municipal councils as unworthy of confidence." The commission rejected this attitude, saying that it felt that "the public holds a more positive view of politics as a healthy resolution of community issues through the democratic process. Municipal politics are no exception." The commission argued that "if it is contended that some local public services must be 'protected from politics,' then it is up to the proponents of that view to demonstrate why some services are needful of this protection, while others are not." Without explicitly saying so, the commission went on to imply that no such argument could be convincingly made (1977: vol. 2, at 105).

The Waterloo Region Review Commission reiterated many of the arguments put forward by the Robarts Commission, but was more blunt on the subject of the claim that police boards are non-political bodies. In an interim report, *Police Governance in Waterloo Region*, which constitutes a unique contribution to Canadian literature on this subject, the commission argued that the "values and beliefs" of a position which "places great emphasis on the need for keeping an emotional public from influencing police policy directly . . . are, or should be, unacceptable in a democratic scheme of government." The empirical evidence in the region, the commission urged, shows not only that "skillful political behaviour and continuous political processes" are required for "the effective resolution of police issues, often in relation to other public issues," but that the recent absence of it has, in the long run, ill served the community and the police (Ontario, Waterloo Region Review Commission, 1978: 100). In its final report the following year, the commission criticized the argument that a "non-political" board is needed for the governance of municipal police forces. Comparing this with the possibility of governance by a representative regional council, the commission observed:

> The arguments for "keeping politics out of the police" are largely fraudulent. No matter how the system is structured, the police governing body must ultimately be responsible to the public—that is accountability and that is politics. The present system where the Provincial Government, elected

through a party system, appoints the majority of police commissioners is every bit as "political" and more potentially dangerous than a situation in which a government composed of twenty-four separately elected individuals with at least three different political stripes and seven different factions appoints the police governing body. Recent allegations of impropriety against provincially appointed police commissioners in York and Halton suggest that no structure is immune from such accusations."[95] [Ontario, Waterloo Region Review Commission, 1979: 156]

In its interim report, the commission also attacked the notion that the concept of police independence makes the police "simply not manageable to the extent that other municipal departments are." The commission asserted that it is "somewhat spurious" to suggest that the legally independent character of the individual policeman's authority in law enforcement "is itself a major problem in management of the police force." The commission commented that:

> The broadest area of police activity is designed to prevent the breaking of law. This includes the way the force is organized and the amount of patrol duty itself. This is not legally subject to the discretion of the individual policeman as is his behaviour on patrol. Hence, the police are eminently "manageable" by the police governing authority. [Ontario, Waterloo Region Review Commission, 1978: 91]

To the argument that municipal policing must conform to provincial rather than local standards and policies with respect to law enforcement and the administration of justice, the commission countered that this fact, by itself, cannot justify the removal of governance of municipal police forces from the local elected municipal council, any more than it can justify it in the case of other municipally controlled municipal services which share a similar need for provincial (e.g., education), or even federal (e.g., welfare) input. Such necessary provincial influence, the commission argued, can be accomplished in more direct ways than through provincial control of the police governing authority. One such way, the commission suggested, would be to expand, where necessary, the supervisory powers of the provincial police commission (Ontario, Waterloo Region Review Commission, 1978: 95).

In addition to these review commission reports, police boards in Ontario have come under criticism recently from a variety of other sources. Two major commissions of inquiry into the Metropolitan Toronto Police Force have recommended the removal from the police board of certain of their responsibilities with respect to the disposition of public complaints against the force (see Maloney, 1975; Ontario Royal Commission into Metropolitan Toronto Police Practices, 1976), and a bill to put their recommendations into effect is currently before the Ontario legislature.[96] More recently, mounting confrontations between the Toronto police and certain minority groups in that city have led to an unprecedented public censure of the police board by city council,[97] and further calls for the return of control over the force to municipal authorities.

Ontario is not the only jurisdiction, however, that has recently experienced controversy over the institution of the police board. In Winnipeg, as a result of a dispute between the city's police board and city administrators, the city council took action in 1978 to strip the board of most of its major functions in governing the police force, and placed these responsibilities in the hands of city administrators responsible to the city council.[98] In New Brunswick, an attempt by the provincial government to introduce legislation in 1973 which would have required municipal police forces in the province to be governed by police boards rather than by local municipal councils,[99] as at present, met with what one document summarizing reaction to the proposal at the time described as "almost universal opposition," and was subsequently withdrawn as a result. The bill which was introduced in its place, and finally passed in 1977, provided that such boards would be optional only.[100] This legislative provision was only proclaimed in force in December 1980, so it remains to be seen whether any municipalities in that province will opt for this form of municipal police governance.

Conclusions

Police boards have had an uncertain and controversial history as institutions of municipal police governance, and continue today to be the subject of a good deal of quite highly charged debate in some quarters. As an institution they epitomize fundamental differences not only over the nature of the police function, but also over the appropriate means of ensuring the accountability of this function in a democratic society. The defenders of police boards stress the judicial (or at least quasi-judicial) nature of the police function, and point to the original judicial responsibility for the police. This "judicial location" of the police, as McDougall (1971a: 31) has described it, is said to require the removal of direct political supervision for its preservation, and police boards, it is argued, fulfil this need for "non-political" governance of the police. Many advocates of police boards, citing what is claimed to be a historic independence of the law enforcement function, and the growing "professionalism" of modern police personnel, go further to argue for a restricted role in governing the police even for such a "non-political" governing authority, contending that a substantial portion of police activity should be subject only to supervision by the courts rather than by any governing authority. An extreme statement of this view may be found in the now-famous reply of Prime Minister Trudeau, in 1977, to the journalist who asked him: "Just how ignorant does a minister have to be before . . . some responsibility is applied to the advisers who seem to have kept him ignorant?" Trudeau is reported to have responded:

> The policy of this government . . . has been that they, indeed—the politicians who happen to form the Government—should be kept in ignorance of the day-to-day operations of the police force and even of the security force. . . . That is our position. It is not one of pleading ignorance to defend the Government. It is one of keeping the Government's nose out of the operations of the police force, at whatever level of government. On the criminal law side, the protections we have against abuse are not with the Government, they are with the courts.[101]

The courts, in their turn, have on occasion pushed this line of reasoning still further to suggest that there may be areas of police discretion in which even they should not interfere.[102] And in the heat of the debate, those who favour the institution of the police board will invariably recall the "bad old days" when policemen were so obviously the willing henchmen of the most blatantly self-serving factions engaged in the crassest political partisanship (Fogelson, 1977; Tardif, 1974).

Yet the detractors of police boards can find much to criticize in such justifications. Their critique ranges from the moderate to the extreme, but despite this it usually shares the same starting point—that the municipal police function is more essentially a municipal service than a judicial or quasi-judicial function, and that its comparability and relationship to other municipal services is of greater significance (in terms of how it should be governed) than any unique "judicial" characteristics it may have.

The moderates, while conceding that the police function includes some quasi-judicial elements which need to be protected from partisan control, argue that such requirements can be met within the framework of normal democratic processes for the control and accountability of municipal services, as they are in the case of many other municipal employees whose role includes a law enforcement function (e.g., building inspectors). Any need for the imposition of standards (be they provincial or federal in scope) which transcend the local jurisdiction can be accomplished, they argue, through directly increasing the authority of relevant provincial or federal agencies, without the need to remove the governance of municipal police entirely from responsible municipal authorities. And they question why, in the case of other services the control of which has been assumed or retained by provincial authorities because of their perceived linkage to the administration of justice (e.g., prosecutorial functions, maintenance and administration of the courts, etc.), the provinces have also assumed the cost of such services, whereas by far the lion's share of municipal police services continues to be paid for out of locally raised funds. They point to the growing sophistication of municipal government, and to the absence of any very clear evidence that modern municipal police forces which are currently directly or primarily governed by municipal authorities are demonstrably inferior to those which are governed by police boards.

More radical critics, however, will challenge the whole notion of municipal policing as a "non-political" function which needs to be protected from the normal political processes of democratic control. In doing so, they will point to the ambiguity of the historical evidence for this position, and particularly to the doubtful nature of the claim that the historical control of the police by the lower judiciary is any real indication of their essentially "judicial" character. The law, they will argue, is itself essentially "political," in the sense that it favours some interests over others. Under these circumstances, they continue, it is simply naive and misleading to suggest that law enforcement (or any other police function) can be essentially a non-political function (see, e.g., Fogelson, 1977: 111–12.) They will point to the doubtful historical origins of the notion of police independence in this regard, and to its uncritical acceptance as applicable to contemporary Canadian municipal policing. The notion that the supposed independence of the police requires their governance to be "removed from politics" is, they will claim, no more nor less than a superficially attractive item of packaging for what has always in reality been an attempt to shift an essentially political control of the police from local to central (provincial) authorities. In this connection they will point to the inconsistency of the requirements for police boards (only certain municipalities are required to have them), to the lack of any clearly non-political criteria of eligibility for police board membership, and to the lack of any clear empirical evidence that the members of such boards and their governance of police forces are in fact any less "political" than those of other, more locally controlled, police governing authorities.[103]

Some will go further and argue that the notions of police independence and of police professionalism, and the postures of restraint and passivity which they engender on the part of police governing authorities, are in reality no more than strategies to legitimize the denial of real conflicts in society in order to ensure that the municipal police function is operated for the benefit of certain elite political interests, at the expense of others (see, e.g., Brogden, 1977).

The advocates of police boards will often respond to such arguments by drawing a distinction between the partisan and the non-partisan interpretation of the term "politics." The purpose of the institution of the police board, they argue, is to protect the police from politics in the partisan sense of the term, and not from politics in a more general sense (see, e.g., Edwards, 1980: 70). The response of the critics to such a distinction tends to take two forms, a practical one and a theoretical one. On the practical level, critics point out that even if the validity of the distinction is assumed, there is still an absence of any clear evidence that police board members in their governance of municipal police forces are any less partisan than municipal councils which govern police forces. In particular, they point to the fact that the powers of appointment of members of police boards are always in the hands of partisan politicians, and that legislation governing the composition of such boards not only includes few, if any, prohibitions on partisan appointments, but also typically provides that police board members hold office "at the pleasure" of those politicians who are responsible for their appointment. Furthermore, they point out that in its need to be protected from crass, self-serving political partisanship the police service is essentially no different from a host of other municipal services, and that in this sense all municipal services should be dedicated to the service of the general public interest rather than personal or partisan interests of those who are responsible for their government. Taken to its logical conclusion, they would claim, this argument in favour of police boards would deny legitimacy to almost all forms of direct municipal government by locally elected representatives.

Others, however, would go further to suggest that the theoretical distinction between partisan and non-partisan politics, while superficially attractive, is in reality an unworkable one. The very question as to what is or is not a partisan political decision, they point out, is itself likely to present itself as a political question which will often engender substantial partisan political disagreement. While from an academic point of view this may not be a necessary conclusion, in practical terms it will always be, because the only forum in which the question of whether a police governing authority has acted from partisan motives is in practice resolved is an institution (Parliament, a provincial legislature, a municipal council, or even a government itself) which is entirely committed to the resolution of all political questions through the medium of partisan politics. Indeed, proponents of this view argue that partisan politics are a fundamental condition of our current democratic political system, in which the definition of actions or policies as being "in the public interest" depends entirely on the ability of their partisan proponents to convince a majority of the partisan elected representatives that this is the case.[104]

Yet over their 122-year history, and throughout the period in which such debates over their legitimacy as institutions of municipal police governance have raged, police boards in Canada have displayed a bewildering diversity of form and function which seems to defy the simple application to them of such ideological labels. In form, they have ranged (and continue to range) from the highly representative to the highly bureaucratic, and in function they range from those which are highly active in the shaping and supervision over the implementation of police policy, to those which appear to be little more than agencies of almost rubber-stamp approval and public relations for the policy and operational initiatives of highly autonomous chiefs of police. They range from those which place a high priority on their public accountability (or at least on the appearance of public accountability), to those which are perhaps best epitomized by the remark made to the author by one police board chairman to the effect that his board actively discourages public participation in its meetings because its members are of the view that the municipal council is the proper forum for "that sort of thing."

At the present time, however, only the most superficial and tenuous empirical evidence is available on the actual role played by police boards in the governance of Canada's municipal police forces. Indeed, the sparsity of the literature on this subject prompts legitimate questions as to why legal as well as political science scholars have devoted so little attention to the control and accountability of municipal policing, given its considerable political and constitutional significance. That, however, would be subject-matter for an essay which others would undoubtedly be more qualified to write.

For the moment, it seems that in our understanding of the institution of police boards in Canada, we have advanced little from the insights of Fosdick, who in 1920 wrote of the American experience with such boards, that "in the kaleidoscopic variations and adaptations which followed upon the adoption of the board plan of control, it is difficult to trace the line of police development" (1969: 80). Fosdick's difficulties in this regard did not dissuade him from a blunt and negative assessment of the American experience with police boards. In Canada, 60 years later, however, much work remains to be done before truly informed judgments can be made about the role of police boards and commissions as institutions of municipal police governance.

NOTES

1. For a brief summary of these, see Freedman and Stenning (1977, chap. 2); Kelly and Kelly (1976, part 2).
2. R.C.M.P. Act, R.S.C. 1970, c. R-9.
3. Ontario Police Act, R.S.O. 1970, c. 351, Part IV; Quebec Police Act, S.Q. 1968, c. 17, Division III.
4. The relevant provincial statutes are listed in note 54, below.
5. E.g., National Harbours Board Act, R.S.C. 1970, c. N-8, section 5; Railway Act, R.S.C. 1970, c. R-2, sections 400–406; Ontario Northland Transportation Commission Act, R.S.O. 1970, c. 326, section 24(6); British Columbia Railway Act, R.S.B.C. 1960, c. 329.
6. Municipal police governing authorities described in this essay are variously named in different jurisdictions. While in most jurisdictions they are called boards of commissioners of police, in some they are called police commissions. Furthermore, whatever their official designation, they are frequently referred to colloquially as either "police boards" or "police commissions." In order to avoid confusion in this essay the term *police board* or *board* will be used throughout to refer to such municipal police boards or commissions. The adoption of this terminology is not intended in any way to derogate from the official nomenclature of municipal police governing authorities in some jurisdictions, but is merely for the purpose of minimizing the reader's possible confusion between these institutions and the *provincial police commissions* to which reference is also made in the essay.

7. In 1855, commissioners in Quebec appointed "to investigate and report upon the best means of re-organizing the militia of Canada and upon an improved system of police," recommended that all municipal police forces in Quebec be replaced by members of a newly created provincial police force organized along military lines: see Quebec (1855: 15–20). This recommendation was not implemented, however, and the Quebec Provincial Police Force, which was established in 1870 (by S.Q. 1970, c. 24) was not given anything like such hegemony as the commissioners had recommended.
8. See, e.g., section 15 of Nova Scotia's Townships and Officers Act, Rev. Statutes 1864 (3rd Ser.), c. 47.
9. The first such board was established by An Act to establish a Police in the Town of Brockville, 2nd Wm. IV, c. 17 (1832).
10. Statutes of Upper Canada, 4th Wm. IV, c. 23 (1834). See in particular sections 22, 57, 65, 74, 77, 78.
11. Vestiges of powers such as this are still to be found today, e.g., in section 2 of the Criminal Code, R.S.C. 1970, c. C-34, which provides that the term "peace officer" includes a "mayor, warden, reeve," etc. Section 212 of Ontario's Municipal Act, R.S.O. 1970, c. 284, still endows mayors with the authority to "call out the posse comitatus to enforce the law within the municipality."
12. The Upper Canada Municipal Corporations Act, 12 Vict., c. 81 (1849).
13. The relevant provisions are: 1873, c. 48, section 333; 1874, c. 16, section 10; 1936, c. 35; 1938, c. 23, section 4; 1943, c. 16, section 7; 1947, c. 77, section 5; 1960, c. 84, section 1; and 1965, c. 99, section 2.
14. City of Charlottetown Incorporation Amendment Act, 1941, c. 24, section 4.
15. 1858, c. 99. See in particular sections 347–53 and 369–80.
16. Section 348 of the Act, however, clearly provided for the possibility that a city might not have a recorder.
17. 1867, 30–31 Vict., c. 3 (U.K.); reproduced, as amended, in R.S.C. 1970, App. II, No. 5.
18. British Columbia Police Act, 1974, c. 64, sections 19–21, and Alberta Police Act, 1973, c. 44, section 18.
19. Law Reform Act, 1868-69, c. 6, section 15.
20. This was effected through the reform of the magistracy including the abolition of the "police magistrate" as a locally optional office: see Magistrates Act, 1936, c. 35.
21. Police Act, 1946, c. 72, section 6(2).
22. Police Amendment Act, 1958, c. 79, section 1.
23. See *Toronto Globe and Mail*, May 8, 1979, "Judges to continue on police bodies."
24. Police Amendment Act, 1979, c. 74.
25. R. Roy McMurtry, letter to the editor, *Toronto Globe and Mail*, July 23, 1979.
26. There are currently ten regional police forces (including Metropolitan Toronto) in Ontario.
27. Municipality of Metropolitan Toronto Act, R.S.O. 1970, c. 295, section 177.
28. City of Brandon Incorporation Act, 1882, c. 35, sections 119–31; City of Winnipeg Incorporation Act, 1882, c. 36, sections 121–32.
29. Municipal Institutions Act, 1886, c. 52, sections 352–75.
30. Brandon Charter Amendment Act, 1949, c. 79, section 3.

31. Vancouver City Incorporation Act, 1886, c. 32, sections 171–84A; New Westminster City Incorporation Act, 1888, c. 42, sections 165–75.
32. Municipal Act Amendment Act, 1893, c. 30, section 63.
33. Municipal Clauses Act, 1896, c. 37, section 217.
34. See British Columbia Police Act, 1974, c. 64, sections 19–21.
35. City of Moncton Police Commission Act, 1907, c. 97 (repealed by the City of Moncton Incorporation Act, 1946, c. 101, sections 113–26 of which transferred control of the city's police force back to the city council).
36. City of Fredericton Police Commission Act, 1908, c. 42.
37. Saint John City Police Commission Act, 1960–61, c. 133. Apparently no board has ever been established pursuant to this statute, and the city police force is still governed by the city council.
38. The Marysville Police Commission Act, 1971, c. 82, also provided for the creation of a police board for that municipality, but the municipality became a part of Fredericton shortly thereafter. New Brunswick's new Police Act, 1977, c. P-9.2, provides for optional police boards for municipalities having their own police forces. These provisions were proclaimed in force in December 1980.
39. Cities Act, 1908, c. 16, section 79.
40. Cities Act, 1915, c. 16, section 92.
41. City of Charlottetown Incorporation Amendment Act, 1938, c. 29, section 2. The new P.E.I. Police Act, 1977, c. 28, Part V, provides for the establishment of police boards in the province's municipalities; the Act, however, has not yet been proclaimed in force.
42. City Act, 1951, c. 9, sections 81–91. Provisions for a police board for the city of Calgary, however, were enacted in 1934 in section 309 of the Calgary Charter, 1893, c. 33, as amended by 1934, c. 72, section 9.
43. Municipal Government Act, 1968, c. 68, sections 94–101.
44. Police Act, 1971, c. 85, sections 9–23.
45. Montreal Urban Community Act, 1969, c. 84, sections 196–241. See now the Public Security Council of the M.U.C. Act, 1977, c. 71.
46. Police Act, 1974, c. 9, sections 19–21.
47. E.g., the Fredericton Police Commission from 1908–11: see Fredericton Police Commission Act, 1908, c. 42.
48. E.g., existing police boards in Alberta: see Alberta Police Act, 1973, c. 44, sections 23–27. Also the Vancouver and New Westminster police boards from 1888–1906 and 1890–1900 respectively: see note 31, above. Also police boards in Saskatchewan from 1908–15: see note 39, above.
49. E.g., the police boards in some British Columbia municipalities (other than Vancouver) from 1917–57: see Municipal Act Amendment Act, 1917, c. 45, section 61.
50. A more detailed description of this variety will be found in Stenning (1981: part 1, chap. 1).
51. Information supplied to the author by the Ontario Police Commission.
52. See, e.g., section 11 of the Ontario Police Act, R.S.O. 1970, c. 351.
53. See, e.g., sections 462–71 of the City of Winnipeg Act, 1971, c. 105.
54. The following is a list of the relevant provincial statutes governing existing and proposed police boards in Canada: B.C., Police Act, 1974, c. 64, sections

19–21; Alberta, Police Act, 1973, c. 44, sections 23–27; Saskatchewan, Police Act, R.S.S. 1978, c. P-15, sections 27–36; Manitoba, Brandon Charter Amendment Act, 1949, c. 79, section 3, and City of Winnipeg Act, 1971, c. 105, sections 462–72; Ontario, Police Act, R.S.O. 1970, c. 351, sections 8–17; Quebec, Public Security Council of the M.U.C. Act, 1977, c. 71; New Brunswick, Police Act, 1977, c. P-9.2, sections 7–9, and Fredericton Police Commission Act, 1908, c. 42, as amended; Nova Scotia, Police Act, 1974, c. 9, sections 19–21; P.E.I., Police Act, 1977, c. 28, Part V. Ten statutes providing for regional governments in Ontario (including Metropolitan Toronto) also provide for police boards for these regions, but are too numerous to be listed here.

55. The Metropolitan Toronto Board, however, which administers the largest municipal police force in Canada (5,384 policemen and 1,126 other employees in 1979), has a separate staff of seven, consisting of an executive secretary, a secretary, an assistant secretary, two clerks, a liaison officer (who investigates minor matters for the board), and a civilian labour relations officer. The board however, can call on the ad hoc assistance of any member of the force.
56. The Toronto and Regina boards, for instance, meet once every two weeks. The Public Security Council in Montreal meets every week.
57. As an example of such a "crunch issue," he cited the decision as to whether his force's patrol cars should be equipped with shotguns.
58. In Ontario, however, and possibly in other jurisdictions too, it sometimes happens that a person is appointed to a board by the provincial authorities on the clear understanding that that person will be elected chairman. The only way in which such an understanding can be ultimately enforced, of course, is through the power which the provincial authorities have over the appointment of the majority of members of the board. Another practice which has occurred on at least two occasions in Ontario is that of the provincial authorities appointing a person to be a judge for the express purpose of immediately appointing him to membership of a police board.
59. *Re a Reference under the Constitutional Questions Act*, [1957] O.R. 28 at 30 (Ontario Court of Appeal).
60. Nova Scotia Police Act, 1974, c. 9, section 20; City of Winnipeg Act, 1971, c. 105, section 465.
61. A brief account of these changes will be found in Stenning (1981: part 1, at 33–34, and part 3, at 74–78).
62. In the event of a dispute between a police board and a municipal council over a municipal police force budget, section 14(3) of the Ontario Police Act, R.S.O. 1970, c. 351, gives authority to resolve such dispute to the Ontario Police Commission. This power, however, was only first formally exercised in 1981, in a dispute concerning the budget of the Niagara Regional Police force. A similar provision is to be found in section 23 of the British Columbia Police Act, 1974, c. 64.
63. See City of Winnipeg By-Law No. 2150/78, section 7. Recently, however, there have been recommendations to re-establish the Winnipeg Police Commission with a much broader mandate: see Ross (1980: 40–42).
64. See note 62, above.
65. This is an illustrative, rather than an exhaustive, list. Police board rules and regulations are not normally public documents, and during the research in

preparation for this essay, the author neither sought nor was offered access to such documents in most instances.

66. See, e.g., Maloney (1975).
67. See, e.g., *Toronto Globe and Mail*, September 12, 1979, "Godfrey joins Sewell, backs review of complaints over police."
68. See, e.g., sections 377–86 of Ontario's Municipal Act, R.S.O. 1970, c. 284.
69. E.g., *Glasbrook Bros. v. Glamorgan County Council et al.*, [1925] A.C. 270; *Fisher v. Oldham Corporation*, [1930] All E.R. Rep. 96; *A.-G. for New South Wales v. Perpetual Trustee Co.*, [1955] 1 All E.R. 846; *R. v. Metropolitan Police Commissioner ex parte Blackburn*, [1968] 1 All E.R. 763.
70. E.g., *Nettleton v. Prescott* (1908), 16 O.L.R. 538; *Bruton v. Regina Policemen's Association* (1945), 3 D.L.R. 437; *R. v. Labour Relations Board ex parte Fredericton* (1955), 38 M.P.R. 26; *Myers v. Hoffman*, [1955] O.R. 965; *The King v. Labour Relations Board (N.S.)* (1951), 4 D.L.R. 227; *Re St. Catharine's Police Association and Board of Police Commissioners for the City of St. Catharine's* (1974), 1 O.R. 430; *Re Nicholson and Haldimand-Norfolk Regional Board of Commissioners of Police* (1979), 88 D.L.R. (3d) 671.
71. Great Britain, Royal Commission on the Police (1962a: chap. 4).
72. See Great Britain, Royal Commission on Criminal Procedure (1981: 2–4).
73. See, e.g., Anderson (1929); Marshall (1965); Cull (1975); Plehwe (1974); Mitchell (1962); Gillance and Khan (1975); Leigh (1975); Milte and Weber (1977); Edwards (1980).
74. [1968] 1 All E.R. 763 at 769.
75. See note 70, above.
76. Examples of the uncritical acceptance of the applicability of the English notion of police independence to the Canadian situation abound: see e.g., Ontario, Task Force on Policing in Ontario (1974: 15); Canada, Canadian Committee on Corrections (1969: 45); Kelly and Kelly (1976: 201–2).
77. (1981), 17 C.R. (3d) 193.
78. See, e.g., *Toronto Globe and Mail*, January 19, 1973, "30% abused bail law last year, Bick says."
79. See, e.g., *Toronto Globe and Mail*, January 25, 1973, "Political control of commission would hinder police, chief says."
80. Interview with the author, July 1979.
81. Interview with the author, July 1979.
82. 1946, c. 72.
83. Quebec in 1968, Manitoba and Alberta in 1971 (the Alberta Police Commission was disbanded two years later, however), British Columbia in 1974, Saskatchewan in 1975, Nova Scotia in 1976, New Brunswick in 1978.
84. The functions of the Alberta Commission, disbanded in 1973, are now essentially performed by a Director of Law Enforcement (who is a member of the provincial solicitor general's department) and a Law Enforcement Appeal Board: see Alberta Police Act, 1973, c. 44, sections 4–17.
85. Police Act, 1977, c. 28, Part I.
86. A more thorough description of provincial police commissions will be found in Stenning (1981: part 2).
87. R.S.O. 1970, c. 101.
88. This, at least, is clearly the way it has been interpreted by provincial attorneys general: see, e.g., Bales (1973).

89. Edmonton City By-Law No. 4188, section 12, however, imposes reporting requirements (to the city council) on the Edmonton police board. Some provincial Police Acts also require boards to report certain information to provincial police commissions.
90. See, e.g., section 10(3) of the Ontario Police Act, R.S.O. 1970, c. 351.
91. *Re McAuliffe and Metropolitan Toronto Board of Commissioners of Police* (1976), 9 O.R. (2d) 583.
92. A notable example of how these various indirect pressures may come to bear on a municipal police board is the recent series of events surrounding Chief Brown and the Waterloo Regional Police Force. A description of these events will be found in the court decision in *Re Brown and Waterloo Regional Police Commissioners Board and Ontario Police Commission* (1979), 13 C.R. (3d) 46, and in Stenning (1981: part 2, at 80–88).
93. See Ontario, Ottawa-Carleton Review Commission (1976); Ontario, Royal Commission on Metropolitan Toronto (1977); Ontario, Waterloo Region Review Commission (1979).
94. See Ontario, Hamilton-Wentworth Review Commission (1978).
95. With respect to these allegations, see *Toronto Globe and Mail*, February 6, 1978, "Investigator's Status on Police Board Probed," and ibid., December 6, 1978, "Ex-Halton Police Commissioner Won't be Charged, Officials Say."
96. Bill No. 68 (1981).
97. See *Toronto Globe and Mail*, September 18, 1979, "Council Censures Police Commission." In May 1980 the executive of Metropolitan Toronto Council voted in support of a proposal that the Toronto board should be enlarged from five to seven members, the majority of whom should be appointed by the Metropolitan Toronto Council: see *Toronto Globe and Mail*, May 28, 1980, "Metro to Seek Majority on Police Board."
98. For an account of this dispute, see Stenning (1981: part 3, at 74–78).
99. 1973, Bill No. 43. See also 1975, Bill No. 89.
100. Police Act, 1977, c. P-9.2, sections 7–9.
101. See *Toronto Globe and Mail*, December 12, 1977, "Trudeau: Keep Politicians Ignorant of Police Actions," and the critique of Trudeau's statement by Edwards (1980: 94–97).
102. See, e.g., the passage from Lord Denning's judgment in *R. v. Metropolitan Police Commissioner ex parte Blackburn*, [1968] 1 All E.R. 763 at 769, quoted above at 187–88.
103. Edwards (1980: 72), however, has argued that in the debate over police boards the onus is on their detractors to produce evidence that police boards display "subservience to the will of the Provincial Executive."
104. The so-called "Nicholson Affair," which involved the resignation of the Commissioner of the RCMP in 1959, may be viewed as a classic illustration of this point: see, Canada, House of Commons Debates, March 16, 1959, at 1959–66 and 2005–7. The incident is discussed in Stenning (1981: part 3, at 35–39).

REFERENCES

Aitchison, J. H.

1949. "The Municipal Corporations Act of 1849." *Canadian Historical Review* 30: 107–22.

Alberta, Board of Review
1975. *Administration of Justice in the Provincial Courts of Alberta: Report No. 2.* Edmonton.
Anderson, J.
1929. "The Police." *Public Administration* 7: 192.
Arthurs, H. W.
1971. *Collective Bargaining by Public Employees in Canada: Five Models,* chap. 4: "The Formal Public Sector Model: Collective Bargaining by Police Forces in Ontario." Ann Arbor: Institute of Labour and Industrial Relations, Wayne State University–University of Michigan.
Bales, D.
1973. "Address to the Association of Municipal Police Governing Authorities." *Crown's Newsletter* (June 1973): 1–7.
Barot, D., and N. Bérard
1972. *Etude Historico-Juridique: Organisation et pouvoirs de la police.* Montreal: Centre International de Criminologie Comparée, Université de Montréal.
Brogden, M.
1977. "A Police Authority—The Denial of Conflict." *Sociological Review* 25: 325–49.
Canada, Canadian Committee on Corrections
1969. *Toward Unity: Criminal Justice and Corrections* (the Ouimet Report). Ottawa: Queen's Printer.
Canada, Statistics Canada
1978. *Police Administration Statistics 1977.* Ottawa: Statistics Canada.
Critchley, T. A.
1978. *A History of Police in England and Wales.* London: Constable.
Cull, H. A.
1975. "The Enigma of a Police Constable's Status." *Victoria University of Wellington Law Review* 8: 148–69.
Edwards, J. Ll. J.
1980. *Ministerial Responsibility for National Security.* Ottawa: Department of Supply and Services Canada.
Fogelson, R. M.
1977. *Big-City Police.* Cambridge, Mass.: Harvard University Press.
Fosdick, R. B.
1969. *American Police Systems.* Montclair, N.J.: Patterson Smith.
Freedman, D. J., and P. C. Stenning
1977. *Private Security, Police and the Law in Canada.* Toronto: Centre of Criminology, University of Toronto.
Gillance, K., and A. N. Khan
1975. "The Constitutional Independence of a Police Constable in the Exercise of the Powers of his Office." *Police Journal* 48: 55–62.
Great Britain, Royal Commission on the Police
1962a. *Final Report.* London: HMSO.
1962b. *Appendix II to the Minutes of Evidence.* London: HMSO.
Great Britain, Royal Commission on Criminal Procedure
1981. *The Investigation and Prosecution of Criminal Offences in England and Wales: The Law and Procedure* (Cmnd. 8092–1). London: HMSO.

Gregory, G. F.
1979. "Police Power and the Role of the Provincial Minister of Justice." *Chitty's Law Journal* 27: 13–18.
Harrison, R. A. (ed.)
1859. *The New Municipal Manual*. Toronto: Maclear and Co.
Kelly, W., and N. Kelly
1976. *Policing in Canada*. Toronto: Macmillan/Maclean-Hunter.
Leigh, L. H.
1975. *Police Powers in England and Wales*. London: Butterworths.
Maloney, A.
1975. *The Metropolitan Toronto Review of Citizen-Police Complaint Procedure*. A Report to the Metropolitan Toronto Board of Commissioners of Police, May 12, 1975.
Marshall, G.
1965. *Police and Government*. London: Methuen and Co.
McDougall, A. K.
1971a. "Law and Politics: The Case of Police Independence in Ontario." Paper presented to 43rd Annual Meeting of Canadian Political Science Association, June 1971 (unpublished).
1971b. "Policing in Ontario: The Occupational Dimension to Provincial-Municipal Relations." Doctoral thesis, University of Toronto, 1971.
Milte, K. L., and T. A. Weber
1977. *Police in Australia*. Sydney: Butterworths.
Mitchell, J. D. B.
1962. "The Constitutional Position of the Police in Scotland." *Juridical Review* 7 ns: 1–20.
Moir, E.
1969. *The Justice of the Peace*. Harmondsworth, U.K.: Penguin Books.
Ontario, Hamilton-Wentworth Review Commission
1978. *Report*. Toronto: Queen's Printer.
Ontario, Ottawa-Carleton Review Commission
1976. *Report*. Toronto: Queen's Printer.
Ontario Police Commission
1978. *Report on an Inquiry into Police Practices of the Waterloo Regional Police Force*. Toronto: Ontario Police Commission.
Ontario, Royal Commission into Metropolitan Toronto Police Practices
1976. *Report* (the Morand Report). Toronto.
Ontario Royal Commission on Metropolitan Toronto
1977. *Report* (the Robarts Report). Vol. 2: *Detailed Findings and Recommendations*. Toronto: Queen's Printer.
Ontario, Task Force on Policing in Ontario
1974. Report, *The Police Are the Public and the Public Are the Police*. Toronto, 1974.
Ontario, Waterloo Region Review Commission
1978. *Police Governance in Waterloo Region*. Toronto: Queen's Printer.
1979. *Report*. Toronto: Queen's Printer.
Plehwe, R.
1974. "Police and Government: the Commissioner of Police for the Metropolis." *Public Law*: 316–35.

Quebec, Commissioners appointed to Investigate and Report upon the Best Means of Re-organizing the Militia of Canada, and upon an improved system of police
1855. *Report*. Quebec: Derbishire and Desbarrats.
Reiner, Robert
1978. *The Blue Coated Worker*. Cambridge: Cambridge University Press.
Ross, P. S., and Partners
1980. *A Review of the Operating Efficiency and Effectiveness of the Winnipeg Police Department: Final Report*. Edmonton: P. S. Ross and Partners.
Stenning, Philip C.
1981. *Police Commissions and Boards in Canada*. Toronto: Centre of Criminology, University of Toronto.
Swan, K.
1980. "Interest Arbitration of Non-Economic Issues in Police Bargaining" in B. M. Downie, and R. L. Jackson (eds.) *Conflict and Co-Operation in Police Labour Relations*. Ottawa: Department of Supply and Services Canada.
Tardif, G.
1974. *Police et Politique au Quebec*. Montreal: editions de L'Aurore.